THE BOOK OF THE YEAR

THE BOOK OF THE YEAR

THE WEIRDER SIDE OF 2017

James Harkin, Andrew Hunter Murray, Anna Ptaszynski
and Dan Schreiber

Illustrations by Adam Doughty

BOOKS

For Bean, Fenella, Molly and Polina

And for Littlefoot

*who, just like this book, was conceived,
assembled and delivered in 2017.*

---

5 7 9 10 8 6

Random House Books
20 Vauxhall Bridge Road
London SW1V 2SA

Random House Books is part of the Penguin Random House
group of companies whose addresses can be found at
global.penguinrandomhouse.com.

Penguin
Random House
UK

First published by Random House Books in 2017

www.penguin.co.uk

A CIP catalogue record for this book is available
from the British Library.

ISBN 9781847948199

Printed and bound by Clays Ltd, St Ives plc

Penguin Random House is committed to a sustainable future
for our business, our readers and our planet. This book is made
from Forest Stewardship Council® certified paper.

MIX
Paper from
responsible sources
FSC® C018179
FSC
www.fsc.org

INTRODUCTION

On 20 January 2017 Donald Trump became the 45th President of the United States (see **Inauguration**), making him the *second* former *Apprentice* host to have been sworn into office this year (*see* **You're Fired!**). From that moment on, his name would dominate the year's headlines, along with Brexit, North Korea and Russian hacking. With these events towering over the news, it would be easy to forget the lesser-known, equally fascinating episodes that made 2017.

For it was also the year that the reincarnation of King Arthur went to court to challenge a parking fine he got at Stonehenge (see **Kings**), that German scientists revealed the best way to avoid slipping over on ice is to walk like a penguin (see **Penguins**) and that the Russian website that regulates the banning of websites accidentally banned itself (see **Internet**).

This book collects the extraordinary, bizarre and amusing moments that didn't quite make it to the front pages. Over the course of the past year we have read every publication we could get our hands on, from the *Washington Post* to the *Liverpool Echo*, and from the *Aurorasaurus* blog to the *Olive Oil Times*. We made a note of everything we found fascinating along the way – the mysteries (see **Toilet Paper, Used**), the regrets (see **Public, Don't Ask The**) and the triumphs (see **Failures**) – and split them up into essays, lists and occasional extracts of conversation between the four of us (see **Article 50**).

Our thanks are due to the thousands of reporters, investigators, bloggers and curious minds all over the world who dug out all the facts in this book first-hand. Long may they continue to do so, with or without bags on their head (see **Journalists**). We're also grateful to the adventurers, scientists, crocodile-punchers (see **Dickheads**) and recluses (see **Hermits**) who made the news happen in the first place. Because of their fine work there was never a shortage of material, or indeed a shortage of shortage material (see **Food and Drink**).

So here it is – in a year when the world stood on the brink of nuclear war (see **Korea, North**), when governments wobbled (see **UK General Election**), protesters protested (see **Protests, Non-Dirty**), and the only things that stayed strong and stable were the sales of fidget spinners (see **Fidget Spinners**), we present *The Book of the Year*: 365 different ways to look back on the utter madness that was 2017, the weirdest year since last year.

Dan, James, Anna and Andy
Covent Garden

THE BOOK OF THE YEAR

In which we learn …
How Brexit was triggered in a space egg, whether
computers or humans are better at Pac-Man, why
Australia is air-dropping kangaroo sausages, which
king doubles as an airline pilot, and who's
invented an underwater warehouse.

AARDVARKS

A zookeeper performed mouth-to-snout on an aardvark for an hour.

Only five aardvarks were born in Europe in 2016, so when one was born in the Polish city of Wrocław this year and struggled to survive, the head of the Small Mammals Division at the zoo there, Andrzej Miozga, did all he could do keep him alive. We spoke to Wrocław Zoo, and asked how you perform CPR on an aardvark. This is what they said:

'Mr Miozga acted on instinct, he cut the cord, placed the baby on his fleece jacket and started rubbing it vigorously but gently with a towel. He then placed the baby's snout in his mouth and blew the air in. At the same time he was doing chest compressions using his fingers and continued rubbing with a towel. After a few rounds the little heart started beating, but the cub still wasn't breathing. So Mr Miozga went on with the mouth-to-snout ventilation. Finally the baby started breathing on his own. All together it took about one hour after he came out.'

Meanwhile, in South Africa, scientists finally caught aardvarks having a drink, 250 years after the species was first described. It had long been assumed that they get all the water they need from the juicy bodies of termites, but a zoologist at Nelson Mandela Metropolitan University in Port Elizabeth, Graham Kerley, and his team announced that evidence exists for aardvarks drinking from puddles.*

* It was a big year in animal-puddle-drinking news. Researchers in Australia found that koalas, which were assumed to get all their water from eucalyptus leaves, have begun drinking from puddles – probably due to climate change.

If you're a human who wants to drink like an aardvark, a bar in Exeter is selling an 'aardvark cocktail', served with real ants. The drink is made with rum, lemongrass and lime, and is served with an ant chaser. The bar owner, Patrick Fogarty, describes it as 'crunchy yet satisfying'.

ABDICATIONS ▶

The Japanese Emperor wanted to abdicate, but wasn't allowed to tell anyone.

Japan's Emperor Akihito is banned from making political statements – including any that suggest he wants to abdicate. As a result, he had to make a speech very delicately hinting at his concerns about being able to fulfil his duties. The government eventually worked out what he meant and voted to allow him to step down.

But Akihito still has the problem of a distinct lack of heirs. Once the new emperor takes over, there will only be three heirs in total (emperors have to be men, although there is now some debate about this). Some experts are worried that if the youngest heir, Prince Hisahito, has no sons, the 2,600-year imperial line will be broken. Hisahito is only 11, so it's a little early to tell how this will play out.

As a young man, Emperor Akihito had a list of 800 candidates for marriage prepared for him, but rejected them all in favour of someone he met playing tennis. His main interest is marine biology and he's an expert on the goby fish. Interestingly, when the goby equivalent of an emperor (the dominant male) dies, he is replaced by the next in line; but if there are no males, then a female changes its sex and takes the 'emperor's' place.

The Japanese royal family has a claim to be the smallest royal family in the world (even Liechtenstein's is bigger, though its population is 3,400 times smaller). Strictly speaking, the Vatican is technically a monarchy – arguably making the Pope a one-man, elected royal family. The *largest* royal family is that of Saudi Arabia, with 4,000 princes and 30,000 other assorted relatives.

ABKHAZIA

A country that most of the world doesn't think exists, had an election that assumed most of its population didn't exist.

Abkhazia, a self-declared republic that's trying to break from Georgia, is currently recognised only by Russia, Nicaragua, Venezuela and, bizarrely, the tiny Pacific island of Nauru. Still, despite the lack of more general recognition, parliamentary elections were held there this year. Technically, elections in Abkhazia are deemed invalid if less than 25 per cent of people vote. But although only 21 per cent of the population voted on this occasion, the election was still declared valid as it was decided that any citizens who hold Georgian passports should not be regarded as Abkhazian nationals.

The country was also the subject of a critically acclaimed Romanian documentary this year, called *Ouale lui Tarzan*, or 'Tarzan's Testicles'. It told the story of the world's oldest primate centre, the Institute of Experimental Pathology and Therapy, in the Abkhazian capital, Sukhumi. The institute provided the monkeys that the Soviet Union sent into space in the 1980s and was founded by a man called Ilya Ivanov whose lifetime obsession was creating an ape-human hybrid.

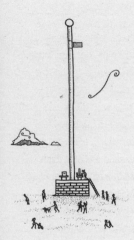

The head of the Lithuanian tourist board resigned after a social media campaign was found to be using pictures of other countries in its advertising. The campaign was called 'Real is Beautiful'.

ADVERTISING

The advertising for the newly opened Trump International Hotel & Tower in Vancouver claims it is six floors taller than it actually is.

Trump Hotels claim that the building is 69 storeys high when actually it is only 63. They arrived at their total by including below-ground storeys (which are mostly used for parking) in their calculations. In the course of his career, Trump has claimed that a 67-storey tower has

78 floors, that a 43-storey building has 46 floors, that a 44-storey building has 52 floors, that a 31-storey building has 41 floors, that a 70-storey building has 90 floors, and that he lives on the 66th floor of a 58-storey building.

Meanwhile, the Trump International Hotel & Tower in Toronto paid a reported $6 million *not* to advertise itself as a Trump hotel. The hotel decided to part ways with the Trump name following many years of construction delays, lawsuits and, more recently, because it had become a gathering point for protests against the president. The agreement they reached allows the management to remove all of Trump's branding from the 65-storey building (which, incidentally, has only 57 floors).

For more on Trump's towers, *see* **Trump Tower**.

AI ▶

The world champion of the ancient Chinese game of Go was beaten by a three-year-old Brit, who then immediately retired.

One way and another, it's been a bad year for humankind. We've been defeated by Artificial Intelligence at no-limit Texas hold 'em poker, Ms Pac-Man and the fighting game Super Smash Bros. And an AI has been developed that can write AI software better than humans. But perhaps the most crushing defeat came when AlphaGo, an AI program developed by Google's DeepMind Technologies, beat the world champion, China's Ke Jie, 3–0. AlphaGo was born in 2014, and was classed as British in the Go rankings as the team behind it is based in London. After beating the world champion it immediately retired. Deep-Mind CEO Demis Hassabis said that winning these games had been 'the highest possible pinnacle for AlphaGo as a competitive program'.

Owing to its incredible complexity, Go had been one of the final games at which humans could still beat the

In the game of Go, in which players take turns putting pebbles on to a board to win territory, there are $10^{10^{171}}$ possible combinations of move. If every grain of sand on Earth each contained the number of stars in the Milky Way, and each of those stars had a hundred planets, each with 10 billion humans, then the number of cells in all those humans would be *fewer than the number of zeros* in the number we're talking about.

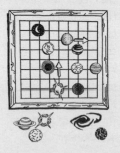

machines. Ke Jie later said, 'Last year, it was still quite human-like … but this year, it became like a god of Go.' Ke Jie's Chinese fans didn't see the interview, though: China (presumably for reasons of national pride) wouldn't allow the match to be shown on television or streamed online.

AIRDROPS

Australia is dropping sausages over its outback.
They come in two flavours: toad and kangaroo.

For years Australia has had a problem with cane toads (which are not indigenous to the continent). Many of its native animals eat them, and because the toads are toxic they tend to kill their predators. To combat this, scientists are dropping cane-toad-flavoured sausages, laced with a chemical to make predators feel sick, over the outback in the hope that it will deter them from biting real toads in the future. Rather more brutally, the Aussie government is also dropping poisoned sausages to deal with their feral cats, who are apparently partial to a kangaroo wiener.

This year Canada also combated an environmental issue with airdrops – of pregnant bison. Banff National Park has not had any bison for more than 100 years, and the ecosystem suffers from their absence. Conservationists collected pregnant bison from the nearby Elk Island and took them to the pastures of the Rocky Mountains. They spent the last 25 kilometres of their journey packed into shipping containers, dangling underneath a helicopter by a rope. Their horns were covered in plastic hoses to stop them injuring each other in transit.

For another flying sausage, *see* **Drones**. For a walking sausage, *see* **Stick Insects**.

Eleven 'promising' alien signals were reported this year. Unfortunately, they all turned out to be from mobile phones on Earth.

The Green Bank Telescope in West Virginia listens for radio signals that might indicate signs of intelligence from 692 of the nearest stars to Earth. It turns out, however, that the signals that aliens might send are very similar to those given out by mobile phones.

This wasn't the only 'alien' mystery that may have been solved this year. The Wow! signal was named in 1977, when an anomaly was found in a list of data, and astronomer Jerry R. Ehman was so impressed that he circled the numbers on the computer printout and wrote the comment 'Wow!'. Antonio Paris, an astronomy professor at St Petersburg College in Florida, has now suggested that the signal didn't come from an alien life form but from a couple of comets that were passing by at the time. Not everyone is convinced. Alan Fitzsimmons, a scientist at Queen's University Belfast, has described the theory as 'rubbish'.

The hunt for ET moved up a gear after the Five-hundred-meter Aperture Spherical Telescope (FAST) – the world's largest – joined the search. FAST is so vast that you could fill its dish with enough cornflakes to supply every person on Earth with one bowl's worth every day for a year – and still have some left over. Sited in Guizhou Province, south-west China, it hasn't proved universally popular: its construction involved the forcible displacement of 9,000 villagers.

Tom DeLonge, the former frontman of the band Blink-182, was named 'UFO Researcher of the Year' at the 2017 International UFO Congress. It came after emails leaked by WikiLeaks showed he had discussed aliens with Hillary Clinton's campaign manager, John Podesta. 'There's a lot that I can't say, but there's some that I can,' he said in his video acceptance speech. 'My job has only just begun on this subject matter and there's some big shit planned.'

AMAZON

The founder of Amazon.com became the world's richest person for just four hours.

———— ▼ ————

Donald Trump caused Amazon's value to plummet with a single tweet, in which he criticised their tax policies and said they robbed 'tax-paying retailers' of business. Immediately after he published the tweet, the company's share price dropped by $5.7 billion.

A surge in Amazon stock on 27 July increased Jeff Bezos's net worth by $1.1 billion, to $90.9 billion, which meant that he overtook Microsoft's Bill Gates (who is worth a measly $90.7 billion). However by the middle of the next day, Bezos's stock had fallen back, and a few days later he was down to third place behind Amancio Ortega, the owner of fashion company Zara.

Amazon's stock performance was largely thanks to increased sales. In the early days of the company, a bell would ring every time there was a sale, and staff would gather around to see if they knew the person who had made the purchase. They don't do that any more. If they did, then on their biggest sales day in 2017 (Amazon Prime Day, 11 July), a bell would need to be rung more than 80,000,000 times.* Each second is very important to Amazon. They have calculated that if their pages loaded just one second slower, it would cost them $1.6 billion in annual sales.

Amazon expanded beyond the online sector this year, opening a physical bookshop in New York. The company recognises that people have a habit of browsing in shops before buying their books online, and so registered a patent that stops customers in Amazon shops (including Whole Foods, which they acquired this year) from checking out competitors as they look around.

It's not the only patent application that Amazon has filed in the past few months. They have also invented an underwater warehouse, in which everything is stored in watertight boxes at the bottom of a lake. Each is assigned a unique sound, which, when triggered, inflates a balloon that floats the box to the surface. The idea is that this will be more efficient than having people or machines

* That's the equivalent of every church bell in England being rung 2,400 times.

8

fetch the packages, because they'll be transported by the water buoyancy instead. Amazon also holds a patent for a flying warehouse.

ANTARCTICA

The Foreign Office warned Britons to look out for terrorists in the Antarctic.

The population of Britain's 660,000 square miles of Antarctic Territory may only be 250 but, as the Foreign Office points out, you can never be too careful. According to official guidelines it issued in May, 'although there's no recent history of terrorism in the British Antarctic Territory, attacks can't be ruled out.' Visitors should therefore 'be vigilant', but they'll probably be fine: the last crime to be committed anywhere on the continent was back in 2003, and involved computer hacking. Even that wasn't home-grown – it was done remotely from Romania.

Scientists from the University of Edinburgh discovered 91 new volcanoes under the ice of Antarctica, meaning that part of the continent may be the most densely packed area of volcanoes in the world.

One Briton who braved the terrorist threat was Patrick Bergel, great-grandson of Ernest Shackleton, who made the first ever crossing of Antarctica by car. It was a month-long, 3,600-mile trip, sponsored by Hyundai, in a normal family car (although it was adapted to run on jet fuel). To avoid littering, the team had to drag all their excrement behind them in a huge fuel drum.

When he was first asked to make the journey, Bergel hadn't even taken his driving test. He modestly insisted that 'compared to what my great-grandfather did, this was one thousandth as hard'.

As if going on four wheels wasn't hard enough, Canadian Hank Van Weelden attempted a 700-mile bike ride on a custom-made, £10,000 bicycle across Antarctica. He was meant to complete the journey in 30 days, but, after six days of pulling a 90-kilo pack in minus 40°C temperatures, he dropped out. He later said, 'I got a taste of it … and I got my ass kicked by it.'

APOLOGIES

For a Cambodian actress who was just too sexy, *see* **Bans**; for a politician who wrestled a journalist to the ground, *see* **Body Slams**; for a priest who made a fashion faux-pas, *see* **Carnivals**; for mistakenly banning a Roman God, *see* **Censorship**; for a name worth apologising for, *see* **Donalds**; for accidentally invading a country, *see* **Gibraltar**; for a bouquet of flowers from the taxman, *see* **HMRC**; for hiring interns via a bikini competition, *see* **Nuclear Power Plants**; for speech-stealing in Ghana, *see* **Plagiarism**; for planting over a children's football field, *see* **Trees**; and for breaking a passenger's nose but denying freezing a giant rabbit to death, *see* **United Airlines**.

APPS

If you want to make an emergency confession, there's an app for that.

A new app, developed in Spain and called Confessor GO, tells you where your nearest priest is for confession, and maps the best route to him. Handily, it also tells you the priest's name and the year he was ordained. In addition, it includes the Ten Commandments to prompt you to recall what you might need to confess. Unlike Uber, the priest doesn't come to you, but on the plus side, he doesn't charge extra at busy times.

Other recent apps have been built that will help you if you want to:

▶ Find a celebrity-lookalike partner. The dating app Badoo has added a feature that allows users to look for celebrity lookalikes. Soon after launch, there were 1,405 people on the app who (supposedly) looked like Ed Sheeran.

▶ Find out where the nearest iceberg is, providing you're in Canada.

▶ Stop buying things while drunk. Once you've consumed alcohol up to a self-imposed limit, the app stops your bank card working. However, for the app to take effect you need to be sober enough to inform it that you've been drinking.

Donald Trump has only downloaded one app on to his phone – Twitter. He has, however, *inspired* over 250 apps for Android alone, including one that measures how many times a man interrupts a woman, one where you can draw your own executive order, and a third, DJ Trump, which uses a huge archive of words The Donald has said to enable you to make the US President say anything you want.

ARRESTS, HUMAN

A Mafia boss famous for having a permanent erection was caught in Spain after seven years on the run.

Francesco Castriotta said his priapism was thanks to his out-of-control cocaine habit. As he sat in court during a previous hearing with a bag of ice on his aching groin, one policeman remarked that he could 'expect a stiff sentence'.

Other notable arrests included:

▶ *A man in India was arrested for trying to create a fake ID card using the name Osama bin Laden.* He even uploaded a blurred photo of the former Al-Qaeda leader as the profile picture. Police discovered the man's real name was Saddam Hussain.

▶ *A woman in Bangladesh, who believed she was her husband's third wife, had him arrested after discovering she was in fact his 25th, of 28.* Police arrested him at the home of his 27th wife.

▶ *A man was arrested by New York State Police for driving under the influence of alcohol.* This only came to international attention because Joseph Talbot didn't want anyone to know about it. After learning that his local paper, the *Times of Wayne County*, had covered the story, he tried to buy every copy of the relevant edition to stop people finding out. Unfortunately, the fact that he managed to purchase around 900 copies became a story in its own right – and then spread.

ARRESTS, NON-HUMAN

For a box under arrest, *see* **Art**; for a rubber duck under arrest, *see* **Ducks, Rubber**; for a pigeon under arrest, *see* **Iraq**.

ART

A giant snow globe was made using the confetti meant for Hillary Clinton's election night.

It was designed by artist Bunny Burson, whose former works include collages made from 'chads' – the punched-out pieces of ballot paper that famously decided the 2000 Presidential election in favour of George W. Bush. It took Burson two weeks to find the confetti that had been loaded into Hillary's victory cannons ready to celebrate the election result last November, and when she did, she got the company who produced it to write a letter of verification. She then placed the confetti in a glass case with the slogan 'And Still I Rise' which she took from a poem by Maya Angelou, a close friend of the Clintons.

In a less overtly political act, French artist Abraham Poincheval attempted to live like a chicken, and successfully hatched nine eggs. He sat on the eggs in a glass case, in a Paris museum, for a month. They were underneath his bottom on a 'laying table' which had a dug-out section to stop the eggs from being squashed. Poincheval said that his work, *Egg*, 'raises the question of metamorphosis and gender'. Despite animal scientists saying that the task was nearly impossible due to humans' lower body temperature, after 21 days, nine of his original ten eggs hatched. The chicks were sent to a farm.*

In February, Poincheval spent a week inside a 12-tonne limestone boulder slightly larger than he was, with only small niches in which he stored food, water and his excrement. As he emerged, he said he was 'a little dazed', which I imagine is totally normal after one week living in a rock'. Eccentricity runs in the family: his father invented a pill to make farts smell of roses.

In America, Russian artist Fyodor Pavlov-Andreevich faced potential charges of public lewdness, criminal trespassing and disorderly conduct after he was arrested for having himself delivered, naked inside a clear plastic box, to the exclusive Met Gala in New York. This was the fifth time he'd had himself sent to an art event – his aim being to donate himself to institutions that have 'difficulty understanding or accepting performance art'. In a statement, his friends clarified that the box had also been arrested. In their view, the charges were ludicrous. 'Even the policemen were showing signs of having fun.'

ASHES ▶

Carrie Fisher's ashes were placed in an urn shaped like a massive Prozac pill.

The giant pill was one of her favourite ornaments. At her funeral in January her brother said of it, 'We felt it was where she'd want to be.'

ARTICLE 50

Andy: The letter we ended up sending to activate Article 50 was six pages long ... but it was nearly 100 pages long.

Dan: That's a big edit.

Andy: They didn't start with 100 pages and cut it down! Government sources said there were two options, but they eventually picked the six-pager. Maybe they thought sending 100 was a bit excessive.

Dan: Who wrote the letter? Was it Theresa May?

James: Well, she probably had some civil service assistance, but she definitely signed it. She gave it a 'wet signature' – i.e. with pen and ink – but unfortunately, she signed with a Parker pen that was once manufactured in Britain but is now made in France.

Anna: And Article 50 was ratified in Norman French. As a law passes in the House of Lords, the Lords say the words *'La Reyne le veult'*, meaning 'the Queen allows it'.

James: Another thing about the letter is that it was delivered by Sir Tim Barrow, the UK's permanent representative at the EU. He took it from Britain's embassy in Brussels to the EU headquarters, known as the 'Space Egg'.

Andy: 'Space Egg?'

James: That's just a nickname. It's a futuristic oval building, set inside a cube made from recycled window frames from across Europe. But the location is pretty interesting. The back of the building was a Nazi headquarters during their occupation of Europe.

Dan: Ah, speaking of the Nazis, I read that Article 50 was put in place partly because of right-wing politics. The guy who wrote it did so at a time when Austria had a far-right politician called Jörg Haider, and people were worried he might be elected. So Article 50 was written partly to make it easier for a country to storm out of the EU.

James: Yes. The guy actually who wrote Article 50 is called Lord John Kerr, and what I love about that is that in Spain his name would be Juan Kerr.

Andy: But, hang on, nobody in Spain would get that joke. They all speak Spanish. Except for the British expats, and after Brexit they won't be around to explain.

Anna: Well, it's not just expats. We also need to work out what to do with the words 'United Kingdom' in the Lisbon Treaty, which is the document underpinning the whole EU. There are 12 mentions of the UK in it, and at the moment they think they'll leave them in, as it'll be too much bureaucratic hassle to remove every mention.

Dan: Is it true that the Article 50 letter was given a load of fake routes before Sir Tim delivered it to confuse saboteurs?

Andy: Maybe. It definitely did have an armed guard on the Eurostar, and the *Daily Telegraph* reported that his path to the Space Egg was kept secret in case ultra-Remainers grabbed the letter from him.

James: But I went on Google Maps and did the journey from one place to the other and it's extremely short, so there's not much space for alternative routes.

Andy: That's right. It's about 300 metres.

Anna: Or 328 yards, as we'll call it after 2019.

This year people have also chosen to have their ashes sprinkled:

▶ *In the toilet of a baseball stadium.* The ashes of New York plumber and baseball fan Roy Riegel have been sprinkled in baseball stadium toilets all over America by his best friend, Roy McDonald. McDonald said he has sometimes used the toilet at the same time as scattering his friend, but that 'I always flush in between.'

▶ *Over a ferry.* A ceremony on an Australian ferry went wrong when the ashes were blown back on deck and over the passengers. The daughter of the deceased said it was her mother 'having the last laugh'.*

▶ *In a hockey penalty box.* Hockey player Bob Probert had his ashes sprinkled in his team's penalty box (aka the 'sin bin') because, having been involved in 200 mid-match punch-ups in the course of his career, he had spent 3,300 minutes there.

▶ *In two separate places.* A survey of Britain's funeral directors revealed that they're now agreeing ever more frequently to split ashes up to stop angry families arguing over them.

* It could be worse. In late 2016 a man tried to scatter his opera-loving friend's ashes at New York's Metropolitan Opera. Other members of the audience, however, assumed he was a terrorist who was trying to spread anthrax. He apologised profusely, saying it had been 'a sweet gesture to a dying friend that went completely and utterly wrong in ways that I could never have imagined'.

AUSTRALIA ▶

For exotic sausages, *see* **Airdrops**; for a faceful of mum, *see* **Ashes**; for people who are not quite as Australian as they thought, *see* **Citizenship**; for destroying priceless collections, *see* **Cock-Ups**; for punching a crocodile, *see* **Dickheads**; for the world's biggest footprint, *see* **Dinosaurs**; for herding from the air, *see* **Drones**; for giving carp STDs, *see* **Fish**; for what not to put in your ballot papers, *see* **Glitter**; for billboards asking people not to visit, *see* **Immigration**; for a homeless messiah, *see* **Jesus**; for multiple marsupials, *see* **Kangaroos**; for a 'royal' family, *see* **Micronations**; for a patriotic pop song, *see* **National**

Anthems; for old kangaroos, *see* **Paintings**; for dangerous Leons, see **Queensland**; for those happy about hacking, *see* **Ransomware**; for ancient sloths, *see* **RIP**; for a rapper in the sea, *see* **Runner, Doing a**; for milking a killer, *see* **Spiders**; for boobs *see* **Swearing**; and for MPs in khakis, *see* **Ties**.

AVIATION ▶

The King of the Netherlands revealed he's been secretly moonlighting as an airline pilot.

Since ascending the throne in 2013, King Willem-Alexander has been co-piloting commercial flights twice a month, without telling passengers. He only ever pilots short-haul flights, though, and makes sure to always return home the same day, in case he is suddenly needed as king.

Meanwhile, in Afghanistan, two MPs went one better, and took control of a plane they weren't even on. After learning the MPs had missed their flight from Kabul to Bamiyan, supporters of the pair apparently organised a team to stop the plane from landing at Bamiyan Airport by blocking the runway. It was therefore forced to fly back to Kabul, where it picked up the two politicians. According to Al Jazeera, one of them, Abdul Rahman Shaheedani, said, 'Everyone will now know who I am, and what my power is.' Shaheedani added that he hadn't asked his supporters to force the plane to return to Kabul.

A flight in China was delayed on the tarmac after an elderly woman threw nine coins at the engine for good luck. Eight of the coins missed their target and only one actually made it into the engine, but staff nonetheless had to make a full examination and the flight was delayed by five hours.

Another MP embroiled in an aviation scandal was Indian politician Ravindra Gaikwad, who admitted to hitting an air steward 25 times with his slipper, and breaking the steward's glasses. His excuse was that he had been given an economy seat rather than business. Air India explained that Mr Gaikwad had been placed in economy rather than business because there was no business class on this particular all-economy flight.

AVOCADOS

The world's first avocado restaurant, where every dish contains avocado, opened in New York. It ran out of avocados on its first day.

Once all the kinks were ironed out, the restaurant became very popular. They went through 650 pounds of avocado a week, helped, no doubt, by the fact that diners who particularly like avocados can double the amount of avocado on their dish for an extra $2.

Avocados reached peak hipster this year. Millennials were told the only reason they can't afford houses is that they keep spending their money on avocado on toast. They're dangerous, too – they were blamed for a rash of brunch-time hand injuries to people ineptly trying to cut them up. The British Association of Plastic, Reconstructive and Aesthetic Surgeons demanded that warnings should be placed on all avocados.

While demand has increased, supply has fallen. Avocados are an 'alternate-bearing crop', which means that every other year the harvests are smaller. Add that to flooding in Peru and workers' strikes in Mexico, and you have what America's National Public Radio (NPR) has dubbed the Guacapocalypse. And with President Trump planning large tariffs on goods coming from Mexico to pay for his wall, it may be that avocado-lovers will soon be waiting even longer to get on the housing ladder.

Marks & Spencer is lasering barcodes into its avocados. This will apparently save 10 tonnes of paper and 5 tonnes of glue every single year. In early trials the lasers blasted too deep, but now they just take off the top surface of the skin. The store also said they were thinking about lasering pumpkins for Halloween.

In which we learn …
How to turn urine into beer, what to do with a radioactive boar, why the Incognito Bandit was so badly named, who wants to make a wall out of hammocks, and why you shouldn't keep all your cocaine in your helicopter.

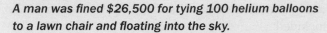

BALLOONS

A man was fined $26,500 for tying 100 helium balloons to a lawn chair and floating into the sky.

Canadian Daniel Boria pleaded guilty to the charge of 'dangerous operation of an aircraft'. In the course of his stunt, which was inspired by a scene in the film *Up*, he was lifted 4 kilometres above the ground, directly into the flight path of commercial aircraft. Two jets actually flew under him before he drifted back down, sustaining minor ankle injuries as he landed. Explaining that he'd done this to promote his cleaning company, he insisted, 'We knew what we were doing,' and added, 'I chose to fly a chair; not because it is easy but because it is hard… [They] didn't charge the Wright Brothers.' The judge was less impressed, telling Boria that he had been 'unconscionably stupid'. Police also confiscated his GoPro video of the stunt.

More legitimately, Google is building a massive network of balloons, known as Project Loon, that travel on the edge of space, providing Internet to rural areas. Project Loon managed to restore Internet access to thousands of people in Peru after huge floods knocked out local networks – although when one of the balloons crash-landed in Colombia, farmers took it to police as a suspected UFO. Even more exciting is NASA's Super Pressure Balloon, currently being tested, which is going to study cosmic rays from 33 kilometres up. Fully inflated, it's four times as big as the *Titanic*.

North and South Korea have been bombarding each other with balloons for years. South Korean activists have sent chocolate snacks across the border (the government wishes they wouldn't), while North Korean balloons carry propaganda leaflets. The current North Korean approach is a step up from the past: until this year, it was sending balloons filled with cigarette butts and used toilet paper.

20

Bank robbers and other bandits sought in America this
year included:

The Shirt Mask Bandit. Wore a shirt as a mask. Still got
caught.

The Incognito Bandit. Nobody knew who he was, until he
was apprehended.

The Bag Trick Bandit. Kept putting his hand in a bag and
pretending to have a gun.

The Coast to Coast Bandit. Only robbed banks in New
York and Los Angeles.

The Texas Butthole Tickling Bandit. Robbed the homes of
single men and poked them as they slept.

The Blueberry Bandit. Stole $100,000 worth of
blueberries and other fruits.

The Foul Mouth Bandit. Swore at people as he robbed
them.

The Lunchtime Bandit. Only robbed banks between noon
and 1 p.m.

The Hangover Bandit. Stank of booze.

The Bedrock Bandit. Stole a large fossil from a Denver
shop by shoving it down his trousers.

The Spelling Bee Bandit. Passed cashiers a note saying
this was a 'robery'.

BANKNOTES

Jane Austen looks too attractive on the new £10 note.

The only completed portrait of Austen in her lifetime
is of the back of her head. Painted in 1804 by her older
sister, Cassandra, it shows Jane sitting by a lake, but

Somalia announced plans to press their first banknotes since 1991 (as a result of this long gap, up to 98 per cent of Somali banknotes currently in circulation are counterfeit). Officials also said that they will upgrade the design from the old one, which featured a woman with a baby strapped to her and waving a rifle, a shovel and a rake.

unfortunately facing the wrong way. We can't even see her hair because she's wearing a massive bonnet. The Bank of England has used a prettified version of the only front view we have of her – a rough sketch, also by Cassandra, about which her niece wrote, 'There is a look which I recognise as hers … though the general resemblance is not strong.' Another niece added that it was 'hideously unlike' her.

It's not the fact that the Bank of England is using an inaccurate portrait that has upset Austen's biographers, though. It's the fact that the Bank has opted for an 'airbrushed' version, based on Cassandra's original sketch and painted after Jane's death by her nephew. Her angry biographers say the portrait makes her look far more attractive than she actually was.

The notes are made of a plastic substance called polypropylene, a material which has also been used in thermal underwear, model planes, Tic Tac boxes, the stickers on Rubik's Cubes, and parts of Tenerife Cathedral. To make it thin enough to be turned into notes it is blown into a giant bubble which grows to the height of a four-storey building, before collapsing in on itself. The result is a thin transparent film that is waterproof, rip-resistant and slippery. Too slippery, in fact – cash machines across the UK have had to be upgraded because most of the old machines couldn't properly handle the plastic notes.

BANKS, NON-SPERM

The World Bank's chief economist refused to sign off the World Development Report if more than 2.6 per cent of the words it contained were 'and'.

Theoretically, the day job of the World Bank is to provide loans to developing countries, but at the moment its management seems to be more concerned with a long-winded style of writing known as 'bankspeak', which the bank worries makes financial statements at best dull and at worst unreadable. In particular, it wants to clamp down on 'and', the overuse of which, according to chief economist Paul Romer, is the reason why only 32 per cent of reports created by the bank are ever read by anyone other than the author. Up until now, the 'and' rate in World Bank reports has been 3.4 per cent, so the institution has a little way to go to achieve its self-imposed limit. Donald Trump's 'and' rate in his inauguration speech, by comparison, was 5.2 per cent. Paul Romer's 'and' rate in the 'about me' section on his personal website is 3.28 per cent.*

The Bank of England is similarly concerned about impenetrable language and is taking steps to address the problem. According to Nemat Shafik, the former deputy governor for markets, she and her colleagues have been studying the prose style of the Dr Seuss books to find ways to make the bank's communications more comprehensible among the general public.

* The 'and' rate in this article is 3.5 per cent, not counting the 'and'† in this footnote. Sorry, Paul.

† Or this one.

BANKS, SPERM ▶

Richard Branson opened the world's first dyslexic-only sperm bank.

The project was launched as part of a campaign designed to remove the stigma of dyslexia, and was inspired by a 2015 news story that the UK's largest sperm bank was turning away donors with the condition. This is surprising, as the UK is currently suffering a severe sperm shortage. The National Sperm Bank – an organisation set up in 2014 to deal with the shortage – closed last year, having attracted only seven donors.

The best place to store human sperm might be in giant tubes inside the moon. That's the conclusion of a team of scientists from the University of Yamanashi, Japan, who managed this year to breed mice from some freeze-dried mouse sperm (*see* **Mice, Space**). They think that storing sperm on the moon might prove a useful safeguard for humankind in the event of a nuclear apocalypse or catastrophic environmental disaster.

Turkish Angora goats also got their own sperm bank this year. The number of goats that produce the finest wool has declined sharply in recent years, but scientists predict that goats inseminated with high-quality sperm from the new bank will give birth to animals that produce three times as much wool.

BANS

Ban-happy countries of 2017 included:

▶ **Country:** Cambodia

Banned: Actress Denny Kwan

Reason: Being – according to the country's Culture and Fine Arts Ministry – 'too sexy' to act. Her ban is in place for one year. Kwan has apologised and said she will try not to be so sexy in the future.

▶ **Country:** Ukraine

Banned: Steven Seagal

Reason: Being a threat to national security. The ban stems from Seagal's association with other post-Soviet countries, notably Russia. Last year, for example, he was personally presented with a Russian passport by Vladimir Putin (Putin's spokesperson claims, however, that Seagal was only given a passport because he would not stop asking for one). The action hero joins a 'banned' list that includes any Russian movie made since January 2014, the lead singer of Limp Bizkit and Gerard Depardieu.

▶ **Country:** Uzbekistan

Banned: A video game that doesn't exist

Reason: Thirty-eight video games have been banned by the government because they conflict with the country's values. The list includes Call of Duty: Black Ops; Dead Space; Left 4 Dead; Left 4 Dead 2; and Left 4 Dead 3. There is no Left 4 Dead 3.

▶ **Country:** Turkey

Banned: Wikipedia

Reason: Turkey is reportedly unhappy with some articles on Wikipedia that associate the state with terrorism. According to the 'Censorship of Wikipedia' Wiki page, the country had previously only censored specific articles, such as 'Vulva', 'Human Penis', 'Vagina', 'Scrotum', and '2015 Turkish General Election Polls'.

BEAUTY PAGEANT WINNERS

For Miss World *see* **Gibraltar**; for Miss Great Grimsby and District, *see* **Journalists**; and for Miss USA *see* **Nuclear Power Plants**.

BEER

A Danish brewery made a batch of beer using 50,000 litres of two-year-old urine from a music festival.

Rather than follow the normal route of using animal manure to fertilise the barley that then makes beer, the Nørrebro brewery opted for music-festival urine instead. The brewery was at pains to point out that no actual urine would end up in the beer (named 'Pisner'). The vital fluid was collected from the Roskilde music festival held two years ago – the brewers were only aiming for

Californian brewery Stone Brewing has developed a beer made from recycled sewage water. It's called Full Circle and tastes 'very clean', according to the man who made it.

25,000 litres and managed to pull in twice as much. At the time, an organiser said, 'We've got urinals right next to the stages … so we're hoping to collect some rock star pee.' Drinkers may therefore now be enjoying beer brewed with the urine of Pharrell Williams, Florence (and her Machine), and Sir Paul McCartney. The batch turned out fine, at least in taste terms: one satisfied drinker said, 'If it had tasted even a bit like urine, I would put it down.'

—— ▼ ——

A 'fake beer factory' was busted in China. Workers were making 600,000 cans of fake Budweiser every month, scooping the beer in from plastic containers with their bare hands.

Meanwhile, in Belgium, MPs were told that they would no longer be served free beer and wine during parliamentary sessions. The decision followed a report by an ethics committee that concluded a) that most workplaces don't give you free alcohol, and b) that the ready availability of alcohol was making some MPs 'quite unpleasant'. Initially, MPs voted against the removal of their booze privilege, but there was such a large public outcry about it that they eventually agreed to pay for their drinks from now on.

BEES ▶

Two thousand bees were stolen in Beeston.

It may not have been the biggest bee heist of the year, but it was the one that happened in the most appropriately named place. One way and another, it wasn't a good year for bees: as well as the ones stolen in Beeston,

Nottinghamshire, 200,000 were stolen in Kent, a million in Austria, a $1 million bee-stealing ring was uncovered in California, and more than 400 independent beehive thefts were reported in New Zealand in just six months.

Why steal bees? Well, firstly, they're very hard to identify: it's hard for a bee owner to look at one and say with any certainty, 'That's my bee.' Secondly they're worth a lot: the price of renting a beehive in California, where almond growers rely on them to pollinate the trees, can be as much as $200 for the season. And the prices have been skyrocketing in recent years, due to abnormally high mortality rates among bees (last year bee deaths in the US fell to their lowest level for years, but even so a third of all bees in the US died).

British bees are also under threat, but Tesco stores in Cornwall and Devon have been doing their bit to help them. They collect any sugar that has been spilt (and is therefore not fit for human consumption) and leave it out for the bees to help them keep going through the winter. It has to be white sugar: brown sugar gives bees dysentery.

BELARUS

The president of Belarus celebrated Freedom Day by arresting 700 protesters in Minsk.

To be honest, Belarus doesn't have much freedom to celebrate at the moment: its press is the second least free in Europe, only beaten by Turkey, which has more journalists in prison than any other country in the world. After President Lukashenko's crackdown on protesters, the headline on the website of the largest state-controlled Belarusian newspaper, *Belarus Today*, was 'Everything is calm in Minsk'. A public outcry led to the headline being deleted two days later.

Belarus invented a fictional country to be the enemy in its war games with Russia, Zapad 2017. Belarusian citizens enthusiastically adopted the idea and made up a foreign ministry, flag, history and Wikipedia page for the nation of Veyshnoria. Hundreds of Belarusians applied for Veyshnorian citizenship on a spoof website.

BHUTAN

India and China clashed over Bhutan, meaning a third of the world's population could have gone to war over a country with the same population as Buckinghamshire.

◆

One reason Indians are worried about road-building in Bhutan is that China is improving its roads in disputed territories much faster than India's specially created 'Border Roads Organisation'. That said, what the organisation lacks in speed, they make up for in poetry. Recent roads built in Bhutan include signs such as 'After drinking whisky, driving is risky'; 'Going faster will see disaster'; and the slightly less successful couplet: 'Don't hurry, be cool, since heaven is already full'.

The dispute was over a region known as Doklam in Bhutan and Donglang in China. When China started building roads in the area, Bhutan asked its friend India for help. India sent troops, who first formed a human chain to stop the construction work and then set up camp in the area. China responded by moving in its own troops. India wasn't acting entirely altruistically: it owns a strip of land nearby called 'the chicken neck' which separates one part of India from the rest. If China were to invade, 50 million Indians would be cut off from the Indian mainland.

So China and India – which have a combined population of 2.6 billion and around 400 nuclear warheads between them – both sent troops to an obscure area in Bhutan. War was not in anybody's interest though, so to avoid conflict the troops were all unarmed. They weren't allowed to strike each other either, and if one side tried to advance, the other could only stop them by chest-bumping and jostling them out of the way. Fortunately, after a 73-day standoff, the leaders of the two countries met and agreed to pursue a peaceful solution.

Meanwhile, Bhutan is dealing with the rise of an alt-right movement, but unlike the nationalism in Europe and America it is mostly interested in diet. The vegetarian-right is a loose coalition of politicians and commentators who think it should be a crime to eat meat in the country. It's already illegal to kill animals for meat in Bhutan, but you can import it to eat, and paradoxically the country is, per capita, the highest meat consumer in South Asia. The veggie-right is pushing to make it illegal both to import meat and to eat it.

BLINK-182, LEAD SINGERS OF

For the one who was named UFO Researcher of the Year, *see* **Aliens**; for the one who believes he successfully cursed a music festival, *see* **Witchcraft**.

BOAR

Hunters in Texas are now allowed to sneak up on wild boar in hot air balloons.

The Texas government – which is currently fighting a two-million strong 'hog apocalypse' – legalised shooting boar from hot air balloons because they're quieter and steadier than helicopters. State representative Mark Keogh said the plan was a 'western, swashbuckling, cowboying type of way to deal with things. It's part of the culture.'

Boar are everywhere. This year they've been wandering the streets of Rome, feeding on the garbage that the new city's mayor has been unable to get removed on a regular basis. Near Vienna, one 'massive' boar chased Britain's ambassador to Austria, while he was walking in the woods. He got away, but injured himself scrabbling up a pile of wet logs. (For the record, the best way to escape a charging boar is to climb up something.)

Since Japan's 2011 nuclear accident, the abandoned town of Fukushima has been overtaken by hundreds of 'potentially radioactive' wild boar. Sadly, this won't lead to a thriving sausage industry – people can't eat them due to the radiation risk. The logical answer – hunting and burying them – has its problems, too, since Japan is running out of grave space. There is a special incinerator that can filter out radioactive materials, but unfortunately it can only handle three boar a day – and 13,000 have been killed in the last two years alone.

In Iraq, three ISIS militants who were preparing an ambush in some reeds were killed by a herd of wild boar. Five others were injured.

BOATS

The world's first zero-emissions boat set off around the world. The trip will take twice as long as the first ever around-the-world voyage.

A family in Scotland launched a Playmobil pirate ship into the North Sea with a note asking anyone who found it to take a photo and send the ship back to sea. It reached Denmark, then Sweden (where it was found in a tree), and it was then picked up by a Norwegian research vessel which took it to Cape Verde so that it could sail the Atlantic.

The boat, *Energy Observer*, is covered in solar panels and wind turbines. As well as powering the ship, they provide energy to take water from the sea and remove the hydrogen, which is then stored in tanks and used for power when it's still, cloudy or night-time. The boat is slow, travelling at an average speed of 10mph, and it will stop at 101 ports along the way to promote renewable energy. The full journey will take six years, which is twice as long as Ferdinand Magellan took in 1522.

It's not the slowest boat of the year, though. That honour belongs to an engineless barge made of recycled material that has been pulled all the way from Liverpool to Riddlesden in Yorkshire by artist and university lecturer Ben Cummins. He hopes to reach London by 2037. 'Some

people get married, or get a mortgage,' he told reporters. 'I've got this.'

Perhaps the pluckiest small boat of the year is called *Undaunted*. It's 42 inches long and looks a little bit like a top-loading washing machine. Its owner, Matt Kent, hoped to cross the Atlantic in it, but had to turn back after just 24 hours when it developed problems. He's planning to try again next year, after the hurricane season. Matt describes *Undaunted* as 'a great storm shelter' but also as 'a terrible boat'.

For Mr Boats Botes *see* **Names**; for *Boaty McBoatface see* **Oceans** and **Public, Don't Ask the**.

BODY SLAMS

A US Republican candidate charged with body-slamming a journalist made his fortune in customer service.

Guardian journalist Ben Jacobs reported that when he asked Republican candidate Greg Gianforte about his party's healthcare plans, Gianforte grabbed him by the neck, slammed him to the floor and broke his glasses.* Gianforte's election campaign was not affected by this incident (largely due to the fact that Montana has an early voting system and half the votes had already been cast) and he successfully won a seat in the House of Representatives the very next day. During his acceptance speech, Gianforte apologised to Jacobs for the attack.

As well as founding RightNow Technologies, which sold software that advised businesses on how best to answer customers' questions, Gianforte has set up a foundation dedicated to supporting the work of faith-based organisations. In 2009 it helped fund a creationist museum in Montana that aims to prove that dinosaurs and humans co-existed. One exhibit features Noah's ark with dinosaurs aboard.

* Ben Jacobs has donated those broken glasses to Washington DC's Newseum, a seven-storey museum dedicated to news – past and breaking. Other exhibits include: the abandoned car left at Dulles Airport by the 9/11 terrorists; a large standing section of the Berlin Wall; and Lady Gaga's meat dress.

BORDER WALL

Anna: Ideas proposed for the US border wall include a trench full of nuclear waste, a one-way mirror and three million hammocks.

Dan: Three million hammocks?

Anna: Well, that one isn't really a serious proposal. After the bidding process started, a lot of people started suggesting ideas and, as well as actual architects, a lot of comedians and artists got involved.

James: For one thing, hammocks wouldn't work because people could just go under them…

Dan: …or over them. It depends how high up the tree they're tied.

Andy: Is the idea that you get to the border, you see the hammock and you think, 'I can't be bothered now, I think I'll just have a rest'?

Anna: I'm not sure. They're the idea of an artist called Jennifer Meridian. She's also proposed a wall of pipe organs and a wall of thousands and thousands of lighthouses.

Dan: Nice. And the one-way mirror is an incredible idea.

Andy: Yes. That's another artist's proposal: meaning you can see Mexico from the USA but they can't see you.

Dan: What's the point in that?

Andy: Well, you could still see someone approaching if they were going to try and climb the mirror, but they don't know if they're being watched.

James: Ah, OK. I thought if people got to the mirror, they might think, 'It looks exactly the same over there as it does over here. I might as well stay.'

Andy: Another proposal involves leaving a 4-inch gap at the bottom of the wall so little animals can cross. More than a hundred species cross the area, so if the wall goes up a lot of them will struggle to mate.

James: I wonder if all the animals will then evolve to be 4 inches tall, so there will be tiny buffalo galloping across the plain?

Andy: Very possibly.

James: Either way, did you know the first ever demarcation between America and Mexico was just a line?

Anna: Really? What did they draw the line with, a marker pen?

James: I'm not sure. I suppose paint.

Andy: You can't paint sand!

Dan: Well, you can, but then you can just nudge the line. So you might arrive one morning and think, 'Hey, my country's smaller than it was yesterday!'

The president of Brazil moved out of his official residence because he thought it was haunted.

President Michel Temer reportedly found the Alvorada Palace too spooky. 'I felt something strange there,' he said. 'I wasn't able to sleep right from the first night. The energy wasn't good.' Luckily he had a spare palace to move into.*

Temer was perhaps right to feel a sense of foreboding. After being recorded allegedly discussing hush money with the Batista brothers, who run the country's biggest meat-packing firm, JBS, he found himself in the middle of a huge corruption scandal that has engulfed Brazilian politics and has led (among other things) to the largest fine in Brazilian history: $3 billion, levied against JBS. Incidentally, the previous record – a $2.6 billion fine paid by the engineering company Odebrecht – also arose from the bribing of politicians, some of whom Odebrecht doesn't seem to have held in particularly high esteem. Their code name for Deputy Congressman Jarbas Vasconcelos was 'Viagra'; Congressman Paes Landim was 'Decrepit'; and Senator Edison Lobão was known as 'Squalid'. Rio de Janeiro's ex-mayor, who is accused of

34

taking millions of dollars in bribes before the Olympics, was called 'the Little Nervous One'.

Some people think the political situation in Brazil is complicated, but it can actually be explained in one sentence:

In 2016, President Dilma Rousseff was impeached, the main charge being that she had massaged the country's accounts to make it appear that it was doing better than it was, the impeachment being led by a guy called Eduardo Cunha, who was then found guilty (after an investigation code-named Operation Car Wash) of hiding $40 million worth of bribes in secret bank accounts, and who was then allegedly paid to keep quiet by Rousseff's deputy president Michel Temer, who took over from Rousseff when she was impeached (despite the fact that he had already been banned from running for president for eight years for financial irregularities), whose aide Rodrigo Rocha Loures was arrested with a bag containing $150,000, and who was busted when he was recorded talking about hush money to the Batista brothers, who are the owners of a meat-packing company JBS, a fact that came to light when JBS was found not only to be selling rotten meat but also discussing $160,000 in potential kickbacks to Aécio Neves (who ran against Rousseff in the last election), as well as paying $150,000 in a suitcase to *another* politician, Rocha Loures (who later returned the money, claiming he hadn't looked in the bag), and paying $500,000 to Aécio Neves's cousin, who then deposited it into the bank account of another politician, Zezé Perrella, whose helicopter was seized in November 2013 and found to be containing 450 kilograms of cocaine.

Brazil's top court spent a lot of time debating whether to annul the results of the last election. If they decide to do so, then the president will likely appeal, a process which will take them to October 2018, when there's another election due anyway.

BREXIT ▸

For a wet signature, *see* **Article 50**; for a history of battlebuses, *see* **Buses**; for ruining a flower show, *see* **Chelsea**; for reporters who can't call Britain 'Britain', *see* **Journalists**; for moving to a rusty platform in the sea, *see* **Micronations**; for Hubert Legal the legal eagle *see* **Names**; for what Gideon did next, *see* **Osborne, George**; for a patriotic colour change, *see* **Passports**; and for how voting to leave the EU has affected your Coco Pops, *see* **Shrinkflation**.

BUDDHISTS

Monks at a Buddhist temple crowdfunded money so that they could hold 'techno memorial services'.

—— ▼ ——

You can now hire a four-foot robot to hold your Buddhist funeral service. Pepper the robot, who can be programmed to read scriptures, chant prayers and tap drums, is being marketed as a low-cost alternative to a human priest.

Hosted in the Fukui City's Shō-onji temple in central Japan, each service features psychedelic lights and a 49-year-old Japanese Buddhist DJ on the decks, who drops heavy beats and Buddhist chants. By holding these memorials, the temple is attempting to make itself more accessible to the public. It started the experiment last year, but the services proved so expensive to stage that only two could be held. The monks therefore turned to crowdfunding. Launching their project on the site Readyfor, they successfully raised 398,000 yen (about £3,000, and 98,000 yen more than they had asked for).

One group of Buddhists not interested in dance music is the Wutaishan Buddhist Association in China, which is threatening to sue anyone and everyone who uploads a video that incorrectly claims to show a collection of its monks partying at a nun's wedding. Anyone who uploads the video can expect to hear from the monks' lawyers.

Meanwhile, three Buddhist monks were arrested in Myanmar after it was discovered they had been stashing more than four million methamphetamine pills in their monastery. The pills had a street value of over £3 million.

BULGARIA

Bulgaria elected a prime minister who was once voted the country's footballer of the year.

In 2011 Boyko Borisov was made footballer of the year, beating Dimitar Berbatov, who that same year had helped Manchester United win the Premier League. Borisov was 51 years old at the time and occasionally turned out for a team that came sixth in the second division. After his victory, he called for the award to be annulled, arguing that his success had been due to a protest vote by fans lamenting the poor standard of Bulgarian football.

This year's election campaign was a bruising one. Borisov sued the leader of the second-biggest party for slander after she called him a thief on national television, while Borisov was himself taken to court by a candidate for implying that she'd taken public money. A national television station, bTV, was censured when it showed a naked picture of 61-year-old Attack Party leader Volen Siderov, naming him the second most attractive naked Bulgarian after former *Big Brother* and Eurovision star Azis. Meanwhile, another candidate, who owns a newspaper, wrote a book entitled *Thieves of Democracy: They Plundered Bulgaria* and then gave away a free copy with every copy of his newspaper. The electoral commission deemed this to be unacceptable. The candidate therefore pulled the book, but proceeded to sell his newspaper with a differently titled book that targeted exactly the same politicians.

Bulgaria's tourism ministry announced plans to post more than 400,000 cards to foreign tourists who visited the country, thanking them for choosing Bulgaria as their destination.

BUSES

Crystal Palace fans vandalised their own team's bus by mistake.

After their game against Middlesbrough, Crystal Palace football fans found what they thought was the team bus of their opponents, and vandalised it by spraying the words 'Crystal Palace FC' on the side. Unfortunately, it turned out that it was their own bus (although at least it may have helped them find it again). Crystal Palace refused to comment on the incident, but the cost of the damage was estimated at £40,000.*

At least the coach *was* a coach, which is more than can be said for the buses used to transport passengers in Omsk, Russia. These were found to have benches instead of seats, and strange, curtained hatches at the back. On investigation, it was found that the bus company was using adapted hearses.

During the UK General Election, as Theresa May travelled the country telling people how Britain would leave the EU, it emerged, to her embarrassment, that her battle bus had been the 'Remain' battle bus during the EU referendum. Back then, it had promised 'More Jobs' and 'Lower Prices' if Britain stayed in the EU. The 'Vote Leave' campaign's bus, on the other hand, was made in Germany.†

† In the lead-up to the EU referendum, the official 'Labour In' battle bus was the one formerly used on tour by S Club 7, while Nigel Farage campaigned for Brexit aboard a double decker that Torvill and Dean rode in a victory parade in 1984.

Nottingham City Council unveiled a fleet of 53 biomethane buses, powered by gases given off by poo and farm waste. The anaerobic digestion industry reckons that animal and human sewage could eventually power half the UK's buses. Sadly, the prototype of Britain's biomethane buses, Bristol's Number 2 bus service, was scrapped last year for lack of funding. With luck it will come back as a political campaign bus.

BUSHES, HIDING IN

US Press Secretary Sean Spicer definitely didn't hide in a bush.

According to reports, when Donald Trump fired FBI Director James Comey, the press secretary to the White House spent several minutes 'hidden in the bushes' in the dark, working out what to tell the press. After the *Washington Post* reported this, White House officials complained, so the *Post* clarified: 'Spicer huddled with his staff among bushes … on the White House grounds, not "in the bushes," as the story originally stated.'

In Japan, a missing giant tortoise was found in bushes. After two weeks of frantically hunting for Abuh, who had escaped from the zoo where she lived, the Shibukawa Animal Park offered a 500,000 yen (£3,500) reward to anyone who found her. The bushes in which she was eventually discovered were 140 metres from the entrance to the zoo.

Spicer joins a long list of people who have definitely not hidden behind foliage to avoid awkward questions. As culture secretary, Jeremy Hunt was once spotted hiding behind a tree to avoid the press when heading to a dinner with media boss James Murdoch. He later firmly denied hiding, telling the Leveson Inquiry, 'There may or may not have been trees.'

There are times where it's worth doing. While walking her dogs, the Queen once hid behind a bush in Buckingham Palace gardens to avoid bumping into communist dictator Nicolae Ceaușescu, who was visiting at the time.

In Nigeria in May, a suicide bomber accidentally blew himself up while hiding in a bush and waiting to attack a university. Nobody else was hurt, although the condition of the bush was not reported.

In which we learn …
Where the Smurfs are considered dangerously provocative,
why cats are more law-abiding than dogs, how the
new £1 coin avoided featuring a full English breakfast,
which dance confused Jeremy Corbyn, and what
to do with a geriatric cow.

CANADA

For pregnant parachuting bison, *see* **Airdrops**; for unusual bangs in official residences, *see* **Brazil**; for glow-in-the-dark money, *see* **Coins**; for a metallic falcon, *see* **Drones**; for a six-storey high bird, *see* **Ducks, Rubber**; for a chunk of ice that went on a nationwide tour, *see* **Icebergs**; for celebrating how great men are, *see* **International Women's Day**; for offensive cars, *see* **Licence Plates**; for the death of a pizza salesman, *see* **Pizzas**; for an anthropomorphic turd called Mr Floatie, *see* **Retirement**; for photos with a runaway moose, *see* **Selfies**; for avoiding a spell in prison, *see* **Witchcraft**; and for what you absolutely can't do with the Prime Minister, *see* **Trudeau, Justin**.

CANNABIS

Since 2010, the number of dogs getting stoned in New York has increased by 144 per cent.

Vets say they treat canine marijuana poisoning every day, and because the owners who have brought the dogs in are often stoned as well, it can be difficult to persuade them to take it seriously. Symptoms, as with humans, include lethargy, wobbling gait, and urine and saliva dribbling, but they're not life-threatening. Dogs constitute 95 per cent of pet marijuana poisonings. Cats, as ever, simply don't seem interested.

Elsewhere in cannabis news:

▶ America's first drive-through cannabis outlet opened in Parachute, Colorado, though, to be honest, it's more of a 'drive-in-and-out'. By law, all marijuana transactions have to happen inside an establishment, so you have to drive your car into a warehouse and wait for the door to close behind you before you can pick up your fix.

A man called Harry Potter appeared in court, admitting to possession of cannabis. The 19-year-old from York said he'd been planning to sell three wraps of the drug to his friends at college.

- At the US–Mexico border, a consignment of what appeared to be 34,764 key limes was discovered, when peeled, to be 34,764 green spheres full of cannabis, totalling two tons in weight. The discovery came days after 3,000 pounds of marijuana was found being smuggled across the border inside fake grapefruits.

- Uruguay became the first country in the world where you can buy weed in pharmacies. To do so, however, you have to register as a marijuana buyer with the government, and submit a digital thumbprint every time you want to make a purchase.

- In Vanuatu, authorities have been giving local youths free gardening tools to encourage them to plant vegetables instead of marijuana. Unfortunately, the scheme has largely backfired. It transpires that the tools are just as useful for cultivating cannabis as they are for cultivating potatoes, and the locals prefer growing the former.

- A Canadian consultant hired to look at how sales might look if the country legalises the drug has reported that they will be 'unbelievably high'.

CARNIVALS

'I want to apologise to anyone who may have been offended' – Father Juan Carlos Martínez

A Catholic priest from Cuntis, Spain, apologised for his choice of float at a local carnival parade. He realised, in retrospect, that it was inappropriate for a priest to be dressed up as Hugh Hefner, travelling on a bed covered with satin sheets, accompanied by two men dressed as *Playboy* bunnies, and having one of them simulate sex with him along the way. Father Martínez was sent on a spiritual retreat by an angry archbishop to reflect on what he had done.

42

CARS, DRIVERLESS

In the first ever race between two driverless cars, one crashed and the other nearly ran over a dog.

The race, which took place in Buenos Aires in February, wasn't the best advert for the new technology. After getting up to speeds of 180km/h, one of the cars, Devbot 2, misjudged a corner and crashed into a barrier. The other, Devbot 1, had to slow down to avoid running over a dog which had wandered on to the track (press reports described this as 'one of the highlights'). It did avoid hitting the dog, no thanks to a race marshal who forgot the car had no driver and frantically waved a yellow flag at it. Justin Cooke, chief marketing officer of Roborace, said, 'We don't learn as much when we do perfect runs.'

In August a mysterious driverless van was seen moving around Washington, DC. In fact, it was taking part in a study by the Virginia Tech Transportation Institute of how people react to driverless cars. It turned out the vehicle had a driver – but he was disguised as a car seat.

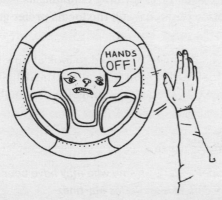

In Greenwich, London, driverless car trials have been taking place, but they're not very sophisticated: the maximum speed the pods are allowed to go is 10mph, and they have to issue constant warning beeps. Rather more ambitious trials were carried out by Nissan in March. Their vehicles managed hundreds of accident-free miles along London's roads. Since there was a human in the driver's seat (who intervened occasionally as necessary), few people would have realised what was going on.

If you're thinking of buying a driverless car the bad news is that that you'll need two insurance policies – one for when you're driving and one for when the car is.

For other driverless cars confused by animals, *see* **Kangaroos**.

CENSORSHIP ▶

Victims of censorship this year included Smurfs, aliens, celebrity gossip, and saying you've been censored.

▶ **Country:** China

Censored: Aliens, from the new *Alien* film. When shown in Chinese cinemas *Alien: Covenant* was found to run six minutes short. Fans noted that the monster only appeared for a minute or two in the whole movie. China's government also cracked down on 'abnormal' beards, the name Muhammad (both moves designed to crush religious extremism), watching computers play games (*see* **AI**) and celebrity gossip websites.

This year, people in China *were* allowed to watch films featuring zombies for the first time. Previously, these had been banned on the grounds that they promoted 'cults or superstition'. In the interests of filling cinemas, audiences were finally allowed to watch zombie-filled movies like the fifth *Pirates of the Caribbean* film.

▶ **Country:** Saudi Arabia

Censored: Families in paddling pools. A Saudi company advertising swimming pools edited a photo of a family in swimming gear so the father and the children were depicted as completely clothed from head to foot. The mother, meanwhile, was removed altogether and replaced with a Winnie-the-Pooh beach ball.

▶ **Country:** Israel

Censored: Overly sexual Smurfs. In the Israeli version of the poster for the latest *Smurfs* movie a Smurfette was removed in order to avoid offending ultra-Orthodox Jews. As the PR company promoting the film explained, they had decided to remove the female Smurf because they didn't want to 'incite the feelings of residents' in the extremely conservative city of Bnei Brak.

▶ **Country:** Tanzania

Censored: Attacks on censorship. Tanzanian rapper Emmanuel Elibariki was arrested for releasing a song that claimed freedom of expression was under attack. He was released after a day and told he had to 'improve' the lyrics.

▶ **Country:** Italy

Censored: The god Neptune. Facebook censored a photo of a 16th-century nude statue of Neptune standing in the city of Bologna on the grounds that it was 'explicitly sexual and … shows to an excessive degree the body, concentrating unnecessarily on body parts'. They later apologised.

For more totally reasonable reactions to freedom of expression, *see* **Belarus** and **Turkey**.

CHEATING ▶

Romanian lexicographers sabotaged their own dictionary to foil cheating students.

Last year, dictionary editors in Romania noticed huge spikes in searches for certain words during a nationwide exam, and spotted that those words happened to feature in the exam. Realising that students were surreptitiously looking them up on their smartphones, they decided to keep an eye out for similar patterns this year. Again, they noticed spikes, this time in searches for three particular words. They assumed the same thing was happening, so they immediately altered the definitions of those three words to be incorrect. Their assumption was justified – two of the words had been set as test questions, and cheating students were duly fooled into thinking that the word for 'spot' meant 'rush' and the word for 'everywhere' meant 'eternal'. The third word had no connection with the exams and was actually just used in a popular blog that day, hence the spike there. Fittingly, it was the word for 'treachery'.

CHELSEA ▶

A Ghanaian priest held a special service to thank God for Chelsea's Premier League victory.

When Chelsea Football Club won the Premier League, it was celebrated not just in west London, but also in West Africa, where a church hosted a special service in honour of the team's victory. Pastor Victor Kpakpo Addo (a former DJ and brand ambassador for a mosquito spray) also gave thanks for Arsenal's FA Cup Final victory, adding, rather uncharitably, 'because it means that Arsène Wenger will stay and they cannot win the league with him'.*

Less than a week after Chelsea FC's victory came a victory for another Chelsea: WikiLeaks whistle-blower Chelsea Manning was released from military prison after serving seven years of a 35-year sentence. She moved into a flat in Manhattan and bought an Xbox. As a precaution, she keeps the remote controls in a microwave when they're not being used, since they contain microphones.

As Chelsea FC and Chelsea Manning were celebrating, Bill and Hillary Clinton's daughter Chelsea released a feminist

If, in their victorious 2016/17 season, Chelsea FC had lost all their players with EU nationalities, they'd have played three-a-side for most of their games, and would have scored a total of only 13 goals, rather than the 108 they actually achieved.

children's book, and the Chelsea Flower Show was under way. There were only eight show gardens present, down from 17. Alan Titchmarsh blamed concerns over Brexit forcing sponsors to pull out. Meanwhile, a survey showed that half of Britons were unable to name a single shrub. One entry for Plant of the Year was the world's hottest chilli – so hot that if you were foolish enough to try it, it could cause a massive anaphylactic shock that would kill you. On the plus side, scientists hope the oil that can be extracted from it may ultimately serve as an anaesthetic for those allergic to conventional drugs.

CHILDISHNESS

See **Uranus**.

CHINA

For a board game that dented national pride, *see* **AI**; for being evicted by a telescope, *see* **Aliens**; for a potential war involving a third of the world's population, *see* **Bhutan**; for an alienless *Alien* film, *see* **Censorship**; for training undercover children, *see* **Espionage**; for blowing up chunks of your own land, *see* **Islands**; for terrorist toys *see* **Lego**; for a number that wasn't so lucky, *see* **Licence Plates**; for an ancient discipline defeated in 10 seconds, *see* **Martial Arts**; for confusing the president with his sworn enemy, *see* **Mix-Ups**; for upcoming missions to the moon, *see* **Potatoes**; for a trackless train, *see* **Railways**; for a giant, jam-loving bug, *see* **Stick Insects**; for a Messi experience, *see* **Theme Parks**; for a high-rise forest, *see* **Trees**; for zombies in taxis, *see* **Uber**; for dangerous toothpicks, *see* **Weapons**; for false friends, *see* **Weddings**; for an un-editable encyclopaedia, *see* **Wikipedia**; for someone who in no way resembles Winnie-the-Pooh, *see* **Xi Jinping**; for a literate scarecrow, *see* **Zhou Youguang**; and for polar bear poos, *see* **Zoos**.

The Ringling Bros. Circus played its final show, after complaining that US politics was bringing the word 'circus' into disrepute.

────── ▼ ──────

In Darwin, Australia, a camel ran away from the circus and wrought havoc on the roads, holding up rush-hour traffic. It eventually made its way to a golf course, where it was caught on the ninth green.

During the presidential campaign, the circus's head clown said, 'You can do and say silly things or slap on colourful ties and pantsuits all you want, but that does not make you a Ringling Bros. clown.' Less than a year later, the circus closed down for good.

In the end it was the symbol of the Republican Party, the elephant, that did for the Greatest Show on Earth, which had been performing since the 19th century. After animal rights protests and multiple lawsuits, Ringling retired its pachyderms, and ticket sales slumped. One televangelist announced that the closing of the circus was a message from God that just as the circus died when the elephants departed, so America would fall if Trump left.

* One act had a safety net: after their final show, the Ringling high-wire act immediately flew to Morocco, where they were finalists in Arabs Got Talent.

The closure left hundreds of circus performers out of work. The brass band got their marching orders, the human cannonball was fired, and the elephants packed their trunks.* And many were left without a home, now that they were no longer able to live on the mile-long circus train that had once taken them from town to town. Resident trombonist Megan O'Malley captured the mood with her tweet: 'Worst. Day. Ever.'

CITIZENSHIP

A senator whose surname means 'foreign sounding' faced losing his job after finding out he might be part-foreign.

Nick Xenophon* is a member of an Australian centrist political party called the Nick Xenophon Team, which was founded in 2006 by Nick Xenophon, and has three members in the Australian senate, one of whom is Nick Xenophon. However when Xenophon made a joke about being part-Cypriot at a book launch in July, it got into the papers, and soon questions were being asked about his nationality.

* Xenophon comes from the Ancient Greek words 'xenos', meaning 'foreigner' and 'phone' meaning 'voice'.

It turns out that Xenophon is not Cypriot, but he might be British (he was born in Australia, but his father lived in Cyprus when it was a British colony). Therefore, unbeknownst to Xenophon, he may actually technically have UK citizenship, and under Australian rules people with dual-nationality cannot be senators. He was forced to go to court to decide if he could keep his job – one of a number of Australians who this year found their nationalities being questioned.

Minister for Regional Development Fiona Nash, Minister for Resources Matt Canavan† and Deputy Prime Minister Barnaby Joyce were all implicated in the scandal; as were Queensland MP Susan Lamb who found she may be part-British, and Green Party MP Larissa Waters who discovered she was part-Canadian. Waters had already hit the news earlier in the year by being the first Australian MP to breastfeed her baby in Parliament. She later said that she had moved a motion only moments after her daughter had 'moved her own motion'.

† Canavan's barrister was quoted as saying that as much as 50 per cent of the population of Australia is technically ineligible to run for parliament.

CLERGY, UNGODLY-SOUNDING

For the priest from Cuntis, *see* **Carnivals**; for an archbishop called Pennisi, *see* **Godfather**.

CLIMATE CHANGE

Andy: Earlier this year, a study on climate change in the Arctic was cancelled. Any guesses as to why?

Anna: Was it due to climate change?

Andy: Basically, yes. A Canadian research trip was scheduled to study melting ice, but high temperatures meant the sea ice was moving so unpredictably that it would be too dangerous for them to go.

Anna: As in, it would be moving so fast it caught them unaware? Surely that's not possible?

Andy: Well, ice can be a problem at sea. I don't know if you've seen *Titanic*.

Dan: Was that a climate-change experiment too?

James: Yeah, but they glossed over that in the movie.

Dan: Extraordinary. Did you guys know that at 12 p.m. on January 20th, the second that Donald Trump officially became president, every single mention of climate change was wiped from the White House website? With one exception: Trump replaced it all with a note promising to abolish Obama's climate-change policies.

Andy: Sounds like he's solved the problem already. Great news.

James: Well, I read an article on that from researchers at Cornell. They found 74.4 per cent of Republicans believe climate change is real, but only 65 per cent believe global warming is happening. And when Trump pulled out of the Paris climate agreement, he tweeted about 'global warming' instead of 'climate change' – maybe because fewer of his supporters believe in it.

Anna: Did you know, there are only two countries – other than America, when they leave – that are not signed up to the Paris climate agreement? And they're Syria, which is in the middle of a war, and Nicaragua. Lots of people criticised Nicaragua when they heard, but actually the whole reason they didn't sign is because they think the Paris Agreement didn't go far enough. Nicaragua is hugely committed to renewable energy, so they're the good guys here.

Dan: When you said that about the Paris Agreement not going far enough, I thought Nicaragua had assumed it only covered the city of Paris.

Andy: I am confident that that wasn't it, Dan.

James: Trump did attract a lot of attention for saying he'd pull America out of the Paris Agreement. Stephen Hawking said that his action will push the Earth over the brink, and we'll become like Venus with temperatures of 250 degrees and raining sulphuric acid.

Anna: OK, I for one think that is a bit alarmist.

James: But he wasn't alone. Even North Korea said it was the 'height of egotism' for Trump to pull out of the agreement. And that's the country which has a 560-metre propaganda sign, visible from space, that says 'Long Live General Kim Jong Un, the Shining Sun'.

Anna: Presumably they meant 'the height of egotism – to which we aspire'.

A NASA rocket launch to create artificial clouds was delayed because it was too cloudy.

Scientists found a planet called WASP-12b, which is covered in ruby and sapphire clouds. The planet's clouds are 2,200-degree Celsius liquid droplets made of a substance called corundum – the material that forms rubies and sapphires on earth.

However, after numerous failed attempts, NASA eventually launched 10 containers the size of soft-drink cans 118 miles into the sky, which then ejected turquoise and red vapour into the air, creating gigantic coloured clouds. The clouds were so large that despite being launched from NASA's Wallops Flight Facility in Virginia, they were visible from the ground 200 miles away in New York.

The rockets – technically called Terrier-Improved Malemute rockets – were launched as part of a large-scale international programme to help scientists answer a rather worrying question: why is the Earth leaking nearly 90 tonnes of air every day into space?

Earth's magnetosphere has two gaping holes in it – called cusps – which allow our atmosphere to escape the planet. Scientists hope to get a better understanding of how this process occurs, by following the colourful clouds as they exit the cusps. Tracking them will also help us understand geomagnetic storms, as well as auroras, and help answer the question of why we actually have a magnetic field. It's a good job we do: without a magnetosphere to deflect the sun's particles, they would batter the Earth, and our planet would be a barren desert like Mars.

COCK-UPS

The biggest blunders of the last 12 months included, but were not limited to, the following:

▶ *Australia was loaned an irreplaceable collection of 18th-century flowers from a Paris museum.*

Cock-up: Owing to a paperwork error, Australia's biosecurity officers incinerated them on arrival.

▶ *A new Polar Fox Military Combat Work Desert Boot was released.*

Cock-up: The boot had to be withdrawn when a customer discovered that the footprints it left included a swastika pattern.

▶ *A Canadian politician sent a reply-all email to 100 civil servants concerning local infrastructure.*

Cock-up: The reply-all message he sent contained nothing but a picture of a naked woman with her legs spread.

▶ *X-rated TV channel Babestation advertised a live sex chatline with an 098 prefix for viewers to call.*

Cock-up: Many Irish viewers forgot to use the international dialling code when calling, and as a result inundated the residents of the small Irish town of Westport in County Mayo, whose numbers began with 098 as well, with sexy late-night phone calls.

▶ *Japanese government officials held a press conference to warn the public about a deadly tick, bringing a live one along with them for the media to see.*

Cock-up: The officials dropped the tick during the press call and were unable to find it. They were forced to spray the entire room with insecticide and leave it overnight.

COINS

The Bank of England's gym lockers wouldn't accept the new £1 coin.

As a result of this blunder, for months, members who tried to use the 'most secure coin in the world' were left with valuables that were not secure.

According to the Royal Mint each new £1 coin contains secret messages, secret images, a hologram and, it is rumoured, an anti-forgery code hidden on the Queen's face. On the coin's 'tails' side is an image of a rose, thistle, leek and shamrock that was drawn by a 15-year-old schoolboy, whose design was chosen following a nation-wide competition set up by the Royal Mint. The Mint decided the winner. Had the vote been left to the public, we might now have a £1 coin with a full English breakfast on it. It featured prominently in the submissions, but was ruled out because, according to the Royal Mint's chief engraver, the design had to be something 'appropriate'.

Another coin released this year was Canada's new $2 piece: the world's first glow-in-the-dark coin. Issued to mark the 150th anniversary of Canada's birth, this coin also carries a design suggested by the public, with an end result that nicely illustrates the difference between British and Canadian tastes. Whereas the British, left to their own devices, would have come up with a £1 bacon-and-egg coin, the Canadians opted for one in which canoeists row across a golden lake beneath the Northern Lights. When viewed in the dark, the aurora borealis glows softly.

Thieves in Las Vegas stole 30,000 condoms, 33 vibrating 'prostate massagers' and 48 vaginal beads. The company affected said in a statement: 'What kind of party are these people having?! We could have done the sponsorship or something.'

CONDOMS

A Chicago zoo tackled mass extinction by giving out free condoms.

Lincoln Park Zoo teamed up with a group called the Center for Biological Diversity as part of the latter's long-running campaign to slow human population growth, which they argue is causing mass extinctions. So the zoo gave out hundreds of condoms adorned with pictures of endangered animals. The front of the packets featured slogans saying things like 'Wrap with care, save the polar bear' or 'Before it gets any hotter, remember the sea otter'. Each package contained two condoms, information about the species depicted on the outside, and suggestions of ways to solve the problem of unsustainable human population growth (such as wearing condoms more).

CONSTITUTION, US

A man who received a C for an essay he wrote in 1982 had it re-marked to an A after successfully changing the US Constitution.

While studying at the University of Texas in Austin 35 years ago, Gregory Watson wrote a paper arguing that a constitutional amendment proposed in 1789 (relating to Members of Congress's salaries) could still be ratified. After getting a C grade, he spent the next decade proving his point by persuading the necessary number of states (38 in total) needed to approve it. He was successful, and it became the 27th, and most recent, amendment to the US Constitution. It had taken almost 203 years to be ratified – 199 years longer than the runner-up.

Watson's old tutor finally got wind of this, and on 4 March this year Watson received a document, signed by her, requesting that his C be changed to an A+. Unfortunately the university doesn't offer plus and minus grades, but it did change his grade to an A.

CORBYN, JEREMY

Jeremy Corbyn is the Parliamentary Beard of the Year champion.

He's won the competition, organised by the Beard Liberation Front (BLF), a record seven times. On the most recent occasion it was with 64 per cent of the vote, slightly higher than he received in that year's Labour leadership contest. The head of the BLF, Keith Flett, wants to see more parliamentary whiskers, and

A Cornish artist started making Jeremy Corbyn garden gnomes. They sold out so fast that the artist said he planned to put the next batch in a superhero costume.

When Corbyn first heard the 'Oh Jeremy Corbyn' song (at Prenton Park, the home of former UKIP leader Paul Nuttall's former team, Tranmere Rovers), he thought the audience were booing him.

commented: 'We always thought that David Cameron would have been vastly improved by having a beard, but there was some doubt as to whether that was ever possible.'

A study published in April by the London School of Economics found that 69 per cent of newspaper articles that attack Corbyn mention his appearance, clothing or lifestyle – often referring to his facial hair. He's the first leader of a mainstream British political party to have a beard since Labour Party founder Keir Hardie, who left office in 1908. This year, he met a beard rival when he took to the main stage at Glastonbury to give a speech. As part of it, he presented Glastonbury founder Michael Eavis with a signed copy of the Labour manifesto. Eavis won Beard of the Decade in 2009, narrowly beating Fidel Castro to the top spot.

It's been a rock and roll year for Jeremy: Paul Weller sent him a copy of his new album, while Grace Chatto from the electronic band Clean Bandit had her T-shirt blurred out by the BBC because it was Corbyn branded, breaching BBC election campaign impartiality rules. When asked by the *Financial Times* what his 'summer soundtrack' would be, Corbyn named Clean Bandit (along with The Farm's 'All Together Now' and Ralph Vaughan Williams's symphonies). He's not entirely au fait with pop culture though. When he attended the Durham Miners' Gala and 'YMCA' was played over the loudspeakers, it became apparent that he didn't know the moves. He tried to dance along and make hand gestures, like those around him, but failed to spell out the letters Y, M, C or A.

COSTUMES

For a priest dressed as Hugh Hefner, *see* **Carnivals**; for schoolboys dressed as schoolgirls, *see* **Heatwaves**; for a runner as a phone box, *see* **Marathon, London**; for a Prime Minister as a hiker, *see* **May, Theresa**; for teddy bears as soldiers, *see* **Noriega, Manuel**; for a White House Chief Strategist as Napoleon, *see* **Paintings**; for a student as Darth Vader, *see* **Schools**; for a White House Press Secretary as the Easter Bunny, *see* **Spicer, Sean**; for an owner as a punter, *see* **Swearing**; for a punchbag as the President, *see* **Unpopular**; for a person as a crayon, *see* **Yellow**; and for a shaman dressed as a Sasquatch, *see* **Zoology, Crypto-**.

COVFEFE

On 31 May, we all woke up and smelled the Covfefe.

In May, Donald Trump tweeted the (non-)sentence 'Despite the constant negative press covfefe', and then retired to bed, presumably unaware that this unusual combination of letters had sent Twitter into meltdown. 'Covfefe' quickly became the number-one trending word worldwide, and the post was retweeted 127,000 times, three times more than Trump's tweet announcing Mike Pence as his running mate.

Entrepreneurs jumped on the word. A man called Per Holknekt registered Covfefe with the Swedish Patent Office soon after Trump's tweet, and got exclusive commercial rights to the term across Europe; while in America Covfefe.com was bought by a printing company who proceeded to sell T-shirts, hoodies and mugs with the word on them. Scrabble-like app 'Words with Friends' added 'covfefe' to its list of acceptable words in the game, and a number of people snapped up COVFEFE driving plates (but not in Montana, where it was deemed an illegal combination of letters due to its political nature).

Even Hillary Clinton joined in. She responded to a tweet by Donald Trump that read 'Crooked Hillary Clinton now blames everybody but herself, refuses to say she was a terrible candidate' with 'People in covfefe houses shouldn't throw covfefe.'

'Fefe' is actually a word – in Samoan. Lagipoiva Cherelle Jackson, a Samoan journalist, wrote that Samoan has no letter 'c', so there's no 'cov', but there is 'ko', which means 'pregnant'. 'Fefe' is an expression of fear, so 'ko fefe' would be 'pregnant but afraid about it'.

One Democratic legislator went so far as to introduce the Covfefe Act, which would preserve Donald Trump's tweets as presidential records. Covfefe in this case stands for 'Communications Over Various Feeds Electronically For Engagement'.

COWS ▶

India announced that all elderly cows should be sent to retirement homes.

Cows are so sacred to Hindus that this year the Indian government banned selling cattle for slaughter (although the courts later suspended the ban, as selling elderly cattle for slaughter is a big part of the rural economy). Not only that, but India's home ministry announced it wanted every region to set up a cow retirement home, and the government announced plans for all 190,000,000 cows in the country to get an ID number for their protection. (India's largest state, Rajasthan, charges 10 per cent extra stamp duty when people buy homes, just to pay for elderly cows' dotage.) Tensions have run so high that vigilante groups have attacked and even killed people suspected of eating beef.

Elsewhere in India, the state of Uttar Pradesh launched an ambulance service for sacred cows, the Cattle Healing Mobile Van Service, and a cricket tournament gave the winning team a cow each as their prize. One of the players, Raju Rabari, said he and his colleagues were delighted to receive the cows.

In Switzerland, 12 cows died after mysteriously throwing themselves off a cliff. A 13th cow also fell but survived, possibly because it landed on the others. One farmer said, 'One or two cows falling off, that's possible. Thirteen, that's a new and incomprehensible phenomenon.'

———— ▼ ————

A scientific review by a German university found no evidence that homeopathy works on cows. And in America, a (somewhat disputed) survey of 1,000 adults found that 48 per cent didn't know where chocolate milk comes from. Seven per cent thought it only came from brown cows.

In which we learn …
How not to impress a woman with a crocodile, the dark
meaning of 'Smoochy Woochy Poochy', what T. rexes
used their noses for, which power couple's name means
'Dark Ruler of the World', how Doomsday came to
the Doomsday Vault, and why Russian police
have been arresting bath toys.

DATING, ANIMAL

For 'looking for love' in Dorset, *see* **Penguins**; for 'would like to meet' in the Netherlands, *see* **Orangutans**; and for a rhino with a GSOH *see* **Tinder**.

DEBTS

Cuba offered to pay off its outstanding Cold War debt in rum.

Cuba owes the Czech Republic £220 million, but it's a bit short of cash, so offered to pay instead with various commodities, including some of its famous rums. That would amount to about 116,000 tonnes of the spirit. Unfortunately, the citizens of the Czech Republic drink so little rum that if the whole debt were to be serviced in this way, it would take the population 138 years to get through it.

A 'granny gang' of elderly Chinese women who intimidated people into paying debts were imprisoned for up to 11 years. Their tactics included swearing, spitting, and stripping off their own clothes or those of other people. One said she had joined because 'I had nothing to do ... also, a key point is that we were given free meals.'

The Czech deputy finance minister, Lenka Dupakova, politely said that it was 'an interesting option'. The Czech finance ministry was less keen, arguing that 'at least part of the debt should be dealt in cash'. They also pointed out that the rums on offer were rather obscure ones and that they would require an advertising budget to shift them. An alternative Cuban plan – to pay the debt in pharmaceutical drugs – didn't go down too well either. Cuban drugs don't have EU certification.

This is not the first time that the Czech Republic has been offered payment in kind rather than in cash. Back in 2010, North Korea offered to pay some of its £8 million debt to the Czechs by sending them 20 tonnes of ginseng – again far more than the Czechs could get through. The then deputy finance minister, Thomas Zidek, said, 'We have been trying to convince them to send, for instance, a shipment of zinc.'

DENMARK

Denmark was supplanted as the happiest country in the world by Norway, and was very happy for the new champions.

'Good for them,' said Meik Wiking of the Happiness Research Institute in Copenhagen, 'I don't think Denmark has a monopoly on happiness.' But why are Danes so happy? It could be that for the fifth consecutive year Denmark has been named the least corrupt country in the world by Transparency International; or maybe it's because it was crowned the best place in Europe to do business by a survey from the business interest group EuCham; or it just might be due to another poll it tops – in 2017, Danes were found to shop for sex toys more regularly than anyone else.

Police in Denmark told a group of fun-runners that, because the event they were running crossed the Danish–German border, they would have to carry passports or other valid travel documents with them as they ran.

DICKHEADS

Brisbane launched a 'Don't Be a Dickhead' campaign to cut down on antisocial behaviour.

The slogan was displayed on posters and billboards all over Queensland's Fortitude Valley. Simon Turner, one of the men behind the state-sponsored initiative, said, 'Dickhead is a term that means your behaviour is unacceptable. You're either a decent bloke or you're a dickhead.'

In January, Twitter users searching for the term 'dickhead' were directed to Donald Trump's profile, thanks to the website's powerful search algorithm, which directs viewers towards results other people have searched for. Other searches which suggested Trump – before they mysteriously disappeared – included 'racist', 'asshole' and 'tiny hands'.

While this campaign was running, 18-year-old Queensland banana farm worker Lee De Paauw tried to impress a girl by jumping into a river after drinking 'about 10 cups of goon' (boxed wine), only to be immediately mauled by a three-metre crocodile. He managed to fight it off but failed to win over 24-year-old Sophie Paterson from Somerset, who said, 'Being attacked by animals doesn't really do it for me' and 'I'd have to be quite twisted to be impressed by that.' Eventually she said she'd go and see a film with him, if her schedule allowed.

Speaking from his hospital bed, Mr De Paauw described his actions as 'stupidity', adding, 'I don't want that crocodile harmed ... I want it to have a happy life.' When Jason Costigan, an Australian MP, was asked if something could have been done to avoid such an incident occurring, he replied, 'We can't legislate to protect dickheads.'

DICTIONARIES

'Kodak moment' was finally accepted as a phrase in the English language by Oxford Dictionaries, five years after the Kodak company went bust.

It was one of 300 words added by Oxford, alongside 'aquafaba' (chickpea water used in vegan cooking), 'sausage party' (an event in which the majority of participants are male), and 'craptacular' (remarkably poor or disappointing).

Merriam-Webster, meanwhile, announced that 'sheeple' had made it into its dictionary – it means people who tend metaphorically to follow the flock. Merriam-Webster cited those who buy Apple products to illustrate how the word might be used, though it could have reasonably cited itself, as the word has been in the *Oxford English Dictionary* since 2008 and in *Macmillan's Dictionary* since 2003.

62

America's Drug Enforcement Administration published a dictionary of slang drug terms this year, designed for police who find the hundreds of slang terms used by drug users confusing. Words included:

Whiffle Dust: Amphetamines

Bernie's Flakes: Cocaine

Aunt Hazel: Heroin

Smoochy Woochy Poochy: Cannabis

And the International Anthony Burgess Foundation uncovered a hitherto unknown dictionary of slang that was started by the author of *A Clockwork Orange*. Unfortunately, he never got beyond the letter B, and some of his definitions perhaps lack the rigour to be found in most dictionaries. His entries included:

Abfab: Obsolescent abbreviation of absolutely fabulous, used by Australian teenagers or 'bodgies'.

Abyssinia: I'll be seeing you. A valediction that started during the Italo-Abyssinian war. Obsolete, but so Joyceanly satisfying that it is sometimes hard to resist.

Arse: I need not define.

A Liverpool English dictionary was published covering more than 2,000 Scouse words and phrases. They included 'bumstarver' (a short jacket), 'egg-shell blond' (a bald man) and 'desert wellies' (sandals).

DINOSAURS

The largest dinosaur footprints ever discovered were found in Western Australia. They were as long as Marc Bolan, the lead singer of T. Rex.

The 1.7-metre prints belonged to herbivores that lived about 150 million years ago and stood 5.5 metres tall at the hip, which, as one palaeontologist clarified, is 'enormous'. Locals in the region have long known about the prints. In Aboriginal lore, they belong to Marala, a giant

The largest creature ever to walk the earth, a dinosaur whose 100-million-year-old fossil was found in 2012, was finally named. Its genus is *Patagotitan*, named after Patagonia, where it was found, and *titan*, the Ancient Greek word for 'giant'. The species name of the 76-tonne creature is *mayorum*, which is (coincidentally) an anagram of 'your mam'.

emu-man who travelled the realm, dispensing laws to the people.

Back in the UK, the country's most famous dinosaur, Dippy, is going on tour. The diplodocus plaster cast, the Natural History Museum's most famous attraction, will visit eight venues between 2018 and 2020, having spent a year being dismantled, polished, vacuumed and upgraded. While travelling between venues he will be flat-packed, with each body part carefully labelled so that it ends up back in the right place.

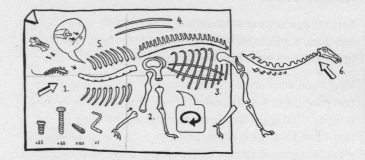

In other dinosaur skeleton news, a head was reunited with its body almost a century after they were torn apart. Palaeontologists at the University of Alberta studied the decapitated skeleton of a corythosaurus, excavated in 1992, and found that it was a perfect match for a skull on display in their museum. The skull had been discovered in 1920 at a time when 'headhunting' was popular among dinosaur hunters: they often took the more exciting skulls, tail spines and claws for their collections, and abandoned the rest.

One clue that led scientists to believe the two parts belonged together was that newspaper fragments found at the site where the skeleton was unearthed dated back to the same year that the skull was taken. It wasn't uncommon then for palaeontologists to wrap their finds in newspaper.

Palaeontologists also concluded this year that Tyrannosaurus rex was partial to a bit of pre-coital nose-rubbing. An analysis of a particularly well-preserved tyrannosaurid skull revealed that the snout was covered in enough nerve endings to make it as sensitive as human fingertips. Authors of a study in the journal *Scientific Reports* speculated that this may have played a crucial role in T. rex foreplay, as the dinosaurs would have rubbed their faces together before sex.

DISCOVERIES

Science made great leaps forward this year, but sadly we only have space to record the most vital findings. And so, in no particular order, scientists have discovered:

Why shoelaces untie themselves; that eating yogurt can cure depression in mice; why water splashes when it lands; that dogs' favourite music genre is reggae; that chimpanzees have no interest in music at all; that elephants poo six times faster than dogs; that humans' oldest known ancestor didn't have an anus; why pandas are black and white; why LSD trips take so long; that ants navigate by the sun, and rescue their wounded; that bees can be taught to play football; beetles that disguise themselves as ants' bottoms; why bird eggs are egg-shaped; a parasite that controls fish from inside their eyeballs; a new continent just off the coast of New Zealand; a new organ in your body; 467 million hectares of previously unreported forest; 3.6 million more Adélie penguins than they thought existed; that *Tyrannosaurus rex* had no lips; a 2,600-year-old demand to 'send wine' inscribed on a shard of pottery; a shrimp whose claw makes a noise so loud that it can kill other fish; the only species of crab known to spend its whole life in trees; that male great tits build their homes next to birds with similar personalities to their own; an extinct ancient turkey the size of a kangaroo; the first new antibiotic since 1987; five new

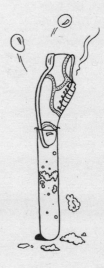

species of truffle, one of which has been named after Oreos because of its sweet smell; 12 new types of cloud; a worm that eats plastic; that people who swear more are more honest than those who don't; that being 'liked' on Facebook doesn't make you happier; that Internet withdrawal increases blood pressure; a meat-eating sponge; why pugs have flat faces; and that 98 per cent of British people think they're in the nicest 50 per cent.

DIVORCE

A Palestinian judge banned divorce applications during Ramadan on the grounds that we all make bad decisions when we're hungry.

An American couple got divorced, and blamed President Trump. Lynn and David Aronberg married in 2015, but a statement from Lynn's firm said that Lynn is a 'supporter of President Donald Trump', while David is a Democrat.

The judge, who is head of the Palestinian Islamic sharia court system, said he based his decision on previous years' experiences. His point was borne out earlier this year when newspapers in Jordan reported that a hungry husband divorced his wife in a restaurant because each time he wanted to eat something, she made him wait until she'd taken a photo of it for Snapchat.

The Chinese government is also currently trying to deal with high divorce rates, most notably in the village of Jiangbei, where the government wanted to demolish 160 homes. It offered to compensate residents with new houses, but the couples living there realised that if they were divorced they would qualify for a new house each, rather than one between them. This prompted a mass divorce. Technically the regulations stipulate that couples should have been divorced for at least five years to qualify for the scheme, but one law firm in the area convinced residents that they can overcome that detail, and cases are ongoing.

In America, Alex Jones, the founder of controversial alt-right website Infowars, attempted (unsuccessfully) to win a court case against his wife for the custody of his three children by trying to prove to a divorce court that his on-screen persona wasn't the real him. His attorney said that to judge him on his on-air persona would be like judging Jack Nicholson on the basis of his performance as the Joker in *Batman* and that he was simply playing the role of an angry Obama-hating conspiracy theorist who wants to break Alec Baldwin's neck.*

His case was not helped, however, by the fact that he was unable to remember basic details about his children's day-to-day life. Nor did telling the judge that the reason he'd forgotten was that he had just had a big bowl of chilli for lunch.

DOGS, HOT

For airborne, *see* **Drones**; for puffy, *see* **Inventions**; for bony, *see* **Recalls**; and for metaphorical, *see* **Tunnels**.

DOGS, NON-HOT

For taking drugs in New York, *see* **Cannabis**; for being nearly run over by a robot, *see* **Cars, Driverless**; for favourite musical genres, *see* **Discoveries**; for a long game of 'fetch', *see* **Drones**; for scaring wealthy teenagers, *see* **Fyre Festival**; for being abandoned in a palace, *see* **Korea, South**; for assuming political office, *see* **Mayors**; for watching their weight, *see* **Obesity**; for looking good for the camera, *see* **Passports**; for not being named Doggy McDogface, *see* **Public, Don't Ask the**; for no longer being eaten, *see* **Taiwan**; for not doing a very good job of guarding, *see* **Theft**; and for falling out of a plane, strapped to a person, *see* **Venezuela**.

One of the people who disagreed with Alex Jones's lawyer was Alex Jones himself. The same night his lawyer claimed he was actually a 'perform-ance artist', Jones himself released a video saying, 'They've got articles out today that say I'm fake, all of this other crap. Total bull … I 110 per cent believe what I stand for.'

DONALDS

Fewer American babies were named Donald than Odin, Atticus or Augustus.

Indeed, the name Donald has slumped to an all-time low in the US. When The Donald was born, in 1946, it was the 13th most popular name in the country, but now it's the 488th. The situation is even worse in the former heartland of Donalds – Scotland – where only seven babies were named Donald in 2016. That's the lowest number since records began and a 200 per cent drop from 2014, the year before Donald Trump announced his candidacy for the presidency. Donald Anderson, former leader of Edinburgh Council, suggested, 'We need a character called Donald on *Game of Thrones* to make it popular again.'

'Donald' comes from the Gaelic name 'Domnhall', which means 'ruler of the world'. 'Melania' derives from the Greek for 'dark'. Together, therefore, the names of the US power couple make 'Dark Ruler of the World'.* Yet for others, the association with the leader of the free world seems to be problematic. In an interview with Slate.com, Donald Bell, a 38-year-old from California, said, 'I'm more sensitive about my name when I say it out loud to people. You can tell that people will flinch almost, not even meaning to, but just hearing the name, it produces such an emotional reaction in people. I'm just going to Starbucks for a cup of coffee, they ask me for my name, I have to say my name and then kind of apologise for it.'

* Theresa comes from the Greek for 'to harvest' – which is appropriate, given May's love of running through fields of wheat.

DOOMSDAY

The Doomsday Vault – one of our last defences against climate change – was flooded thanks to climate change.

The 'Doomsday Vault' is the Svalbard Global Seed Vault, located on a frozen archipelago in the Arctic. Built by the Norwegian government in an abandoned coal mine, at the end of a 130-metre tunnel, it stores the seeds of almost a million varieties of plant at a temperature of minus 18°C. In the event of crop failures, a nuclear war or environmental crisis, the seeds can be used to regenerate plant species and restore diversity to the planet's crops. There are other backups around the world, but this is the ultimate one.

Unfortunately, last October unseasonably warm weather caused melted permafrost to flood into the tunnel. The melted water then froze, leaving a big ice plug blocking the vault's entrance. This keeps happening – a little water gets in every single year, but never this much before. Thankfully the seeds were unharmed, and the vault is now being fitted with extra waterproofing.

In March 2017, a Norwegian company opened a *second* Doomsday vault on Svalbard – for data. The Arctic World Archive is 300 metres below the surface in another converted mine. Norway, Mexico and Brazil have archived copies of their constitutions and important historical papers there on photosensitive film. The archive is offline (and therefore unhackable) and it's apparently nuclear-proof, so it should offer peace of mind for the next 1,000 years. The firm responsible for the vault is called 'Piql', because they pickle your information like a gherkin.

Donald Trump's presidency prompted atomic scientists to adjust the Doomsday Clock – the imaginary clock that records how many minutes we are from nuclear apocalypse. It's now at two and a half minutes to midnight, the closest it's been since 1960. The scientists who set the clock said this was thanks in part to Trump's 'intemperate statements [and] lack of openness to expert advice'.

In his will, a Ugandan man asked to be buried along with 200 million Ugandan shillings (£42,000) with which he hoped to bribe God to forgive his sins on Judgement Day. Within a month, fellow clan members dug up his coffin to claim the money for themselves.

DRAGONFLIES

Female dragonflies avoid male attention by faking their own deaths.

This drastic strategy was observed for the first time this year in Switzerland by a researcher who saw it employed by 27 of the 31 dragonflies he studied. When being chased by an undesirable suitor, he reported, a female would suddenly plummet out of the sky, crash-land into the ground and lie motionless on her back until the male departed. She would then dust herself off and fly away.

Scientists created cyborg dragonflies by hitching tiny solar-powered backpacks on to live dragonflies and connecting the devices to their nervous systems. The scientists controlled the insects remotely, via the backpacks.

They do this because if a female's eggs for that particular cycle have already been fertilised, further copulation is not only fruitless but could damage their reproductive tracts. Twenty-one of the 27 females who attempted the ploy were successful. In the other six cases, the males were simply too persistent.

DRIVING

Police in Bath launched a crackdown on bad drivers, but only managed to find one.

As part of Operation Close Pass, a national campaign to make motorists aware of the dangers of driving too close to cyclists, Bath Police got plain-clothes officers to ride along the city's Lower Bristol Road, with instructions to pounce on drivers who passed them too closely. Unfortunately, the day they selected happened to be one when traffic congestion was so bad that, most of the time, cyclists were overtaking motorists. Only one driver was stopped.

Undaunted, the police moved to a different road. However, this one was rather wider and motorists gave them all plenty of room. The police admitted that the operation hadn't caught many people out, but noted that 'there was lots of passing interest'.

Another nationwide crackdown, on drivers using their mobile phones at the wheel, was a bit more successful. Among the 8,000 stopped were: a driver who was texting about her lost puppy; a van driver who was swerving because he had his pet parrot perched on his steering wheel; and a journalist who was caught using her phone while on her way to cover the launch of the crackdown.

DRONES

Drones were used to trace a chihuahua, herd sheep, and spy on the Lannister family.

Following a failed search party by dozens of volunteers for a chihuahua that had been lost on a Welsh mountain for five days after running off to fetch a stick, a heat-seeking drone found the animal within 20 minutes. Meanwhile, over in Australia, farmers started using drones to a) herd their sheep, and b) find them in the first place. Drones were used for espionage, too: *Game of Thrones* actor Liam Cunningham revealed that while shooting in Spain, 'We were being live-streamed while we were filming…Everything we've done has been infiltrated, which is terrible.'

Elsewhere:

▶ Edmonton Airport in Canada installed a drone painted like a falcon, with fast-flapping wings, to clear birds from flight paths. (It's been programmed to make sure it doesn't accidentally fly into flight paths itself.)

Authorities in Nigeria started testing bad drivers for signs of insanity. Drivers in the capital, Abuja, who jumped red lights were pulled over, put into ambulances and given a one-hour test of their mental competency. The acting director of road traffic services, Wadata Aliyu Bodinga, said, 'To my great surprise, none of them has actually been found to be mentally unstable.'

Any modern army needs to be able to deal with the threat of drones. France now employs golden eagles to attack them (they train the birds by having a drone deliver all of their meals) while America takes out drones in the most American way possible: with a massive flying bomb. General David Perkins told a military symposium that a drone, worth around $200, had recently been intercepted by a Patriot missile, worth around $3 million.

▶ Scientists in India tried using drones to drop 'seed bombs' that will generate entire forests.

▶ And in Sweden, a team experimented with flying defibrillators to people who are having heart attacks, and found that it's four times quicker than sending an ambulance.

One of the more bizarre ideas of the year came from tech firm Windhorse Aerospace, which announced it was looking at making a prototype of an edible drone. If it works, the one-way drone could deliver food and medicine to famine-hit areas and then be eaten itself. Founder Nigel Gifford said the frame might be made of honeycomb and the landing gear possibly from salami.

Also in drone-sausage news, hot-dog firm Oscar Mayer launched what it called 'the first unmanned hot-dog-carrying aircraft designed for remote location delivery' as a publicity stunt (realistically, the drone could only carry a single sausage and would be much slower than land-based distribution systems). It wasn't the very first in the field, however: last November an Australian man called Tim got in trouble for having a sausage sandwich delivered to him by drone – ordered from a nearby restaurant – as he sat in his hot tub. The Internet called him a 'Goddamn Australian legend'; the Civil Aviation Safety Authority pointed out that his actions contravened

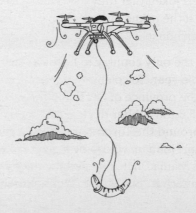

rules governing drone use in public areas and fined him AUS$900. To add to his woes, the local council saw the video, spotted that he didn't have a proper fence around his hot tub, and forced him to put one up.

DUCKS, RUBBER

A rubber duck was arrested in St Petersburg.

That, at least, was the claim of Pussy Riot member Nadezhda Tolokonnikova, as Russian Special Forces confiscated a giant duck that was being paraded by anti-corruption protesters. As it was taken away, protesters yelled, 'Not the ducky! Don't arrest the ducky!'

The background to this is a video posted last year by opposition leader Alexei Navalny showing a luxurious summer home, used by Prime Minister Dmitry Medvedev, and paid for by the public, which boasts, among other things, three helipads, a ski slope and a 'house for a ducky'. Ever since the video was released, rubber ducks have become a de facto symbol of the opposition. Protesters in St Petersburg, for instance, keep putting a duck house outside a building owned by the company financially connected to Medvedev. Each time the company removes it, the protesters simply put another in its place. When the story of Medvedev's mansion first broke, Russians joked that they'd be willing to quack and dive for bugs, if the prime minister allowed them to live in his luxury duck house.

Russia wasn't the only country to have rubber duck issues this year. To celebrate Canada's 150th anniversary, the province of Ontario hired a six-storey-high, 13.6-ton rubber duck called 'Mama Duck' to sail around the Toronto waterfront. Dutch artist Florentijn Hofman, whose own giant rubber duck predates Mama Duck, claimed the duck was an 'illegal counterfeit'. But Mama Duck's owner, Craig

Samborski, an events producer who calls himself the 'world's largest rubber duck owner', replied that the studio had 'zero rights to the concept of enlarged bathroom toys', and that Hofman had charged 'exorbitant prices for rudimentary drawings of a duck'. All the while, lots of people thought that, fake or not, the duck was a waste of taxpayers' money – the Canadian Taxpayers Federation's Ontario Director, Christine Van Geyn, said, 'This giant rubber duck isn't all it's quacked up to be.'

DUTERTE, RODRIGO

The president of the Philippines can't control his duterte mouth.

In May, Duterte appointed a pop star and sex blogger as his assistant communications secretary. Mocha Uson is lead singer of the band Mocha Girls and known for performing lap dances on stage. Duterte described her as 'a little bit sexier' than others who supported his election campaign, but said this shouldn't be held against her.

In 2016 Rodrigo Duterte, the Filipino president who has been condemned around the world for his brutal and murderous campaign to rid the country of organised crime, made a promise to God that he would never swear again, after he heard a voice threatening to down the plane he was travelling on if he did not stop.

He didn't stick to his promise. In January 2017, when asked about a UN investigation into his activities, he responded, 'I do not care if you are Obama or Ban Ki-moon. You just don't reprimand me in public [...] I will kick you out, you son of a bitch.' When the *New York Times* criticised his human rights record, he retorted, '*New York Times*: Asshole.' He dressed down the national police live on television, saying, 'Don't dare me to a gunfight [because] I will not back down, you sons of bitches.' And when the European Union rebuked him for his deadly war on drugs, he called them 'sons of bitches' too, adding, 'Why don't you mind your own business? Why do you have to f*** with us, goddamn it?'

God's opinion of these outbursts is unknown. But this year, perhaps sensibly, Duterte turned down an offer of a private jet from the former owner of Philippine Airlines.

In which we learn …
How much it costs to get crucified in Manchester,
why we should power the world with kites, how 8,800
sheep thwarted Russian spies, and why the
dinosaurs were just unlucky.

Bunnies were banned for Easter.

Police in Nice arrested a man during Easter Mass because he was waving something that 'looked like a sausage'.

Pets at Home, Britain's biggest pet retailer, announced it wouldn't be selling any rabbits between Good Friday and Easter Monday because so many of them are abandoned every year in the subsequent weeks. It seems that people infected by the Easter imagery buy bunnies on impulse and then are unable to look after them; shelters take in 67,000 abandoned rabbits each year.

In Manchester, organisers of a performance of an Easter passion play* tried to fund it by offering to crucify people in exchange for money. Their crowdfunding page declared that for £750, donors could get 'the full cruci-fixion experience' – which, it transpired, would have involved hoisting them on to a cross for a few minutes then lowering them back down again. The idea was shelved after Reverend Canon Falak Sher, chairman of the play's organising committee, got wind of it and argued that it was blasphemous, dangerous and – perhaps most importantly – very tasteless.

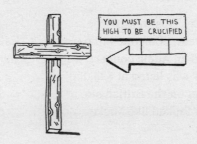

YOU MUST BE THIS HIGH TO BE CRUCIFIED

* Passion plays are dramatic presentations of Jesus's suffering, but Jesus isn't actually the thing that people most associate with Easter. In a YouGov poll, the son of God was beaten into fourth place by Easter eggs, bank holidays and hot cross buns.

Meanwhile, an off-licence in Ireland started selling Buck-fast Easter eggs this year, packaging up chocolate eggs with a bottle of the notorious tonic wine. The Devon-based monks who make Buckfast Tonic Wine advised people against buying the boxes, arguing they might encourage children to drink. Ironically, despite being made by monks, Buckfast has an ungodly reputation in

Scotland, where the vast majority of it is consumed. A 2009 report found that 43 per cent of Scottish prisoners had drunk Buckfast just before committing their last offence, even though it accounts for only 1 per cent of Scotland's overall alcohol sales.

EBAY

eBay users sold Cheetos shaped like laser guns, Bart Simpson, the Virgin Mary and penises. Lots of penises.

The craze for selling snacks that look like something else began in February, when a Cheeto resembling Harambe the gorilla (killed at Cincinnati Zoo in 2016) appeared to have been sold for $99,900. In fact, the buyer pulled out before completing the transaction, but that part of the story didn't reach a lot of people, so they searched through their snack packets hoping to strike Harambe-shaped gold. Over the following months, many more Harambe-shaped Cheetos came on sale, along with snacks shaped like all sorts of other objects. For some reason, Cheetos seem to lend themselves to looking like penises.

Odd-shaped Cheetos weren't the weirdest things on sale on eBay this year. Someone bid more than $1,500 for a bag of air from an Adele concert; a slice of toast with an image of Jesus was listed at $25,000; a 14cm-long bran flake was listed on the British site at £1,000; and a mouldy sandwich that looked like Mickey Mouse was on sale for $30,000.

ECUADOR

Ecuador elected as president the author of a joke book entitled World's Best Jokes.

Lenín Moreno believes that laughter can help the body to heal. And it isn't the only book he wrote on the subject:

The Tajikistan president, Emomali Rahmon, wrote and published a book of his own quotes this year. It's called *Wise Thoughts and Sayings of the President of Tajikistan, Founder of Peace and National Unity*, and is 464 pages long.

as vice president he was the author of another called *Being Happy Is Easy and Fun*.

His narrow victory in this year's election makes Moreno the world's first paraplegic head of state. He says that his disability helps him as a politician: 'When you don't have legs, you look down. That's what I learned: that there's another life, another existence, that there are other human beings that need a lot from us. For me, this is a novel experience that I thank God for.'

ELECTIONS, GENERAL

For an election in a country that doesn't exist, *see* **Abkhazia**; for a footballer of the year turned president, *see* **Bulgaria**; for a country that voted by marble, *see* **Gambia**; for a party with a milk packet as its logo, *see* **Kenya**; for a president who claimed victory a month before voting opened, *see* **Rwanda**; for a president called Mr Cheese from Buffalo, *see* **Somalia**; for a singing dentist turned president, *see* **Turkmenistan**; for a corpse becoming president, *see* **Zimbabwe**.

For General Elections, *see* **UK General Election**.

ENERGY

The Kentucky Coal Mining Museum converted to solar power.

The museum, which celebrates all things coal, installed 80 solar panels on its roof, hoping to save up to $10,000 a year. The man who installed the solar panels said he was surprised to get the job, saying, 'I was like, are you for real?', while the museum's communications director, Brandon Robinson, admitted to reporters that 'It is a little ironic.'

Meanwhile, in Britain, a windy couple of weeks in June made the the country's wind turbines so productive that there was little need for coal-powered electricity. However, because it costs so much to turn coal power stations on and off, they were all kept online, and people were actually *paid to take electricity* for a short while, meaning that their final energy bills were lower than they would otherwise have been. Earlier in the year, the UK went a full day without needing any energy at all from its coal power stations for the first time since 1882. This was partly due to low electricity demand after the Easter holidays, and again, a few particularly windy days.

Also cashing in on the breezy conditions, a British firm is planning a massive wind farm to be powered by giant kites flying higher than London's Shard building. As they pull at a tether, they will generate power by rotating a drum on the ground.

In Germany, scientists built what they called the 'world's largest artificial sun': effectively 149 film-projector spot-lights that can produce light 10,000 times as intense as the sun. When all the lamps are swivelled to point at a single spot, temperatures of up to 3,500°C can be generated. It is hoped that such power will one day produce hydrogen fuel. The project manager, Kai Wieghardt, said, 'I had tears in my eyes today. It's my baby.'

In other energy news:

Waitrose introduced trucks fuelled by rotten food.

A smartwatch was invented that is powered by body heat alone.

The pop group Gorillaz created the first music studio powered entirely by the sun.

ESPIONAGE

China offered a cash prize to catch spies.

In April, Beijing's government promised 500,000 yuan (about £60,000) to anyone who could expose a foreign agent. And in what state media described as an attempt to mobilise young people into 'a huge, counter-spy force', publishers inserted a game called 'Find the Spy' into school textbooks.

While China was recruiting child spies, German children were allegedly being spied on. The My Friend Cayla toy doll was classified as 'illegal espionage apparatus' and banned. Cayla responds to user's questions by accessing the Internet via a bluetooth connection embedded in her body. A German government watchdog ruled the connection could be hacked and used to eavesdrop on, and speak directly to, the user via the doll's microphone system.

Even more surprising than a children's doll, the late Richard Whiteley – former host of Channel 4's *Countdown* – was accused of top-level espionage. Ricky Tomlinson, star of *The Royle Family*, alleged that Whiteley worked for the intelligence services in the 1970s, when he was involved in a plot to jail Tomlinson and other trade unionists. Whiteley's partner insisted the allegations were nonsense, not least because he was terrible with technology and 'very indiscreet'.

EVEREST

Climbing Everest may have got easier: by nearly one inch.

Indian scientists mounted an expedition to see whether an earthquake in 2015 had taken an inch off the height of Mount Everest. The potential height reduction may be good news for tired climbers, but the bad news is that tectonic plate movement makes Everest (and the rest of the Himalayas) 3–4 millimetres taller each year – so even if it has lost it, Everest will be back to its old height by about 2022.

In May, Indian mountaineer Anshu Jamsenpa became the first woman to climb Everest twice within a week. A week later, 29-year-old Spanish mountaineer Kilian Jornet Burgada *also* climbed Everest twice within a week, without oxygen, *and* while suffering food poisoning. He modestly said it was 'a mountain like any other – albeit taller'.

Unfortunately, the less dedicated have now started cheating their way up Everest. Last year an Indian couple photoshopped their faces on to someone else's photo from the summit, to trick the Nepal authorities into giving them their official Everest completion certificate. They were banned from climbing mountains in Nepal for 10 years. The authorities are now considering giving GPS belts to climbers to track whether or not they've told the truth about their ascent.

The downside of all the people climbing Everest (at least, those who do actually climb it) is the huge mountain of litter they leave behind. So much rubbish, like abandoned tents and supplies, has been left on the mountain that this year the Nepalese government had to recruit sherpas to fill huge canvas bags with 80 kilos of waste each. They were then taken by the 'bin men' – helicopter pilots – who winched it away. The Sherpas received a bonus of $2 for every kilo of rubbish they brought back to camp.

The entire country of Estonia will get up to 9 inches taller next year, after deciding to change the way it measured its height above sea level. The country will now be on a European-measured system, rather than a Russian one. As a result of the change, the highest peak in the country will grow 20 centimetres to 317.4 metres above sea level – about 3.5 per cent the height of Everest.

EXCUSES

To find out why an alt-right commentator forgot basic information about his children, *see* **Divorce**; why some employers don't pay their staff fairly, *see* **HMRC**; why the residents of Nashville were late for work, *see* **Mayors**; why a 'thunder master' lost a fight in 10 seconds, *see* **Martial**

Arts; why Kentish commuters were delayed, *see* **Railways**; why almost 900,000 litres of alcohol mysteriously went missing, *see* **Rats**; and why a real-life Jaws made someone late for dinner, *see* **Shark Attack**.

EXTINCTIONS ▶

If the Chicxulub asteroid had hit the Earth 30 seconds later, we'd all still be speaking dinosaur.

NASA carried out a computer simulation to see what would happen if a giant killer asteroid approached the Earth, and concluded that there wouldn't be time to stop it before it wiped out the whole of humanity. However, there *would* be time to send up a satellite to take photos of the event. NASA researcher Dr Joseph Nuth said, 'The biggest problem, basically, is there's not a hell of a lot we can do about it at the moment.'

Chicxulub was the asteroid that landed in present-day Mexico 66 million years ago and obliterated the dinosaurs. Theoretically, it shouldn't have been able to do so – it was only 9 miles across, the equivalent of a grain of sand hitting a bowling ball. But this year, geologists finally worked out how it caused such devastation: it hit the Earth in 'the worst possible place'.

Scientists drilled into the crater where the asteroid struck, and found that the rock there was full of sulphur. At the moment of impact, this would have vaporised, exploded upwards and turned into a cloud that reflected all the sun's heat back into space, cooling the Earth to temperatures dinosaurs couldn't handle. Since the asteroid struck at 40,000mph, matter from the Earth's crust would have flown higher than the Himalayas, and a 10,000°C fireball would have formed and incinerated everything within 600 miles. It would also have made a hole 111 miles wide and turned the surrounding sea into steam. Had Chicxulub arrived 30 seconds later, it would have met the Earth at a different point in its rotation, avoiding that sulphur-filled spot, and the dinosaurs might still rule today.

In which we learn …
The difference between fake fake fur and real fake fur,
the duties of a sex tsar, how God is like a fidget spinner,
why you shouldn't sleep with an Australian carp, and
what happened in the Great Japanese Crisp Shortage.

A Ming-dynasty temple started using robots to ration toilet paper.

China is on a massive face-recognition drive. Some traffic junctions now spot jaywalkers and display their faces on giant video screens to embarrass them; companies use facial recognition to let customers access vending machines or make deposits; and this year a Beijing marathon installed scanners to make sure people didn't take short cuts.

What's more, the lavatories at Beijing's 15th-century Temple of Heaven are scanning visitors' faces to make sure they don't take too much toilet paper. The change was instituted because the authorities had found that people were stealing huge lengths of toilet paper by stuffing it into backpacks. Customers now have to stare for three seconds at a machine outside the cubicle, which then spits out a single two-foot length of paper. If customers want more, they have to wait nine full minutes, then return. A temple spokesman told a local newspaper, 'If we encounter guests who have diarrhoea or any other situation in which they urgently require toilet paper, then our staff on the ground will directly provide the toilet paper.'

The technology behind face-recognition software is good – it can even tell if you've had plastic surgery. But it's not yet perfect. Last year, Wang Yuheng, a Chinese man with a photographic memory, defeated a face-recognition machine in a trial that involved matching women with their childhood photos. Wang's skills are extremely rare: on a TV show he once successfully identified a specific glass of water out of 520 identical glasses of water.

The Mexican Museum in San Francisco was informed by a team of independent inspectors that 96 per cent of its oldest exhibits could be fake, and that only 83 items out of 2,000 in the museum's pre-Columbian collection were definitely genuine. The other 1,917 will now probably be given away to local schools or smaller museums. 'I was surprised,' said the chair of the museum's board. 'I thought we'd have more that are of museum quality.'

This is a Monopoly-esque board game released in 1989. The museum director said it was 'vile; it's got a huge Donald Trump picture on the front, it's got Donald Trump pictures on the money and on the cards – everywhere. We tried to play it the other day and it's impossibly dull.'

FAILURES

Sweden's Museum of Failure was a huge success.

The museum, which opened in June in the small town of Helsingborg, contains over 70 exhibits, all of them commercial products which turned out to be disastrous failures. They include:

- A rejuvenating face mask that gave the wearer electric shocks
- The Bic for Her: a range of pens with floral patterns on them
- Heinz's experimental green ketchup
- Coffee-flavoured Coca-Cola
- Colgate Lasagna, from the 1980s
- A cologne by Harley-Davidson called Hot Road
- The TwitterPeek, a handheld device whose sole purpose was to show Twitter messages, but that could display only the first 20 characters of any given Tweet
- Trump: The Game*

The museum also hosted 'Nights of Failure', such as a renowned classical pianist performing the early, 'far from perfect' versions of Beethoven's 5th.

In press terms, the Museum of Failure was a massive success. Explaining the reason for the museum, director Samuel West said that he was 'tired of all the success stories … failures never get any attention and they are so much more fascinating'. When he first registered the domain name for the website, West managed to misspell the word 'museum'. He later said, 'That could happen to anybody after a few beers.' When asked why the museum was located in the town of Helsingborg, he said, 'It's where I live.'

FAKES

People in Britain have unwittingly been buying fake fake fur.

People who thought they'd been responsibly buying fake fur in British shops found that they had actually been purchasing fake fake fur – in other words, real fur. Sky News bought items labelled as artificial fur from multiple shops, and found the fibres came from such animals as rabbits, foxes, raccoons and cats. One father told the BBC, 'You don't want a raccoon pom-pom on your daughter's head.'

As well as fake fake fur, this year saw fake fake food. People in Nigeria were warned to be careful after police seized 2.5 tonnes of artificial rice made of plastic. Similar stories cropped up elsewhere in Africa, and in India news reports said more than 30 people had been arrested for selling plastic rice and eggs. However, all this news of fake food was itself fake. There is such a thing as 'plastic rice', but it's something that is used in shipping and it's never found its way into the food chain. For one thing, so-called fake rice is more expensive than real rice.

Both the fake fur and the fake rice turned out to be fake fakes, but one real fake that made the news was an entire US embassy in Ghana. Late last year, news broke that for 10 years Ghana had had two US embassies – one real and one fake. The fake one, complete with a Stars and Stripes flag outside, was a money-making scam which sold people a range of false ID documents, fake visas and fraudulently obtained real visas. Possible giveaways included the fact that the 'embassy' was located in a shabby two-storey building with a corrugated iron roof, and that it was staffed by Turkish people pretending to be Americans. The organised crime ring that ran the embassy was so confident that it advertised it on billboards across West Africa. It also ran a fake Dutch embassy in case anyone fancied visiting the Netherlands.

FAKE NEWS

Andy: Fake news is about to get much worse.

Anna: How?

Andy: Researchers from the University of Washington have worked out how to make fake news videos. So in future, instead of seeing a made-up newspaper headline, you'll see videos of people saying things they haven't said. They've just made an artificial Obama.

Dan: A robot Obama? A Robama?

Andy: Well...nearly. They've taken footage of Obama and used software to make him say whatever they want. Essentially they've trained software to 'watch' videos of people speaking, then it learns the mouth shapes they make to go along with particular sounds, and they've taken his voice from previous words he's said.

Dan: So it's like one step up from wearing a party mask of Obama and impersonating him.

James: Well, it's more like four normal steps up. Or one enormous step, I suppose.

Anna: Facebook has recently circulated ways to spot fake news. Have you guys read their ten-point checklist?

James: One: It's on Facebook so it's probably fake news.

Anna: Not far off. It's all very obvious stuff. Points include: 'Check the evidence', 'Check for unusual formatting' – I'm not sure what that means – and then 'Is this a joke?'

Dan: They should have said, 'Would Obama really be talking about a secret trapdoor in the White House?' Because that's one I fell for. I saw a story about an escape route under the president's desk which he could use to escape.

Anna: Sounds legit. What was wrong with that?

Dan: Well, it turned out to be from a site called 'Not the White House', and I just missed the 'not'.

Anna: Everyone's acting like fake news is a new thing. But in 1828 Andrew Jackson started a rumour that his presidential rival John Quincy Adams had procured an American prostitute for the Russian tsar to appease him. And that was almost 200 years ago. So it's always been around.

James: A lot of today's fake news came from a certain town in Macedonia called Veles. According to some reports, teenagers in this town were writing fake stories so they'd get more clicks to make advertising revenue. They've stopped doing that now, but they have found a new way to make money.

Dan: What's that?

James: They broadcast long silent clips on Facebook that show a question like 'What do you think of Donald Trump?' and people click on the smiley face, or the angry face, or whatever, and those clicks turn into revenue. So they don't have to go to the trouble of writing news, they can just put silence up there.

Dan: We should get in on that. Would save us having to write this book.

Old MacDonald had a sex change, E-I-E-I-O

Switzerland relaxed
laws governing the sale
of insect-based foods.
Previously, shops had to
have special authorisa-
tion to sell grub-based
grub; now, they can sell
any food that includes
mealworms, locusts
or crickets. Delighted
by the news, the Swiss
supermarket chain
Coop announced they
would be launching
worm meatballs and a
wormburger.

The British charity LEAF (Linking Environment And
Farming), which promotes sustainable agriculture,
has come up with a new, up-to-date version of 'Old
MacDonald's Farm'. The first verse of the new version
goes:

> Young MacDonald had a farm
> Yo, yo, yo, yo yo!
> And on that farm she had a drone
> Yo, yo, yo, yo, yo!
> She flew it here, she flew it there
> Checked the farm, from in the air
> Young MacDonald had a farm
> Whirr, whirr, whirr whirr, whirr!

In Kenya, Old MacDonald's cows probably go 'clunk clunk
clunk', as farmers there are using giant mechanical cows
called anaerobic digesters, which work rather like bovine
stomachs. They take plant matter in at one end and fire
out manure from the other.

These at least are real farms, but it emerged this year
that in Britain farms are not always what they seem.
Waitrose's 'British ready meals' range was found to
include lamb from New Zealand farms. The supermarket
explained that while the lamb may indeed have been from
the other side of the world, the recipe was 100 per cent
British. After a storm of outrage, the company caved and

relabelled the range 'Waitrose Classic'. A spokeswoman said, 'We understand why confusion has arisen.' Waitrose isn't the only guilty one: last year Tesco launched a range from the non-existent 'Nightingale, Redmere and Rosedene farms'. They were all invented by the supermarket, offering food that may sound British but in many cases has been grown abroad.

FAT LEONARD

US navy officers were bribed with prostitutes by a man called Fat Leonard.

Malaysian businessman Fat Leonard is so nicknamed because he weighs more than 350 pounds and is called Leonard. He bribed US officials with luxury goods, travel expenses and prostitutes in order to get them to direct their boats to his ports, where he could bill them for overpriced fuel, barges, water, sewage removal and tugs. Twenty-seven people have now been charged over the scandal, and this year one of them, Robert Gilbeau, became the first US navy admiral ever to be charged with a federal crime in connection with his military service.

It's not the only waste of US army money this year. The Pentagon spent $28 million on forest camouflage uniforms for Afghan troops. Afghanistan has only 2.1 per cent tree cover.

FERTILITY

Spain now has a Minister for Sex.

The Spanish government tackled the country's low fertility rate by employing a 'sex tsar'. Edelmira Barreira Diz, the senator who has stepped into the newly created role, has been tasked with reversing the country's declining population trend. She will be working with communities to help them understand the urgency of

A high court judge in Rajasthan claimed that peahens get pregnant by drinking the tears of peacocks.

━━━━━ ▼ ━━━━━

One traditional method of increasing fertility is to flush the fallopian tubes with poppy seed oil. The practice is more than 100 years old, but was assumed to be an old wives' remedy until a study this year found that 40 per cent of women got pregnant after having their tubes flushed with the oil, compared with 29 per cent who'd had them flushed with water. It's thought that the oil is more effective than water in dissolving debris or mucus in there, and that this aids conception.

the problem and the need to procreate. This year, Spain registered more deaths than births for the first time since 1941.

In an attempt to solve its own underpopulation problem, the Swedish town of Övertorneå considered the idea of giving employees an hour a week to go and have state-subsidised sex. The politician who proposed it, Per-Erik Muskos, did acknowledge it would be hard to enforce the idea, and impossible to know if employees hadn't used the time to take a walk in the country instead. The town's council turned down the idea, saying, 'If sexual congress is considered a valid activity, then other activities should be approved, such as cleaning.'

The French village of Auge also has a problem with low fertility. This year, a new baby was born there for the first time in 50 years, and it was such a rare occurrence that no one knew how to register the birth. A few days after having a baby in her garden – a location that pleased the father, who is a landscape gardener – mother Cyrielle Brugère took her newborn daughter to the town hall to get a birth certificate. This flummoxed the mayor, who admitted that she wasn't sure how to fill in the form for a birth, and that the birth register had become so redundant that it was now used to register deaths. Happily, she successfully navigated her way through the paperwork, and said that she hoped news of the newborn would attract other families to the village.

FIDGET SPINNERS ▶

Fidget spinners were used to explain the Holy Trinity.

For those not already in the know, a fidget spinner is a piece of plastic with three arms that you hold between your fingers and spin. You can either do tricks with it or just let it rotate for long periods of time. It's been claimed, with little scientific evidence, that fidget spinners help children with ADHD to concentrate. What is certainly the case is that they quickly became the craze of the year. Teachers across the world were driven mad by them and many schools banned them.

In May 2017, all top 25 toys on Amazon.co.uk were fidget spinners, and they accounted for 17 per cent of daily online toy sales. Overall, the fad generated somewhere in the region of half a billion dollars. However, they were almost completely unknown until this year, and their origins are uncertain. Many newspapers reported that they were invented in 1997 by a woman named Catherine Hettinger, that she was unable to afford the patent renewal fee of $400 in 2005, and that she therefore made no money from the craze. But the toy she invented is somewhat different, and it seems more likely that, as online magazine *Inc*. reported, the spinners evolved from the Torqbar, a high-end spinning office toy launched on GoFundMe.com in 2015. The popularity of fidget spinners in general was apparently boosted by New York teenagers Cooper Weiss and Allan Maman, who began printing their own versions of the toy on their school's 3D printer at the end of 2016.

Soon everyone was in on the act. Trendy priests suggested that the three arms of the fidget spinners could be said to represent God the Father, the Son and the Holy Spirit, all spinning through heaven together… or something.* Celebrities as diverse as Kim Kardashian, Brazilian footballer Ronaldinho and rock band Arcade Fire marketed their own. NASA announced it would take some into space, to see how long they spin for. And during the UK general election, one newsagent in Devon sold red and blue fidget spinners alongside one another, thinking that their relative sales would reflect the final result. It didn't quite work. Forty-seven per cent sold were Labour red and 43 per cent were Tory blue. Labour's spin doctors were, of course, unable to replicate that result.

* Fidget spinners are actually satanic. So claims a Paraguayan pastor, who says the spinning action forces children to make the 'horns' gesture, which is often referred to as the 'sign of the devil'.

FIGHTS

For India vs China, *see* **Bhutan**; for journalist vs politician, *see* **Body Slams**; for man vs crocodile, *see* **Dickheads**, for Kuratas vs Eagle Prime, *see* **Japan**; for monk vs monk, *see* **Jesus**; for boxer vs 'thunder master', *see* **Martial Arts**; for McGregor vs Mayweather *see* **Mayweather vs McGregor**; for centurion vs tourist, *see* **Rome, Ancient**; for man vs shark, *see* **Shark Attack**; and for politicians vs water balloons, *see* **Taiwan**.

FINLAND

Finland started handing out free money.

———— ▼ ————

Finland held the 22nd World Air Guitar Championships this year. It was won – for the second time – by Matt Burns, whose stage name is Airistotle. The stated aim of the championships is to bring about world peace with no guitars. Burns said of his victory, 'You do not have to be in good shape for this, which is a huge plus.'

The idea behind what is known as 'Universal Basic Income' is that if you give everyone in the country a certain amount of cash, it will reduce poverty, increase individual freedom, and also cut down a lot of admin in the welfare department. Basic income may well become necessary if robots take over all of our jobs, and it was presumably welcomed by Helsinki's bus drivers: the city got a fleet of driverless buses this year.

Finland's trial initially applied to unemployed people, and the deal is that they will keep receiving $600 a month even if they get a job. It seems to be working, with people on the scheme reporting lower levels of emotional (as well as financial) stress. Pierre Omidyar, the billionaire founder of eBay, also likes the concept; he is giving more than 26,000 people in Kenya a regular salary through the charity GiveDirectly. Not everyone thinks it's a great idea, though: critics have suggested people may lose the motivation to work, and that the lack of personalisation of welfare may hurt the most needy. Last year, the people of Switzerland actually voted against receiving free money every month.

*Scientists discovered that you can save your life by
slamming your body into a chair.*

People can now perform the Heimlich manoeuvre on
themselves. Doctors from London's Royal Brompton
Hospital wrote in the journal *Thorax* that if you start
choking on food you can self-Heimlich by thrusting a
hand into your abdomen or by pressing yourself sharply
on to a chair. They tested both methods after swallowing
pressure sensors to measure the effects.

Dr Henry Heimlich, the man who first popularised the
technique in 1974, died in late 2016. He had campaigned
against slapping people on the back when they were
choking, saying that it was dangerous (it's not). The
American Red Cross thought his campaign against what
he called 'death blows' was so dubious that it reinstated
back slaps as its first recommended option, advising the
Heimlich manoeuvre only if that didn't work. Heimlich
was so angry to be associated with back-slapping that
he asked the organisation to remove his name from its
training procedures. The American Red Cross therefore
renamed the manoeuvre 'abdominal thrusts'.

Heimlich developed his technique to deal with what was
sometimes known as the 'beefsteak disease' (because it
often involved people choking on large lumps of meat).*
He and his team worked out the answer after two years
of experiments that involved putting balloons down the
throats of anaesthetised beagles. The last time he used
his technique was at the age of 96, when he saved an
87-year-old woman who was sitting next to him at dinner
in his retirement home. She later wrote to him, 'God put
me in this seat next to you,' although she didn't suggest
why God had made her choke on her burger in the
first place.

A Bristol woman saved a
stranger's life imme-
diately after finishing
a three-day first aid
course. A few hours after
Rachelle Miller had been
practising CPR on a
dummy, real-life human
Lewis Bond, who had
driven over to collect a
fish tank, had a heart
attack outside her front
door. She kept him
alive until paramedics
arrived.

** Carrie Fisher once
choked on a Brussels
sprout on set while
filming* The Blues
Brothers*. Dan Aykroyd
saved her life with the
Heimlich manoeuvre,
then proposed
marriage a few
minutes later.*

Australia gave its carp herpes.

In January, a Japanese
man known as the 'Tuna
King' spent £500,000
on a single 470-pound
bluefin tuna. A regular
purchaser of large tuna
(in 2013 he spent over
£1 million on one), he
uses them to publicise
his restaurant, and
reckons he makes
back his investment in
additional customers
who come to see his
massive fish.

Ninety per cent of the fish in the Murray River are carp, which is an invasive species. They were introduced into Australia in the 1800s, and have out-competed native species ever since. They're worth little to fishmongers, as due to Australia's strict biosecurity laws they can't be sold overseas, and so the government wants to kill as many as possible. According to the coordinator of the National Carp Control Plan, Matt Barwick (who one politician has dubbed 'The Carpinator') the best way to do this is to give them the fatal koi herpes virus, so Australia started testing the idea.

The move has worried scientists, especially, it seems, Professor Cock van Oosterhout of the University of East Anglia, who told the *Daily Telegraph* that it was an 'irreversible high-risk proposal'. The Australian government claims its tests have shown that other species in the rivers can't contract the virus, but van Oosterhout says the herpes could evolve to attack other animals.

Meanwhile in Sweden, Gothenburg's anti-bomb team were called out to defuse a fishy package that turned out to be 10 kilos of frozen cod. 'This could only happen in Gothenburg,' one reporter wrote, but he's wrong: in the past couple of years fish have been mistaken for bombs in both Hamburg and Manila. In 2013, an actual bomb was found in the belly of a squid in Guangdong, China.

** There is, of course,
no such thing as a fish.*

FOOD AND DRINK

People in Japan started panic-buying crisps.

After a series of typhoons destroyed the country's potato crop, people started stockpiling packets of crisps, for fear of running out. They were selling for ¥8 a bag – six times their normal price. This was not the year's only food shortage:

▶ *Courgettes in Europe.* Bad weather in Spain – one of Europe's main courgette producers – ruined the crop and led to prices quadrupling across the continent. The inclement conditions damaged other super-market staples, too. Tesco temporarily banned their customers from buying more than three iceberg lettuces each, and Morrisons customers were limited to three heads of broccoli per trip.

▶ *Milk in Qatar.* One consequence of the diplomatic dispute between Qatar and neighbouring Saudi Arabia (*see* **Qatar**) has been the cutting of all dairy trading links between the two countries. In an attempt to counter the effects of this, one Qatari businessman flew 4,000 cows to his motherland in order to bring milk to the masses.

▶ *Croissants in France.* Falling milk yields led France to announce a butter shortage. Even more worryingly, this threatened to cause a croissant shortage (crois-sants are typically 25 per cent butter).

▶ *Bacon in the USA.* The Ohio Pork Council prompted alarm when it reported that US bacon reserves were at their lowest level since 1957. It later suggested that there was no need to panic-buy, as America still had 8.2 million kilos of pork belly reserves. The BBC summed up the overreaction with the headline 'Aporkalypse No' (for other aporkalypses, *see* **Boar**).

▶ *Vanilla ice cream across the planet.* Madagascar grows 80 per cent of the world's vanilla, so when a cyclone in March destroyed huge numbers of vines, the price rocketed and vanilla ice cream disappeared from shelves. In September, vanilla was 20 per cent more expensive than silver, costing £530 a kilo to silver's £440. In 2012, a kilo of vanilla cost just £23.

In a bid to encourage German tourists to visit Mexico, the Mexican government partnered with a creative agency to build an artificial cloud that rains tequila, and then installed it in a Berlin gallery. Thanks to some clever technology, the cloud emitted a thick tequila fog when-ever it rained in Berlin.

Monks in the earth-quake-hit town of Norcia in Umbria released a limited-edition beer that was fermenting in the vats when the quake hit, claiming that the vibrations gave the beer a unique flavour.

The England women's team reached the semi-finals of Euro 2017, thanks to one player paying attention in a meeting.

—————— ▼ ——————

A non-league footballer in Aberdeen missed the goal so badly the ball ended up 1,800 kilometres away in Norway. His shot went into the River Dee and floated into the North Sea. Sometime later, the footballer's club, Banks O'Dee FC (whose name was on the ball), received an email from Vanna, a small island off the coast of Norway, saying the ball had washed up on their beach. Club secretary Tom Ewan said, 'We lose about two balls a month. We just never realised this is where they might be ending up.'

With the game between England and Spain on a knife-edge, English defender Ellen White slipped, causing the ball to bounce off her leg and hit her arm. The referee gave a penalty for handball. However, another English player, Lucy Bronze, calmly explained to the referee that she'd got the rules wrong. Before the tournament, UEFA held meetings with the players to clarify the rules, and in one of those meetings UEFA said that if the ball deflects on to someone's arm then it couldn't be hand-ball. The referee had forgotten this, but Bronze said, 'I really paid attention [in those meetings]. I had my book out and everything, making sure if I was playing I knew exactly what was a yellow card and red card.' The referee reversed her decision, and England went on to win the match, before proving themselves the equal of the English men's team by getting hammered in the semi-finals.

In the European Women's Under-17 Championships, FIFA turned to Abba for help in their penalty shoot-outs. There's long been a set approach to shoot-outs: a coin toss to see which team will take the first penalty, and then five penalties each taken in the sequence Team A, then Team B, then Team A, then Team B again, and so on. The problem is that whichever team goes first tends to have a psychological advantage – indeed the statistics suggest that Team A will end up winning 60 per cent of the time. A new, theoretically fairer system has therefore been trialled, which, rather than going ABABABABAB, follows the tennis tie-break pattern of ABBAABBAAB. It's hoped this will make penalties fairer, but the first time it was ever used things went pretty much as you would expect – the shoot-out was won by Germany.

FORTUNE COOKIES

The world's leading fortune cookie writer retired after 30 years due to writer's block.

Wonton Food Inc. is the largest supplier of fortune cookies in the world, producing over 4.5 million every day. For the last 30 years most of the fortunes have been written by one man, the Chief Fortune Writer, Donald Lau. He initially got the job because no one else in the company could speak good enough English.

Unfortunately, he is now stepping down as he can no longer think of what to write. 'I used to write 100 a year,' he told *Time* magazine, 'but I've only written two or three a month over the past year.'

A fortune that Lau wrote back in 2005 led to the company being investigated. It seemed innocent enough: the encouraging words 'All the preparation you've done will finally be paying off', and a series of lucky numbers, 22, 28, 32, 33, 39, 40. The numbers turned out to be a bit too lucky, though: Lau had unwittingly predicted five out of six winning balls in that week's lottery. One hundred and ten fortune-cookie readers who had taken his advice were able to claim their share of a huge payout. Sadly, Donald Lau was not one of the 110 winners.*

* The new fortune writer, James Wong, revealed that some years ago, a man who was sharing a meal with his wife before a business trip opened a fortune cookie to find the prediction: 'Romance is in the air for your next trip'. The couple eventually divorced, blaming the cookie.

FRANCE

For the French artist who became a chicken, *see* **Art**; for why Paris will probably never lend Australia anything again, *see* **Cock-Ups**; for a birth in the death register, *see*

Fertility; for croissant shortages, *see* **Food and Drink**; for grandmothers delivered to your door, *see* **Old Age**; for an international booze battle, *see* **Wine**.

FRENCH PRESIDENTIAL ELECTION

Emmanuel Macron won the presidency of France, narrowly beating 'nobody at all'.

Here's how the top five ranked:

▶ *5th place – Jean-Luc Mélenchon*

The far-left candidate, Jean-Luc Mélenchon, won almost 20 per cent of the votes cast in the first round of the French presidential election. He proposed a top rate of tax of 100 per cent, addressed multiple rallies simultaneously through a hologram,* and campaigned via a computer game called Fiscal Kombat, where players picked up bankers and then shook them upside down so money came out of their pockets. One of his slogans was 'Can't Stenchon the Melénchon', which a lot of French people didn't understand. It turned out to be a play on Donald Trump's line 'Can't Stump the Trump', using the supposedly common English phrase 'stench on'. English people didn't understand it either.

* Actually it wasn't technically a hologram, but a 'Pepper's Ghost', a 19th-century magic trick that projects an image on to a transparent surface. It's not a true hologram because the image it creates is 2D, whereas holograms are 3D.

▶ *4th place – François Fillon*

François Fillon won just over 20 per cent of all votes cast. He was dogged by scandal throughout the campaign. His wife, who described herself as 'very English' despite being born and raised in Wales, was accused of falsifying documents related to her job – an allegedly fake job working as Fillon's parliamentary assistant. Fillon then got into even more trouble for failing to declare nearly 50,000 euros' worth of suits from a Paris tailor.

▶ *3rd place – Marine Le Pen*

Marine Le Pen beat Fillon by just over 1 per cent, and so went into a run-off with the eventual winner, Emmanuel Macron. Until it became a drag on her campaign, she was president of the far-right National Front, founded by her father, Jean-Marie Le Pen, whose other claim to fame is that he popularised the duffel coat in France. The two fell out in 2014 when Jean-Marie's Dobermann killed Marine's Bengal cat.

▶ *2nd place – ennui*

Marine Le Pen may technically have come second in the election, but some commentators pointed out that if you counted the four million abstentions, blank and spoiled votes, and the 25 per cent of the electorate who didn't vote at all (unusually high for France) she actually came third. The apathy was probably due to the fact that neither of the leading candidates was particularly popular. The most common reason given for voting for Macron was to oppose Le Pen. Only 16 per cent said that they voted for him due to his policies.

▶ *Winner – Emmanuel Macron*

This was the first time Macron had won any kind of election, and his victory might have surprised some of his old teachers; he wasn't a great student, recalling many years later that he was 'terrible at maths and statistics', despite later becoming Minister for the Economy. He was much better at literature, theatre, and finding a future wife – he met his partner, Brigitte, aged fifteen, when she was a teacher at his school. He was in the same class as her daughter and according to his biographer, when he began to act lovesick, Macron's family believed he had a crush on the daughter.

When Marine Le Pen wanted to ring and concede the election to Emmanuel Macron, nobody had his number. Eventually one of her aides had to get it by ringing a talk-show host.

Scientists discovered a glow-in-the-dark frog.

————— ▼ —————

Scientists in Turkey published their new discovery that frogs hitchhike on the backs of water buffalo for warmth (and to eat flies on the buffalo). Nobody has ever seen amphibians exhibiting this kind of relationship with large mammals before. Most of the buffalo observed had between two and five frogs on their back, although one was coated in 27.

The polka-dot tree frog (*Hypsiboas punctatus*) lives in Argentina and is the first naturally fluorescent amphibian ever seen. Scientists aren't sure why it glows; they guess it could be to help the frog communicate.

Elsewhere in South America, scientists in Ecuador identified a new species of glass frog, so named because many are partially transparent. *Hyalinobatrachium yaku* is so clear that you can see its heart beating through its chest, and its bladder is transparent, too. The new species was (sort of) discovered on Facebook. It was first caught in 1998, but was left in a glass jar and forgotten, until the scientist who first found it spotted photos his colleagues had posted of identical specimens they'd picked up. Scientists suggest that being see-through might help the frog hide from predators or save energy. Sadly, even though the frog was identified only this year, it is endangered already, because its habitat is threatened by oil drilling.

A third of the world's amphibian species are either in decline or recently extinct. This is bad news not only for frogs but also for humans, as the animals can often have medical uses. It's just been discovered, for instance, that some South Indian frogs may have life-saving snot (*see also* **Nose, Picking Your**). There's a chemical in their bogeys which can kill some influenza viruses. This means they can't catch the flu, and their snot could possibly be turned into medicine for humans.

FYRE FESTIVAL

The Fyre music festival was criticised for, among many other things, having no music.

Created by rapper Ja Rule and entrepreneur Billy McFarland, the Fyre Festival was meant to be the ultimate elite music-festival experience for rich millennials. Addressing staff before the festival opened, Ja Rule made a toast to 'living like movie stars, partying like rock stars, and f***ing like porn stars'. Ticket holders also looked forward to sleeping in luxury tents and eating gourmet food on a private island in the Bahamas.

Instead, attendees reported sleeping in disaster-relief tents, eating cheese sandwiches from polystyrene boxes, fighting each other for the island's inadequate supply of water and electricity, dodging packs of feral dogs, and crying for rescue via their social media channels.

Following the disaster, the festival organisers published an apology on their website saying, 'We thought we were ready… but then everyone arrived.'

Scientists recently discovered a frog which startles would-be predators by flashing its bright orange groin at them – nobody has thought of any medical applications yet.

One group who didn't arrive were 90s rockers Blink-182 who were booked to play but pulled out the day before the festival. Lead singer Matt Skiba credited himself with the disaster. 'I consider myself a pagan and a witch,' he said. 'With every inch of my energy I wanted Fyre not to happen. I put all the electricity and energy in my body against that thing happening.'

In answer to a question on the refund application form sent out to all ticket holders, 81 per cent of the initial responders said despite all this, they would like to attend Fyre Festival 2018.

In which we learn …
*How Britain accidentally invaded Spain, why you should
wrap a glacier up nice and warm, why you shouldn't leave
old grenades in the fridge, who ate all the pasties, and
what Donald Trump keeps in his golf bag.*

The new president of Gambia once worked as a security guard in a north London branch of Argos.

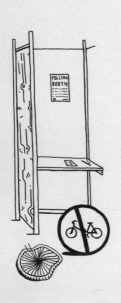

* The Gambian farms coordinator is one of Jammeh's friends, the excellently named Colonel Seedy Baldeh.

After his victory, Adama Barrow almost didn't get to take office. The previous incumbent, Yahya Jammeh, initially refused to accept defeat, arguing that the decision should be left to the country's judges. This was a smart move on his part, given that he had sacked most of them the previous year, leaving an insufficient number to form a ruling panel. Eventually, though, he did agree to go, but not before he is alleged to have taken $50 million from the country's coffers. On the plus side, he wrote to Barrow, who worked at the Holloway Road Argos while studying in London, magnanimously allowing him to keep all the rice that was growing in his fields.*

Gambia's elections are organised according to a unique marble-based voting system. As the country's literacy rate is low, voters are given a marble instead of a voting slip. They vote by putting their marble into a barrel painted with the colours of the party they support. As the marble drops into the barrel it automatically rings a bicycle bell – so there's no way you can sneak two marbles in without polling officers hearing. To avoid confusion, bicycles are banned from the vicinity of polling stations. In the last elections, only two invalid votes were cast, by voters who balanced their marbles on top of one of the barrels instead of putting them inside.

GAME OF THRONES

There is a new world record for 'most stuntmen on fire at the same time'.

This year, the seventh season of *Game of Thrones* included one battle which featured half of all the stunt performers in the UK, and most of them were set on fire.

Emmy-winning stunt coordinator Rowley Irlam said that by igniting 20 actors at one time, the programme makers beat the 13 burning actors in *Saving Private Ryan* and the 18 people partially burned in *Braveheart*. They also beat the record for the total number of people set on fire in a single episode, managing 73, but stressed that all the horses shown on fire were fake. Showrunner David Benioff told *Entertainment Weekly*, 'Our stunt coordinator really wanted to get in the Guinness Book of World Records for this.' Unfortunately they won't make it into the book, as Guinness doesn't recognise the record.

Those who are particularly interested in *Game of Thrones* can now study a history course at Harvard inspired by the show. Not to be outdone, Berkeley University introduced a course called 'The Linguistics of *Game of Thrones* and the Art of Language Invention', where students can learn the fictional language of Dothraki.

Ha vilajerosh ki ador shor tawakof, *see* **IKEA**.

GIBRALTAR

Spain deliberately stationed its most inexperienced police officers at the border with Gibraltar.

This was the claim made by Joseph Garcia, Gibraltar's deputy chief minister, who said Spain had posted rookie police officers on purpose at the territory's border to cause traffic jams. He believes Spain uses traffic jams as a 'political weapon' against Gibraltar.

Gibraltar was a hot topic this year. Police even had to escort two passengers off a plane for arguing about the territory, following discussion in the media over whether Gibraltar should have to leave the EU along with the rest of Britain. But at least the altercation didn't lead to war. The last time that seemed even remotely likely was in 2002 when Britain invaded Spain. Accidentally. Admiral Lord West, then First Sea Lord, revealed this year that during a

A former Miss World became mayor of Gibraltar in April. When Kaiane Lopez won Miss World in 2009, all government employees got to go home at 3.30 p.m. to celebrate, and the government requested that all businesses close between 4 p.m. and 6 p.m.

military training exercise a group of marines charged up a beach in what they thought was Gibraltar, only to discover that they were actually in Spain's La Linea. West received a call from his military commander saying, 'Sir, I'm afraid something awful's happened … I'm afraid we've invaded Spain, but we don't think they've noticed.' Retreat and apologies swiftly followed.

GLACIERS

Switzerland is trying to save its glaciers with fake snow.

The theory is that if you spray enough machine-made 'snow' over a square kilometre of glacier, the sunlight will be reflected back, dramatically slowing the rate at which the glacier melts. The Swiss have now tried this approach on a small test glacier, and if the results are encouraging the government might buy 4,000 snow machines to spray snow over the larger Morteratsch Glacier. It will take an enormous amount of effort: turning all the machines on would use 8,000 litres of water every second. But if it works, the Morteratsch Glacier could grow 800 metres longer in 20 years.

This isn't the only strange method being tried to save Swiss glaciers. The Rhône Glacier – the oldest in the Alps – is now covered in white blankets each year to slow its melt rate. Even so, its ice is 350 metres less thick than it was in the mid 19th century, and the blankets are a temporary solution at best.

Meanwhile, in India, a court ruled that it was granting Himalayan glaciers legal personhood (along with some rivers), meaning anyone harming them can be sued. But the prognosis for most glaciers remains grim. The US Glacier National Park in Montana now has just 26 glaciers left – in the 19th century, it had 150. Many more will disappear soon: there aren't enough snow machines in the world to save them.

Australians were told not to put glitter on their ballot papers.

The country held a plebiscite on marriage equality, conducted via postal ballot. Gay rights campaigners argued the process favoured a negative result, since if the survey returned a 'Yes' to gay marriage, MPs would still be free to vote against it, and if it returned a 'No' to gay marriage, the bill wouldn't be put to parliament at all.

In protest, social media campaigners encouraged people to put glitter bombs in the envelopes along with their 'Yes' votes.* The Australian Bureau of Statistics, which organised the vote, immediately advised against this. The statistician running the plebiscite said that envelopes containing 'extraneous material' risked spoiling the ballots, and glitter would be especially problematic because it could break the scanning machines.

While statisticians were advising against putting glitter in envelopes, doctors were advising against putting it in vaginas, after a product called 'Passion Dust' appeared online. It's a glitter-filled capsule designed to be inserted in the vagina, where it gradually dissolves and spills its contents. According to the website, this generates a sweet-flavoured, sparkly substance called 'magicum' that will liven up the user's sex life. Multiple gynaecologists strongly advised against using the product, saying it could lead to bacterial infections, thrush and inflammation.

Another, less harmful, product available to buy online is the world's glitteriest glitter. It was manufactured by an artist called Stuart Semple as part of an ongoing colour war between him and fellow artist Anish Kapoor. The feud began when a British manufacturer developed the world's 'blackest black', so dark that only 0.035 per cent of light reflects off it. Kapoor snapped up the rights to

There's a dedicated website in Australia that sends envelopes filled with glitter to an MP of your choice for $8.95. In 2015 Liberal MP Craig Lundy received one and called emergency services, fearing it was a dangerous substance. Six fire engines, six police cars and one hazardous materials response van were sent to his office to deal with the glitter.

use it, making him the only artist who can paint with it. Furious that a single artist would 'copyright' a colour, Semple retaliated by creating the world's 'pinkest pink' paint and putting it on sale to everyone except Anish Kapoor. To buy it, you had to promise that 'You are not Anish Kapoor, you are in no way affiliated to Anish Kapoor, [and] you are not purchasing this item on behalf of Anish Kapoor.'

Unfortunately for Semple, Kapoor did get his hands on it, and announced the news in a restrained and adult way: by releasing a photo with his middle finger coated in the pink. Semple retaliated by inventing a substance he dubbed the world's 'glitteriest glitter'. Again, he states on his site that the glitter is available to anyone, except Anish Kapoor.

GLOW-IN-THE-DARK ▶

For the Canadian currency, *see* **Coins**; for the Argentinean amphibian, *see* **Frogs**.

GNOMES ▶

Meth addicts in New Zealand stole garden gnomes to feed their addiction.

It's been a good year for gnomes. After reports in 2016 that the garden gnome was becoming endangered, with only five million left in the UK, vendors reported a resurgence in gnome-buying. Online sales were up by 42 per cent at the beginning of spring, Asda had sold almost 100,000 by April, and eBay was shifting at least 20 of its more niche gnomes every day – including nudist gnomes, homeland security gnomes, and a very popular 'Game of Gnomes' range.

Google jumped on the bandwagon by announcing Google Gnome as an April Fool's Day prank. It was claimed that

—— ◆ ——

A Cheshire man was told by his local council to remove his roadside ornament, a gnome that has its trousers lowered. The council said Laurence Perry's gnome, whose bottom lights up at night, could distract motorists.

Google Gnome would live in your garden and tell you about the temperature, control your garden hose, report which way the wind was blowing, and impart stark realities to your children: 'Really, we're all compost if you think about it,' Google Gnome informed a young boy in the promotional video. 'Almost everything is made up of organic matter, and will return to organic matter.'

Of course, as soon as an item's popularity rises, it becomes catnip for criminals. New Zealand's Sergeant Cam Donnison announced that meth addicts were stealing gnomes and selling them on the black market to fund their narcotic habits. And a survey in Britain found that 80 per cent of British gnome owners had had at least one gnome nicked in the last five years.

GOALKEEPERS

Sutton United's goalie lost his job for eating a pie during a match, only to get a new job as a food taster for a Tex-Mex restaurant.

Known as the 'Roly Poly Goalie', Wayne Shaw was non-league football club Sutton United's 20-stone substitute goalkeeper, plastic-pitch caretaker and unofficial community liaison officer. He lived 80 miles from Sutton, and so often had to sleep at the ground on a sofa when he couldn't get home at night. Because of his considerable girth, he put up with years of chants of 'who ate all the pies' from opposing fans, and so when Sutton United faced Arsenal in the FA Cup, it was no surprise that he was pictured eating a pasty on the substitute bench.

That pasty proved to be his downfall. It turned out that one bookmaker had offered odds of 8–1 that the cameras would catch him eating on the bench. Shaw admitted that he was aware of the novelty bet but didn't place any money himself, instead eating the pie as 'a bit of banter'. Either way, by the end of the week he had lost his job.

Unfortunately for Sutton United, their first-team goalkeeper was injured in the course of the next game. With no substitute on hand, the team had to send defender Simon Downer into goal. Wayne, meanwhile, found himself a new job – as a taster for Chimichanga Tex-Mex restaurant, where he successfully completed the 'Tombstone Challenge', eating a huge pile of ribs, wings and beans in record time.*

GODFATHER

A Sicilian archbishop banned Mafia members from becoming godfathers.

Archbishop Pennisi of Monreale decreed that no Mafia members attending baptisms should be allowed to take on the role of a child's spiritual guide.

Pennisi is trying to reclaim the word 'godfather' for the Church, saying it has lost its religious respectability. He made the move after learning that a parish priest in the town of Corleone (which inspired the surname of the fictional mob family in *The Godfather*) made a Mafia boss his niece's godfather.

GODFATHER: PART II

The number of Mafia members arrested while working in pizza restaurants has risen to three.

This year a fugitive Mafia boss, believed to be the brains behind an international cocaine and heroin-smuggling ring, was arrested while working as a pizza chef in Geneva. But he was by no means the first Mafia boss to have fled to work in a pizza parlour. In 2015, Pasquale Brunese, alleged to be from the Camorra clan, was arrested while working as a waiter in a pizzeria in Valencia. And last year, 73-year-old Rocco Gasperoni, of the notorious 'Ndrangheta Mafia, was found working as a pizza cook in the Dutch seaside town of Scheveningen. Gasperoni's neighbours in the Netherlands said they were really annoyed at his arrest, as he made the best pizza in the area.

Mafia work isn't all cocaine, heroin and pizza. In February, 12 people with links to the Mafia were arrested in Rome, suspected of being involved in a crime ring that shipped cheap olive oil to the USA and relabelled it 'extra virgin' along the way.

▼

Suspected Mafiosi recently arrested include men nicknamed 'Paulie Roast Beef', 'Joey Glasses' and 'Mamma'. Late last year, police found 'Mamma' hiding behind a cupboard in his own house.

GODFATHER: PART III ▷

Monkeys in Indonesia have developed a Mafia-style protection racket.

Long-tailed macaques living at a temple on the island of Bali have come up with an ingenious form of extortion. First they grab valuables from visiting tourists, then they run to the temple staff, who offer them snacks to drop the swag so it can be returned. They've stolen hats, cameras, jewellery, phones and even sunglasses right off people's faces.

The monkeys seem to have been learning from their predecessors, as the crimes have been happening for thirty years. But it hasn't made it elsewhere: this is the only place in the world where human–monkey bartering is known to happen. Some monkeys with more valuable items wait to be offered more food to drop the goods; some demand particular foods and reject others.

It's a phenomenon that has been reported anecdotally for years, but this year is the first time scientists have studied it properly, when a team from the University of Lethbridge in Canada visited and published their findings. It seems as though the monkeys didn't want the findings to be made public. Primatologist Fany Brotcorne told *New Scientist*, 'The monkeys were always trying to steal my hat, my pen, even my research data.'

113

GOLF

Donald Trump spent more days golfing in his first 100 days as president than professional golfer Rory McIlroy.

As well as playing golf with Donald Trump, Rory McIlroy has played a round with Bill Clinton, offered a lesson to Barack Obama and nominated George W. Bush for the ALS Ice Bucket Challenge.

The winner of the medal for best amateur golfer in this year's Open Championship was Alfie Plant. His girlfriend is called Daisy Meadows.

Trump played 19 rounds of golf during the first 100 days of his presidency. In the same period McIlroy played only 12 rounds on the US PGA tour. In fairness, Rory may have played a few more practice rounds that we don't know about, but his recurring back injury makes this unlikely. We do know that the two men played a round together in February, a fixture that led to Rory being called a 'fascist' and a 'bigot' on social media. McIlroy argued that it was a completely apolitical act on his part – all he wanted to do was to see what it was like to play golf with a president, with all the security and hoo-ha that comes with it.

It certainly must have been quite a sight. When Trump sets off in his golf buggy, he has Secret Service agents sitting alongside, in front of and behind him. According to reports in a Florida newspaper, he also keeps high-powered rifles in his golf bag while on the course. McIlroy reported that Trump scored around 80, which is exceptionally good for a man in his seventies. He's probably the best golfer ever to become president, but we can't know for sure: as with his taxes, Trump refuses to release any details of his golf scores.

GRENADES

Fifty thousand Germans were evacuated because the Allies dropped three bombs on Hanover.

In May, experts in Hanover were called to investigate five suspicious objects. Two turned out to be scrap metal, but the other three were unexploded Second World War grenades, and 10 per cent of the city's population had to leave their homes before they could be defused. In the same month, inhabitants of the German town of Hennef were evacuated when 80-year-old grenades bought by a man at a car-boot sale started to explode in the heat. Authorities were called after passers-by heard a series of explosions coming from his garage and noticed it was on fire.

But perhaps the most unusual grenade discovery was made in a nursing home in New York, where two Second World War grenades were found in a 91-year-old resident's fridge. Not surprisingly, the nursing home had to be evacuated.

The Oxford vs Cambridge Boat Race went ahead on the Thames, despite the discovery of a Second World War bomb near the starting line. The last time the race was cancelled was during the Second World War.

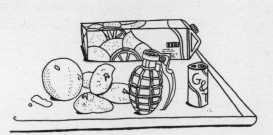

The First World War made its own contribution to grenade news this year. A man in Guildford found one from the Great War while trimming his hedge. He described it as being the size of a large potato, and admitted he was not 100 per cent reassured when the police arrived and told him grenades that old 'hardly ever explode'.

In which we learn …
Why French bus drivers started wearing dresses, which town
advertised for a chatty hermit, how to get the taxman to send
you flowers, why early man looked best in a hat, and
who won big on the 1974 Grand National.

Minutes after the NHS was cyber-attacked, GCHQ tweeted a poem about how good they are at protecting Britain from cyber-attacks.

The poem was as badly written as it was badly timed:

> We're an intelligence agency known as GCHQ.
> Carrying on our mission from Bletchley in World War 2.
> Based in Cheltenham, Manchester, Scarborough and
>   Bude.
> We work against cyber threats, terrorists and those up
>   to no good.
> Because keeping Britain safe is what we do.

The NHS hack was stopped when a computer expert, 22-year-old Marcus Hutchins, inadvertently activated the 'kill switch' in the software. Hutchins was once suspended from school for allegedly hacking into the computer network (an accusation he denies). As a result he was made to take his IT GCSE with a pen and paper. He failed.*

GCHQ isn't the only intelligence agency to be caught off guard by hackers. In June, it emerged that a few years back America's CIA suffered a hack within their own building, carried out by their own contracted personnel. At risk, though, were not the country's secrets, but the CIA's snacks. Apparently the hackers had managed to hack their way into one of the building's vending machines and then proceeded to steal more than $3,000 worth of snacks over a period of six months. When they were finally caught, all those responsible handed in their badges.

* Things later got a bit more serious for Hutchins when he was arrested by the FBI on charges of creating malware software designed to harvest bank details. As at school, Hutchins denied all charges.

LERT ● ● RED ALERT ● ● RE

Britain battled a heatwave by sending gritters on to the roads.

Cows in Japan are being given high-tech shirts to keep them cool. If a sensor in the shirt detects the cow is too dry, it soaks it with cool water. Cows in California have been given chilled water-beds for the same reason.

The UK suffered its hottest June day in 40 years, as the temperature at Heathrow Airport reached 34.5°C. And for the first time since 1995, the mercury hit 30°C for five consecutive days. Exeter schoolboys and bus drivers in France (where temperatures also soared) both protested against a ban on shorts by going to work and school in skirts, and in Cambridgeshire winter service vehicles were sent out to grit the roads, but on this occasion to stop them melting.

Things were worse still in Arizona and California, where the temperature reached 48°C this year. Flights had to be cancelled, as that's hotter than the operating temperatures of some planes. After medics warned that touching hot steering wheels in cars might cause burns, people were spotted driving in oven gloves.

In Iran, the mercury hit 54°C. That's the joint-hottest day anywhere on Earth in recorded history. There was a reported temperature of 57°C in Death Valley in 1913, but most meteorologists now think that it was a mistake, probably caused by someone misreading the thermometer due to the debilitating heat.

Back in Britain, at Royal Ascot horse-racing organisers allowed men to remove their jackets in the Royal Enclosure for the first time ever, and the hashtag #TooHotToSleep trended on Twitter. As Britons melted, and moaned on social media, Australia just laughed. Britain's 34°C heatwave was colder than the temperature on the same day in the Aussie city of Darwin, where it was the middle of winter.

HELIUM

The world suffered a helium shortage, despite a quarter of the universe being made of it.

A third of the world's supply of helium comes from the tiny country of Qatar, and most of it is driven out, by truck, through Saudi Arabia. So when the Saudis accused Qatar in June of funding terrorism (*see* **Qatar**), and closed the border between the two countries, the helium factories were all shut down, and global prices drifted upwards.

In the US, Atlantic City authorities were among those to ban helium balloons. Now if you release one there, you could be fined up to $500.

Helium is used in everything from party balloons to scuba equipment to MRI scanners to the Large Hadron Collider. Helium balloons' days may be numbered though. Fifty local authorities in the UK and various towns in America have banned their release because when they pop their remains are a choking hazard to local wildlife. America's Balloon Council, however, is fighting back. This lobbying group has spent over $1 million in the past five years campaigning to ensure that proposed balloon bans never get off the ground.

For giant sausage-shaped balloons in the Antarctic, *see* **Tunnels**.

HERMITS

An Austrian town appointed a hermit whose job description includes talking to people.

Divorced ex-artillery officer Stan Vanuytrecht beat 49 other applicants to land the job as a professional hermit in Saalfelden. He was surprised to get the job, saying, 'I thought I didn't have a chance.' According to the town's mayor, 'He radiates calm and comes across as well anchored.' His role will include playing host to people who walk up his mountain to confide in him.

Vanuytrecht's 350-year-old hermitage is unheated, has no running water and is only habitable from April to November. TV and computers are banned. Because the job is unpaid, applicants were advised to have a private income in place. To apply they had to post a CV, a covering letter and an 'up-to-date photo', although it was made clear the winning candidate would be selected more for their personality than their looks or any previous hermit experience. Vanuytrecht said that he was well qualified for the role due to his divorce and the poverty he experienced as a result.

His predecessor lasted only one season in the job, claiming that although he'd met very nice people, he'd been criticised by conservative Catholics for not having a beard. Fortunately, Vanuytrecht, who is Belgian, has a beard. A few months into the job he reported that he was content, saying he always had a glass of schnapps ready for visitors.

Europe has very few professional hermits left. Last year the Swiss city of Solothurn appointed one, a divorced ex-policeman (also bearded) who gets £1,600 a month in salary. He needs social skills, too – in 2014, a previous hermit quit, complaining about the number of tourists who visited him.

One of the only hermits in Britain is Sister Rachel Denton (unbearded), who lives in an end-of-terrace house in Lincolnshire with her chihuahua, Mr Bingley. She makes a living selling greetings cards, explaining, 'There's not much call for rush mats and rosaries these days.' She's not completely cut off from the world: she likes listening to *The Archers* and has a website, a Twitter account and two Facebook pages.

HMRC spends £3,000 a year buying flowers to say sorry for mistakes on people's tax bills.

The Times revealed that over the last three years, HM Revenue and Customs has spent £8,500 on apologetic bouquets. One went to a café owner in Manchester, who was told she owed the taxman £1 billion. In fact, she owed £17,000. Another recipient was owed a £800 rebate, and instead received a cheque for £1.

In January, HMRC released some of the excuses they'd been given by employers for not paying their staff minimum wage. These included:

▶ 'It's part of UK culture not to pay young workers for the first three months as they have to prove their "worth" first.'

▶ 'She doesn't deserve the National Minimum Wage because she only makes the teas and sweeps the floors.'

▶ 'My accountant and I speak a different language – he doesn't understand me and that's why he doesn't pay my workers the correct wages.'

▶ 'My workers like to think of themselves as being self-employed and the National Minimum Wage doesn't apply to people who work for themselves.'

▶ 'My workers are often just on standby when there are no customers in the shop; I only pay them for when they're actually serving someone.'

HMRC also released a list of the weirdest stuff that people tried to claim as business expenses, including 'Pet food for a Shih Tzu "guard dog"', 'Armani jeans as protective clothing for painter and decorator' and 'underwear – for personal use'.

HOLLINGWORTH, CLARE

The world said goodbye to the journalist who discovered the Second World War.

Before the war, Hollingworth helped Austrians and Germans who opposed Hitler to flee across the border disguised as peasants. To make them look the part, she supplied them with vegetables, and sometimes a chicken.

During the 60s, Hollingworth once got a colleague freed from guerrillas by telling their leader, 'Monsieur, if you do not release our colleague at once, I will have to hit you on the head with my shoe!'

Clare Hollingworth (1911–2017) died in January aged 105, 78 years after breaking the biggest news story of all time. She was 27, and had been a foreign correspondent for only four days. On her first assignment, driving on a closed road from Poland into Germany in August 1939, she noticed a series of screens along the side of the road, blocking the view of the valley below. A gust of wind lifted one of them, revealing dozens of Hitler's tanks preparing for the invasion. The report that she sent back to London wasn't believed at first, but the *Daily Telegraph* finally ran it under the headline '1,000 tanks massed on Polish border'. A few days later, war broke out.

The Second World War may have been Hollingworth's greatest scoop, but there were plenty more. In 1963, for example, she broke the story of Soviet spy Kim Philby defecting to the USSR. She kept working, too: aged nearly 80 she climbed a lamp post to get a better look at the Chinese government's student crackdown in Tiananmen Square. Once, in Romania, she stripped naked to avoid being arrested by security police, reasoning that they would be too embarrassed to dress her by force so that they could lead her away. It worked, and a friend was then able to put a blanket over her and take her to an embassy. She could fly a plane, kept a pearl revolver in her evening bag, and well into her eighties would sleep on the floor every couple of weeks to stay tough.

For more Second World War news from 2017, *see* **Grenades**.

HOMO SAPIENS

A human from 300,000 years ago would be indistinguishable from one today as long as he wore a hat.

That was one of the two findings that emerged from a study of hominid fossils discovered in Morocco this year. The other was that the textbooks on human evolution would have to be rewritten.

Computer scans showed that the hominids' faces would have looked like ours. They were relatively flat, and had modern-looking jaws. Only their more elongated brain-cases would give them away – hence the need for a hat. But what made these relatively modern humans extra-ordinary was that they were alive 100,000 years earlier than thought possible, and they were found away from the so-called 'cradle of humankind' in Ethiopia. This evidence means the perceived wisdom that our ances-tors became humans and then spread from Ethiopia can no longer be true. 'It is not the story of it happening in a rapid way in a "Garden of Eden" somewhere in Africa,' said Professor Jean-Jacques Hublin, one of the authors of the study. 'If there was a Garden of Eden, it was all of Africa.'

HORNS

Rock star Gene Simmons tried to trademark the 'horns' hand gesture.

Simmons, who claimed he made it popular in 1974 during his band Kiss's *Hotter Than Hell* tour, submitted an appli-cation to the US Patent and Trademark Office along with a sketch of the gesture and a photo of him doing it.

He pulled the application eight days later, after receiving an unexpected backlash from the rock community. They pointed out that:

1. *He didn't invent it* – Not only is it centuries old, even its origins in rock and roll can be traced to a former Black Sabbath member's grandmother.

2. *He was patenting the wrong symbol* – According to numerous rock and metal magazines, Simmons has been doing the 'horns' wrong. By raising his thumb, he's actually doing an impression of Spiderman shooting his web.

3. *It's probably not registrable* – Because what he was inadvertently trying to do was to trademark 'I love you' in American Sign Language.

HORSE RACING ▶

A man won £130 this year by betting on Red Rum to win the Grand National.

This year's Grand National winner was the Scottish-trained One For Arthur, but before that race was run, one man cashed in on a bet placed 43 years earlier. In 1974, Bob Holmes's father-in-law placed a £1 bet at odds of 11–1 on Red Rum to win that year's National, but never collected his winnings. He died in 1979, and it was not until April this year that Bob came across the betting slip while clearing out his house. He called William Hill, who confirmed it hadn't been cashed, and agreed to pay out, even adjusting for inflation.

Meanwhile, in Finland, a new kind of horse racing has caught on – hobby-horse racing. It's like showjumping, but instead of a horse, you get a broom with a head.* It has become popular among teenage girls, and the World Championship attracted more than 1,000 spectators. 'I think hobby-horsing has a feministic agenda,' said one organiser. 'No boys are coming and saying what we need to do, or bossing us around. So I think there is some sort of a feministic point.'

* Serious riders have been known to give their hobby horses names and tuck them up under a blanket at night.

124

In which we learn …
What the 43rd US president thought of the 45th's
inauguration, how the Russian Internet banned itself,
why Iran isn't run by a three-year-old, who put an
iceberg on a bus, and how hard it is to organise
a piss-up in a brewery.

There's an iceberg floating in the ocean 500,000 times larger than the one that sunk the **Titanic.**

Harrods started selling water harvested from melting icebergs. The water is collected twice a year by an icebreaker that cuts blocks off bergs in the Norwegian archipelago of Svalbard. Harrods claims it's the best-tasting water in the world, which explains why it's selling the melted ice for £80 a bottle.

The 'berg, which broke off the Larson C ice shelf, is the second largest ever recorded – it's bigger than Norfolk and twice the size of Luxembourg. When it broke away from Antarctica in July it didn't directly affect global sea levels as it was already floating, but now that it has separated itself from the landmass, other glaciers will be free to slide towards the sea, which will eventually cause levels to rise. The iceberg will float northwards over the next few years, and will eventually break into smaller 'bergs, which could prove to be more of a danger to shipping – smaller icebergs are harder to see by satellite, as they look just like pods of whales. These new icebergs will make a bad problem worse: the brilliantly named International Ice Patrol announced in June that whereas they were usually aware of around 500 dangerous icebergs, this year they counted 986.

Icebergs are not just bad news for ships. They can also pose a threat to oil rigs, which, of course, can't steer out of their way. Energy companies deal with the problem by getting a ship to circle any icebergs that seem to be a threat, and drag a rope around them, like a lasso. They then yank the iceberg out of harm's way.

A company in the United Arab Emirates is also planning to drag icebergs, but for commercial reasons. Its hope is that by pulling a 3km-long iceberg 9,200 kilometres across the Indian Ocean, the company will be able to provide drinking water. Environmentalists are not impressed, pointing out that shipping icebergs requires a lot of fuel and that the meltwater will affect the local ecosystem.

A vodka company in Canada also moved an iceberg around this year. To celebrate the country's 150th birthday, an iceberg was lassoed off the coast of Newfoundland and taken to the coast by boat, before travelling across the country by bus.

ICELAND

Iceland dug the world's hottest hole.

This year, geologists in Iceland finished drilling a hole right into the middle of a volcano. They reached a depth of 5 kilometres, where the temperature reaches 500°C. They hope to find volcanic rock mixing with naturally occurring groundwater, meaning they could use the steam down there to create geothermal energy.

This is not the only way in which Iceland is leading the world. It's also been ranked best for gender equality by the World Economic Forum eight years running. However, Icelandic women point out there is still some way to go. Each year on 24 October, they leave work early to protest the country's continuing pay gap, timing their departure to coincide with the moment each day that, in comparison with their male colleagues, they effectively stop being paid. In 2005, they walked out at 2.08 p.m.; in 2010, it was 2.25 p.m.; and this year they left at around 2.40 p.m. Also this year, Iceland became the first country

A drone takeaway service has begun in Iceland. Unfortunately the drones can only travel six miles, so after the chef puts food into the drone, it flies for six miles before a delivery driver takes it the rest of the way.

to introduce a law that will force all companies to prove that they pay women and men equally, which means that by the time it comes into force, in 2020, all workers in Iceland should theoretically be leaving work at the same time on 24 October.

IKEA ▶

IKEA admitted its mixing bowls can set your grapes on fire.

———— ▼ ————

It was revealed in August that *Game of Thrones* character Jon Snow's capes are made from IKEA rugs.

IKEA customer and mixing-bowl owner Richard Walter was sitting outside one sunny day when he smelled burning. It turned out that due to its parabolic shape, his metal Blanda bowl was focusing sunlight precisely where his grape stalk was placed. IKEA admitted that such an occurrence was possible, but decided against recalling the product, saying, 'It has been established that many different parameters would have to converge for the content of the bowl to overheat and that the risk for this to happen is very low.'

Earlier in the year, IKEA was awarded the Design of the Year award in the prestigious Beazley design competition for its flat-pack refugee shelter that it created in partnership with the United Nations High Commissioner for Refugees (UNHCR). There are now more than 10,000 of these shelters in use worldwide. IKEA also worked with NASA, sending some of its designers into a Mars base simulator. While it is hoped that they might one day make 'tiny domes on a desolate alien world', that wasn't the primary reason for the project – they also hoped that studying the cramped conditions and awkward toilet facilities planned for Mars might help to improve living spaces on Earth.

IMMIGRATION

Australia ran an ad in Baghdad encouraging people not to move to Australia.

Australia's government launched an advert specifically marketing Australia as a place to avoid. The anti-immigration billboards told Iraqis, 'Do not try to come to Australia illegally by boat, you will be turned back,' and featured a tough-looking man in military uniform.

They needn't have worried, however. A new report released by international relocation experts MoveHub showed a 5 per cent decrease in people moving to Australia. Instead, they're all going to New Zealand. In the 12 weeks after Donald Trump won the American presidential race, applications to move to New Zealand from the US grew by 70 per cent.*

Despite its rise in international popularity, not everyone is yet fully familiar with New Zealand. Late last year Chloe Phillips-Harris, a Kiwi tourist, was detained by immigration officials in Kazakhstan for a day and a half because they didn't believe her claim that New Zealand is a country. They told her it was a state of Australia. Unfortunately, the large map of the world that hung in the interrogation room she was taken to didn't help her to make her case, as New Zealand wasn't on it. She was eventually allowed in, and spent six months in Kazakhstan.

* It was reported that lots of the would-be New Zealanders were super-rich survivalists, who were buying properties there in case of a nuclear war or revolt against capitalism. In the week after Donald Trump's election, applications from the USA to New Zealand rose to 17 times their usual rate.

INAUGURATION

Donald Trump's inauguration featured a large number of weird numbers:

1,500,000: The number of people who saw Trump being sworn in as president, according to the President himself.

* In September,
Spicer appeared at
the Emmys, where he
said that the show
would have 'the largest
audience to witness an
Emmys, period.' As it
happens, he was wrong
again. The programme
was watched by 11.4
million people, the
joint-lowest audience
figures on record.

The event was described by Press Secretary Sean Spicer as 'The largest audience to ever witness an inauguration. Period.'*

300,000–600,000: The number of people who attended according to actual crowd scientists. The low turnout isn't surprising, really – Trump got only 4 per cent of the vote in Washington DC.

0.25: Maximum thickness, in inches, of signs permitted at the inauguration by Washington police.

2: The number of cans of beef ravioli confiscated by security staff as a potential security risk. Security also confiscated non-collapsible umbrellas, cigarette lighters, and several bananas, which were deemed a risk because they weren't chopped into pieces. The organisers seemed pretty sensitive: all the portable toilets were provided by a firm called Don's Johns, but the inaugural committee decided the name might prompt jokes, so covered the name labels up with blue tape.

4: Number of poo emojis Charlotte Church attached to her Twitter message to Trump when she declined to perform at the inauguration. Others who declined included Moby ('I'd DJ…if as payment #trump released his tax returns') and rapper Ice T ('I didn't pick up and blocked the number'). One person who did turn up was Lord of the Dance Michael Flatley, which prompted someone to redirect the website 'colossalbellend.com' to Michael Flatley's website.

0: Number of celebrities Trump clarified he had wanted to attend anyway, saying, 'The so-called "A"-list celebrities are all wanting tixs to the inauguration, but look what they did for Hillary, NOTHING.' Performers who did attend included the Mormon Tabernacle Choir and the 2010 *America's Got Talent* runner-up.

16.95: Cost (in dollars) of the official inaugural photo-print of Donald Trump. It contained one spelling mistake: 'No dream is too big, no challenge is to great.'

5: Number of words summarising Trump's inaugural address by George W. Bush, who reportedly turned to friends and said, 'That was some weird shit.'

INDEPENDENCE ▶

Lithuania's missing Declaration of Independence turned up in Germany.

The document was misplaced almost immediately after it was signed in February 1918. Exactly 99 years later, in February this year, a group of Lithuanian companies offered a one-million-euro reward to anyone who could find and return it. One month after that, a professor unearthed it in a Berlin archive. The German foreign ministry released a statement saying, 'What a great find! This is perfect news for our Lithuanian friends. We celebrate together with them' – although as Reuters noted, the statement didn't mention whether they intended to return it.

Meanwhile, another declaration of independence unexpectedly turned up in Chichester. Harvard researchers confirmed that the extremely rare parchment manuscript of the American Declaration of Independence – one of only two known to exist – dates back to the 1780s. It was produced either in Philadelphia or in New York. They could not explain how on earth it ended up in West Sussex.

One area of the globe currently campaigning for independence is the Spanish region of Catalonia, which has a champion in Manchester City football manager Pep Guardiola. In June he led a protest of 40,000 people

India celebrated the 70th anniversary of its independence in August, with ceremonies, a military parade, and an app: citizens were invited to submit suggestions for what they wanted Prime Minister Narendra Modi to talk about in his speech via an official mobile phone app.

through the streets of Barcelona, delivered a speech and read out the Catalan independence manifesto, accusing Spain – whose football team he captained to Olympic gold in 1992 – of political persecution.

INDIA

For slipper-related air rage, *see* **Aviation**; for potential war with China, *see* **Bhutan**; for bovine retirement homes, *see* **Cows**; for gaining an inch, *see* **Everest**; for a new definition of person, *see* **Glaciers**; for a curry button, *see* **Inventions**; for what the prime minister has in common with Darth Vader, *see* **Music**; for standing up in the cinema, *see* **National Anthem**; for high, flying birds, *see* **Opium**; for a diesel-powered solar train *see* **Railways**; for rat-arsed rodents, *see* **Rats**; and for planting a forest overnight, *see* **Trees**.

INSECTS

For a cocktail served with ants, *see* **Aardvarks**; for a hive of criminal activity, *see* **Bees**; for insects that fake their own deaths, *see* **Dragonflies**; for wormburgers, *see* **Farming**; for the bug spray that was made a bit too strong, *see* **Kim Jong-Nam, Assassination of**; for robo-bees, *see* **Pollination**; for the world's largest living stick, *see* **Stick Insects**; for spiders (which aren't insects) that have started walking like ants (which are), *see* **Spiders**; and for the bug that's reinvented the umbrella, *see* **Umbrellas**.

INTERNATIONAL SPACE STATION

The International Space Station is selling office space.

A Finnish company called Space Nation bought a compartment that's only 50cm x 50cm x 30cm, for £17,000.* Its plan is to become a landlord to

At these prices, if the average British new-build property was transported to space, it would cost £41 million.

scientists – it has turned its office into a block of 18 'flats', each measuring 10cm x 10cm x 10cm, and plans to rent out each one to other space agencies that want to conduct small-scale experiments in zero gravity. The first 'tenants' are slated to arrive on the ISS in 2018.

NASA is conducting a number of its own experiments, notably trying to work out how to bake bread that can be consumed on the Space Station. Bread has been banned from space since 1965, when two astronauts sneaked a corned beef sandwich on board and the crumbs ended up getting everywhere. Since then, astronauts have had to eat tortillas. However, a team of German scientists is now developing crumb-free bread.

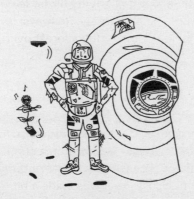

Another problem NASA is trying to resolve is the fact it is running out of spacesuits. All astronauts on board the ISS are wearing hand-me-downs. The space suits they wear date from 1981 and have been worn by astronauts since then, even though they were intended to last only for 15 years.* To date, over 3,400 suit-related incidents have been recorded, including one alarming occasion when a suit started to leak (spacesuits are filled with water for drinking and cooling purposes) while being used on a spacewalk. Had the astronaut not acted quickly, he might well have become the first person to die in space – by drowning.

An error on board the International Space Station was spotted by 17-year-old Miles Soloman from Sheffield, who realised that the radiation sensors were recording incorrect data. NASA said it was more appreciative than embarrassed by this. When asked what his friends thought of his discovery, Miles said, 'It's really a mixture of jealousy and boredom.'

NASA is worried that none of its 11 suits will last the 15 walks planned between now and 2024, and it cannot make new ones quickly enough.

The TV show Loose Women *was cancelled on International Women's Day.*

The ITV show, presented by four women and focusing on women's issues, was replaced on 8 March with coverage of (male) Chancellor Philip Hammond's hour-long budget speech. Women did warrant a mention in his spending plans: viewers had the satisfaction of watching Hammond awkwardly say the word 'tampon' as he explained how the tampon tax would benefit women's charities. He complained that he had planned to reveal three new measures for women, but that Theresa May had given two of them away on Mumsnet a few hours earlier.

* Grégoire Trudeau's surname used to be hyphenated but she removed the hyphen in 2016; no one knows why.

Marking International Women's Day in Canada, the prime minister's wife, Sophie Grégoire Trudeau* posted on Instagram that women should 'celebrate the boys and men in our lives who encourage us to be who we truly are', and share online photos of themselves holding hands with their 'male ally'. Perhaps not surprisingly, she was widely criticised for missing the point of the occasion, though it should be noted that she's heavily involved with more than ten women's charities.

In Russia, where men traditionally give women flowers on International Women's Day, companies offered bouquets for hire. Women could rent flowers for 10 minutes – enough time to take a selfie with them to share on social media – and so give the impression of having a male admirer, without having to fork out on a full purchase.

The Russian website that regulates the banning of websites accidentally banned itself.

Russia doesn't have an overarching firewall to stop access to banned sites. Instead it uses an agency called

Roskomnadzor that creates a blacklist of pages it expects Internet providers to block. Russian anti-censorship campaigners bought up old expired websites from that list and linked them to government sites – with the result that the government sites became blocked. The regulator's own site – https://rkn.gov.ru – was also targeted, leading to a situation in which people could no longer reach the list of blocked sites, because it, itself, was blocked.

Iran similarly seeks to control Internet access, but this year its attempt to block Internet porn went a little too far. Its plan was to remove access to certain sites by effectively forcing computers to look in the wrong direction for the pages. However, neighbouring networks as far away as Russia and Hong Kong were also accidentally blocked, meaning that Internet users in dozens of other countries were unable to access superbigcocks.com and 255 other websites.

INVENTIONS

A new washing machine in India has a button specifically for curry stains.

The StainMaster, released by Panasonic, features five other cycles aimed at Indian consumers, including a button to remove other sauces, one to remove traces of hair oil and one specifically designed to clean saris.

Panasonic has also recently invested in projects including the world's first laundry-folding robot (which can fold individual T-shirts in as little as 10 minutes) and an almost completely invisible television (when switched on it functions as a normal television, but when switched off it becomes a transparent sheet of glass, indistinguishable from a window).

In controversial invention news:

- The US supermarket Trader Joe's claimed to have invented a new product called a 'puff dog'. Critics claim it's just a sausage roll.

- Donald Trump claimed to have invented the phrase 'priming the pump'. The *Oxford English Dictionary*'s first citation is from 1819.

- Historic England spokesperson Celia Richardson claimed that the Cornish pasty was invented in Devon.

- Researcher David Leishman claimed that the Scottish drink Irn Bru was invented in America.

IRAN

One hundred and thirty-seven women and one three-year-old girl unsuccessfully attempted to run for president of Iran.

After the regime removed his government-issue bodyguards, former Iranian President Mahmoud Ahmadinejad turned to crowd-funding to pay for their replacements. He issued a press release saying he wanted 'to thank the great nation of Iran', followed by account details for donations.

Iranian law states that any citizen over the age of 18 can apply to run for president, but that anyone who is not a 'religious and political rejal' will be disqualified. The word 'rejal' is variously translated as 'personality' or, more commonly, 'man'. As a result, all women who tried to run were denied candidacy.

More than 1,600 people applied this year, and all but six were disqualified. Those who missed out included Ghassem Sholeh Sadi, a former lawmaker, who believed that he was banned for wearing a tie, which is often associated with Western decadence (for other political ties, *see* Ties); Abolghassem Khaki, a factory guard who hoped that by becoming president he would realise his dream of competing against Donald Trump in a swimming race; and Hassan Seyedkhani, who announced that if he won he would make his twin brother foreign minister. It's the least he could do: Hassan's brother refrained from running for president out of respect for him since he is older by two minutes.

One man, clearly not fazed by the 'rejal' ruling, or indeed the over-18 law, attempted to register his three-year-old daughter for president. He said that he was doing it to launch her political career. The authorities refused even to register her.

IRAQ ▶

Iraq started importing oil from Huddersfield.

Despite the fact that Iraq produces five million barrels a day, Yorkshire firm Sterling Oil now sells oil back to them. This is thanks to its engineering process, which blends oils together with additives to make the crude more useful and valuable. Sterling already sells oil to the United Arab Emirates, which produces three million barrels of the stuff every day.

The liberation of Mosul from ISIS was a rare piece of good news for Iraq this year. A by-product of the city's freedom was that Iraqis could play football again without the weird rules imposed by Islamic State. ISIS had allowed people to play, but banned referees' whistles in case they made devils gather. They had posted someone with scissors at the pitch entrance to cut any 'idolatrous' insignia off players' shirts, matches had been interrupted for prayers, and the Olympic rings had been sawn off the stadium with an angle grinder for being 'the sign of infidels'.

In some other places under ISIS rule, football referees were banned entirely because they implement the laws of FIFA, rather than Allah. ISIS also brought in the sharia system of 'Qisas' whereby players can exact revenge if their opponents injure them.

Meanwhile, the US forces in Iraq were embarrassed to confess that over the last few years they had lost kit and equipment in Iraq worth approximately $1 *billion*. Amnesty International asked for the details and found

———— ▼ ————

A pigeon in Kuwait was caught carrying drugs across the Iraqi border in its backpack. One hundred and seventy-eight pills of what is thought to have been ketamine were found in a fabric pouch strapped to the pigeon's back. Officials said they knew pigeons had been used to smuggle drugs across the border before, but this was the first time they'd caught one in the act.

that the Department of Defense had not kept records on large amounts of military hardware. The Pentagon claimed the report was 'overblown', which is comforting.

IRELAND

For accidental sexy phone calls, *see* **Cock-ups**; for alcoholic eggs, *see* **Easter**; for a mysterious beach, *see* **Lost and Found**; for what's injuring so many people in Galway, *see* **Selfies**; and for what not to wear in parliament, *see* **Ties**.

IRONY

A Nottingham brewery failed to organise a piss-up in itself.

This year, a brewery in Nottingham failed to organise an event they had called 'Piss Up in a Brewery'. The co-owner of the Black Iris Brewery, Alex Wilson, announced that 'due to a cock-up' they had been unable to get the proper licence. Consequently, they had to move it to a nearby pub. Wilson told punters, 'We'll just have to call it "Piss Up near a Brewery".'

In other irony news:

▶ The UK's Government Digital Service, which is responsible for improving government IT, found itself unable to pay staff because of technical problems.

▶ A 46-year-old worker at the National Rifle Association accidentally shot himself at the NRA headquarters. (He suffered only a 'minor wound'.)

▶ In announcing the US withdrawal from the Paris climate agreement, Donald Trump said, 'I was elected to represent the citizens of Pittsburgh, not Paris.' He then decided to hold a 'Pittsburgh, not Paris' rally in Lafayette Square, Washington DC, which is named after the French general who gave crucial help to the USA in the War of Independence.

▶ And in downtown Albuquerque, a news crew had their truck stolen while they were off gathering footage for a story about the problem of urban crime in downtown Albuquerque.

ISIS

For wild pigs taking on Islamists *see* **Boar**; for the war against referees, *see* **Iraq**; for tasteless toys, *see* **LEGO**; for the mother of all bombs, *see* **MOAB**; and for the former editor of the *ISIS* magazine, *see* **Osborne, George**.

ISLANDS

China blew up islands in one place, while simultaneously building them in another.

China's demolition of its own islands forms part of the country's ambitious 'Silk Road' project launched this year, which aims to establish new trade routes through Asia and Europe. The hope is that by removing some of the small islands that dot the Mekong River, which runs through China, Burma, Thailand and Laos, the route can be opened up for large boats and ships. China describes this rather destructive process as a 'gentling out' of the river.

Environmentalists take a less relaxed view, arguing that such extensive changes threaten the richness of the world's second most biodiverse river (after the Amazon), and that endangered species such as the Mekong catfish, which relies on the islands for feeding and shelter, will suffer.

At the same time as blowing up islands in the Mekong, China is building new ones in the South China Sea in a bid to increase the scope of its territorial waters. This isn't something that's going down well with the country's neighbours. Six Asian governments lay claim to various

Indonesia made a renewed attempt to count its islands. It registered 13,466 with the UN in 2012 but has already counted another 1,700 since. The government now wants to work out how many it has once and for all – which is difficult because many keep sinking and then re-appearing due to sea level fluctuations.

overlapping parts of the South China Sea, and America is none too happy either.* One island, called appropriately enough Mischief Island, has proved a particular bone of contention. Having built on to a natural reef there, China erected large concrete structures that look suspiciously like missile silos. America for its part then carried out military exercises within 12 miles of the artificial island, arguing that it lies in international waters.

In which we learn …
Who is turning turds into trousers, which city introduced
flying firemen, who called for a cat-cuddler, why some
journalists wear bags on their heads, and where
you're not allowed to say 'Britain'.

An epidemic of traffic jams was caused by amorous animals.

Camels in Iran are being fitted with reflective collars and licence plates in an attempt to tackle road accidents.

Drivers in Melbourne had their way blocked by a pair of kinky kangaroos; turned-on turkeys caused a number of accidents in Indiana; and a road was closed in Delaware to stop salamanders from being squashed as they had sex. A huge traffic jam was caused in Dubai by a pair of mating camels. In fairness to them, they only took up one lane; the tailbacks were mostly caused by motorists honking their horns and taking photographs. 'It's undoubtedly the best thing I've seen since I moved to the Middle East,' said one eyewitness.

JAPAN ▶

The Battle of the Giant Robots was held up by health and safety concerns.

In September, the USA and Japan organised a robot duel – between a 13-foot Japanese robot called Kuratas and America's 16-foot Eagle Prime, both piloted by humans sitting inside. The contest came about after a group of American roboticists called MegaBots challenged a Japanese group, Suidobashi Heavy Industry, to a fight, but it initially had to be delayed due to various logistical challenges: namely finding a venue where the floor wouldn't collapse under the weight of huge robots falling over; getting large power supplies into the venue; and no end of health and safety concerns, including learning how the pilots inside the robots could 'figure out how not to die'. The American bot's weapons included a massive paintball gun, grappling claw, a chainsaw and a very large drill.

The *human* Japanese army, founded in 1958, has never fired a shot (or a paintball) in battle, due to constitutional restraints on Japanese military activity. It's not even called an 'army' – it's technically the 'Self-Defence Force'. Japan's prime minister, Shinzō Abe, and his right-wing Liberal Democratic Party are hoping to change this in the next three years with a new constitution that takes a less pacifist approach. That said, Abe probably didn't realise how aggressive his speech on the subject would sound when translated into English, notably the remark, '2020 is the year when a new Japan will kick off.'

Not everyone in Japan shares Mr Abe's hawkish views. One man, Masaki Tomiyama, announced he was suing the Japanese government on the grounds that when his son joined the army, they started training him to kill people. He said, 'I will never allow him to go to war – that's not why he signed up.'

Elderly people in Japan were offered discounts on their funeral if they gave up their driving licence. A company in the Aichi district offered a 15 per cent discount to any drivers who can prove they've handed their licence in at a local police station.

JEANS

An Egyptian politician tried to ban kids from wearing ripped jeans.

Egyptian MP Abdul Karim Zakaria announced he was planning to introduce a motion that, if passed, would impose a dress code on schools and universities. He said recent fashion crazes 'left many of us flabbergasted … most noticeable is the "ripped or torn jeans" fad.' Those supporting him included the dean of Cairo University, who said that women have the right to wear whatever they like, but stressed in a separate statement that parliament must ban the 'socially unacceptable craze' of ripped jeans.

American shop Nordstrom took the craze for tatty trousers one step further by launching $425 jeans covered in artificial mud. The mud doesn't wash out because it's impregnated into the fabric – mostly on the knees, pockets and crotch. The move prompted an angry response from Mike Rowe, the host of TV programme *Dirty Jobs*, who said Nordstrom's jeans 'aren't pants. They're not even fashion. They're a costume for wealthy people who see work as ironic.'

Perhaps the most exciting jeans innovations came from the H&M Foundation's Global Change Award, which offers grants to clothing designers. One prizewinner found a way of recycling the colour from old jeans to dye new ones, which promises to make future jeans manufacturing much more environmentally friendly. Another winner was a firm that came up with a revolutionary new fabric made of cow dung, dubbed 'manure couture'. The poo-fabric, called Mestic, is made by converting the cellulose in cowpats into a tough, biodegradable material (the firm stresses that the resulting jeans don't smell). H&M gave the company a 150,000-euro grant, so turd-derived clothing could soon be arriving on a catwalk near you.

JESUS

Jesus's tomb got a $4 million facelift.

Christ is believed to be buried inside the Church of the Holy Sepulchre in Jerusalem, which has been damaged by pilgrims' footfall over the years. The six denominations that share guardianship of the church therefore agreed to restore the site and split the cost. The fact that they reached any agreement with each other was an impressive achievement. The groups are such bitter rivals that they don't trust each other with the keys, and have had to leave them with a Muslim family since the 12th century. Even this safeguard hasn't prevented violence breaking out. In 2002, a Coptic monk at the church moved his chair from its agreed spot to get some shade, which was interpreted as a hostile move by the Ethiopian denomination. Eleven monks were hospitalised after the resulting fisticuffs.

The chapel Jesus rests in, known as the Edicule, is considered the most sacred monument in Christianity. As part of the restoration, a small window has been carved into its wall, through which you can see the original rock burial bed on which it is thought Jesus's body rested.

The Church of the Holy Sepulchre is also the site of the Immovable Ladder. This is a ladder that's been leaning up against a wall since at least 1728. No one knows who it belongs to, and so no one is allowed to move it, for fear of angering one of the other sects.

▼

A statue of a homeless Jesus has been genuinely homeless for over a year. The bronze sculpture of Jesus sleeping rough on a park bench was given to the Australian city of Townsville in 2016, but the council can't choose where to put it. They finally commissioned a report to make the decision, but in the meantime Jesus is camping out at the Sacred Heart Cathedral.

JET PACKS ▶

Firefighters in Dubai started using jet packs to reach fires.

Dubai's incredibly heavy traffic poses real challenges to any emergency service trying to reach a fire. So the Dubai government has introduced the firefighting jet pack, designed to allow firefighters to arrive at the scene of the incident by jet ski and attack fires from the city's shoreline. The jet pack uses the water pressure from the jet ski to propel the firefighters into the air.*

In Norway, a company has launched a horizontal jet pack for skiers named 'ThrustMe'. It's intended to help power skiers who are travelling horizontally or uphill, potentially eliminating the need for chairlifts. Skiers strap four small jet engines to either side of their waist, helping them to reach speeds of up to 50mph.

* The firefighting jet pack arrived at roughly the same time as Dubai's police launched their first self-driving robot cop car. It can read number plates and scan the faces of passengers to check whether they are wanted criminals. The only drawback is that its top speed is 15mph.

These jet packs weren't the only one-person flying machines to launch this year. In late March, inventor Richard Browning announced his latest innovation – a real-life Iron Man suit that can fly its owner at a theoretical top speed of 280mph (though so far, he has only hovered in it). Unfortunately, the announcement didn't attract much interest. He launched it so close to April Fool's Day that almost everyone thought it was a hoax.

JOBS

Some of the most desirable jobs advertised in 2017 included:

▶ **Job Title:** Cat-cuddler

Job Description: A cat-lover was required to provide petting at Just Cats Veterinary Clinic in Dublin. Applicants needed to have 'gentle hands capable of petting and stroking cats for long periods of time' and an 'ability to understand different types of purring'.

▶ **Job Title:** Minister of Rum

Job Description: Bacardi advertised for a rum aficionado to spread the word about the greatness of rum and 'revolutionise the rum category'. Trinidadian DJ and music producer Jillionaire was selected for the role.

▶ **Job Title:** Chief adventure officer

Job Description: National Rail employed a 19-year-old to travel around Britain and visit all its most exciting and iconic sites, and then to vlog about them in order to encourage people to buy a 16–25 Railcard.

▶ **Job Title:** Chocolate taster

Job Description: The role was advertised by Mondelēz International (the parent company of Cadbury, Oreo and Milka), and required someone to taste their chocolate products and give honest and objective opinions about them.

...and a less desirable-sounding one:

▶ **Job Title:** Cold-blooded and spineless officer

Job Description: The person who got this job had to coordinate the delivery of a project that aimed to record and celebrate invertebrates in the North Pennines.

For other odd jobs, *see* **Goalkeepers**; **Hermits**; and **Osborne, George**.

JOURNALISTS

Newsreaders in Georgia read the news with bags on their heads.

Dissident Azerbaijani reporter Afqan Muxtarli was living in Georgia when, according to his account, he was attacked, abducted, carried back to Azerbaijan and had 10,000 euros stuffed into his pockets so that he could be charged with smuggling cash over the border. The Georgian government denied any involvement in the alleged abduction, but as an act of solidarity several presenters wore bags on their heads on TV shows and at a parliamentary committee session. One wore a bag to interview

A journalist in Belarus promised he would eat his own newspaper if his local hockey team made it to the play-offs. They did, so reporter Vyacheslav Fedorenkov ate his paper, dipped in soup. He only got through half of it.

the deputy interior minister, which annoyed him so much that he walked out.

One journalist who definitely didn't wear a bag on her head was the *Grimsby Telegraph*'s Laura Gooderham. She was sent to interview contestants at the auditions for the Miss Great Grimsby and District beauty pageant, was persuaded to enter by a former title-holder and ended up winning.

In Tajikistan, a new rule came into force requiring journalists to refer to the president by his full official title of 'the Founder of Peace and National Unity, Leader of the Nation, President of the Republic of Tajikistan, His Excellency Emomali Rahmon'. And in Slovakia journalists faced hefty fines for referring to Britain as 'Britain'. A new law states that they have to use official country names in news reports, and so when discussing Brexit they are supposed say 'the United Kingdom of Great Britain and Northern Ireland', and presumably also 'the-United-Kingdom-of-Great-Britain-and-Northern-Irexit'.

In which we learn …
Who used to work at number 666, what happened when
King Arthur challenged his parking fine, who kissed a
car for two days, and which sports star is the only known
friend of both Donald Trump and Kim Jong-un.

KANGAROOS

Volvo admitted that its driverless cars are confused by kangaroos.

The cars can't work out if the marsupials are near or far away, because they use the ground as a reference point to detect the shape and size of objects. Since kangaroos hop up and down, they look smaller when they're in the air and larger when they're on the ground. As far as the car is concerned, this makes them look as though they're getting closer, then further away, then closer, then further away.

Between June and July this year, South Australia's Department of Environment did its annual count of all the kangaroos in the state. The survey is conducted from low-flying planes by observers who literally sit in the passenger seat, looking out of the window, and counting all the kangaroos they can see below.

One 'kangaroo' that won't be included in the census is a rooster which, according to its owners, thinks it's a kangaroo. Ross David West, who lives in Australia's Northern Territory, adopted the cockerel when he found it wandering in the road, and put it in an enclosure with rescued kangaroos. It now imitates the roos' behaviour, kicking like them, biting like them and eating their food. Its owners have named it Cluck Norris.

KAZAKHSTAN

See **Qazaqstan**.

KENYA

Political logos in the Kenyan election included a milk packet, an electricity pylon and a robot.

Kenya's overall literacy rate is 78 per cent, but in rural areas it's much lower. This means political parties need an easily recognisable symbol on their leaflets and posters if they are to have a chance of success. The problem is that all the best ones have already been taken, and so for this year's election independent candidates were forced to adopt objects like baskets, batteries, termites and trowels. One candidate, Sammy Ruwa, had a symbol almost identical to that of the American football team the Miami Dolphins.

Despite the large number of parties, the election was essentially a straight choice between Uhuru and NASA, that is, between the incumbent president Uhuru Kenyatta and the coalition National Super Alliance Party (known by the abbreviation NASA).* Uhuru won it, but Kenya's supreme court ruled the result invalid a month later due to 'irregularities and illegalities'. It's the first time a court has ever overturned an election result in Africa. Kenyatta gave a speech in English saying that the judges' decision must be respected, and then another in Swahili to his supporters, denouncing them as 'crooks' and saying the whole thing was the fault of 'whites' and 'homosexuals'.

* One of Kenyatta's election promises was to cut civil servants' salaries. Half the government's income goes on paying government employee wages even though they number just 2 per cent of population. MPs in Kenya earn 76 times the average GDP per capita. If British MPs were paid at this rate, they'd be on more than £2.5 million each per year.

KIDS

For Chinese child spies, *see* **Espionage**; for English school-boys in skirts, *see* **Heatwaves**; for Finnish teenagers on hobbyhorses, *see* **Horse Racing**; for a three-year-old politician, *see* **Iran**; for a 12-year-old bassist, *see* **Music**; for head-louse sharing, *see* **Phones**; for footwear shaming, *see* **Schools**; and for various children not allowed into the US, *see* **Visas**.

KIM JONG-NAM, ASSASSINATION OF

Kim Jong-un's brother was killed by two women, one of whom was wearing a T-shirt emblazoned with the word 'LOL'.

The incident occurred in Kuala Lumpur airport in February. The women involved claimed they hadn't known they were carrying the deadly VX nerve agent,* believing instead that it was baby oil. They also claimed they'd been paid $90 each to spray the substance on Kim Jong-nam's face as part of a TV-show prank. If the VX had been applied to his face directly the fumes would probably have killed the people applying it. So experts believe the two attackers sprayed separate ingredients that mixed together on his skin.

Until his assassination, Kim Jong-nam was principally known in Western media for being detained while trying to visit Tokyo's Disneyland on a fake passport. The name he chose for his false identity was Pang Xiong, which means 'Fat Bear' in Mandarin.

The South Korean government erected 34 loudspeakers on the border with North Korea so that they could yell news of Kim Jong-nam's death to people in the North. Predictably, they blamed the North. Equally predictably, the authorities in the North deny the charge. It's not the first time in recent years that North Korea has been accused of involvement in peculiar assassination attempts. In 2012, a would-be North Korean assassin was arrested in Seoul carrying a torch that doubled as a gun, a fountain pen that fired a blade, and a ballpoint pen that hid a poison-tipped needle.

There is now only one remaining brother of Kim Jong-un. He's called Kim Jong-chol, and he was passed over for the succession because his father considered him 'too feminine' to lead the regime. Nobody knows his whereabouts; he was last seen in London in 2015, at an Eric Clapton

The substance allegedly used to kill Kim Jong-nam was first synthesised in the 1950s by British scientists who were trying to make an insect repellent. It's 100 times more toxic than the chemical weapon sarin, with the consistency of honey; one droplet of it on your skin is easily enough to kill you.

concert. The previous time he was seen was also at an Eric Clapton concert – the night before.

KIMCHI ▶

Scientists at the World Institute of Kimchi, which can be found in the Kimchi Museum, on Kimchi Street, in Kimchi Town, are trying to remove the smell of kimchi from kimchi.

Kimchi – spicy fermented pickled cabbage – is ubiquitous in South Korea but not nearly as popular in the West. Its makers hope that European and American markets may open up if the dish's pungent smell can somehow be removed.

The World Institute of Kimchi hosts an annual kimchi-ology symposium and a 20-week 'kimchi sommelier' course, and has made space kimchi for South Korea's first astronaut. But younger Koreans don't eat as much of it as their parents did, and South Korean kimchi producers are being undercut by cheap Chinese imports. In a bid for survival, kimchi makers are hoping to make kimchi more marketable in the West not only with the deodorisation, but also by increasing the quantity of good bacteria in the product and selling it as a health product. Not everyone is convinced. Hwang Kyo-ik, a culinary writer in Seoul, called the project 'embarrassing'.

———— ▼ ————

A bacteria found in kimchi could be used to save babies' lives. The biggest killer of newborns worldwide is sepsis. Scientists have recently discovered that by feeding them the microbes found in large amounts in kimchi, their chances of developing the disease are dramatically reduced.

KINGS ▶

The King of Belgium got into an argument with the King of Burgers.

The Belgian royal family contacted Burger King to complain about an advert that asked people to choose who they liked best, Burger King or the Belgian King. Representatives of King Philippe of Belgium complained they had not given Burger King permission to use his image, even if it was in cartoon form. The advert was pulled shortly afterwards.*

In other king news:

▸ King Abdullah of Jordan has been helping to put out fires, literally. A fire started in a forested area on the outskirts of the capital city, Amman, and video circulated of him grabbing a fire extinguisher and plunging into the inferno.

▸ Brazil's president Michel Temer got his kings confused when he visited Norway in June. In a speech intended to convey gratitude for the warm welcome he'd received, he firstly referred to the Norwegian parliament as the Brazilian parliament, and then thanked the King of Sweden rather than the King of Norway.

▸ The self-declared reincarnation of King Arthur went to court to challenge a parking fee he was charged at Stonehenge. Arthur Uther Pendragon (born John Timothy Rothwell) claimed the £15 parking charge for the night of the 2016 summer solstice contravened his human right to worship freely. English Heritage argued that if it waived the charge, this would be discrimination against all those who had actually paid for parking. King Arthur lost the case.

▸ A father of two living on a housing estate in Greater Manchester was named by the Rwandan Royal Council of Abiru as Rwanda's king-in-exile. Emmanuel Bushayija's family was exiled in 1961 when he was a baby, and he worked for Pepsi in Uganda before moving to the UK in 2000. His predecessor, King Kigeli, died in 2016, having spent his final years living on food stamps in Virginia and selling knighthoods to make ends meet.

*Burger King also made a TV advert that featured the words 'OK Google, what is the Whopper burger?', designed to set off Google Home devices. If you were watching the ad and had a Google Home box in the room, the device would immediately start reading the Wikipedia entry for the Whopper burger. Predictably, many complained that this was intrusive.

Europe opened its first sex-doll brothel.

Located in Barcelona, and with only four 'members of staff' (Lily, Katy, Laiza and Aki), the brothel offers sessions to customers at 80 euros an hour. Dolls can be customised in advance (options include three different outfits), and a choice of position on arrival is also available. The website assures customers that the dolls are 'thoroughly disinfected' between bookings.

The brothel initially proved so popular that it provoked complaints from real-life sex workers, who said the dolls were stealing their trade. After the building's owners found out the nature of the business and kicked them out, the brothel eventually moved to a 'mystery location' which was only given out to paying customers.

Meanwhile, in New Jersey a cop called Kristen Hyman was suspended from the force after it was discovered she was a former dominatrix. She was told she could stay on the condition she passed a psychiatric exam to prove she wasn't prone to using excessive force. Officer Hyman has rejected the offer and is on paid leave pending a hearing.

Authorities at Brecon Beacons National Park spent £50,000 installing concrete anti-dogging blocks to stop people having late-night sex in the car parks of local beauty spots. A workman in the area said, 'People living nearby have had enough of this dogging lark.'

A radio station in Texas gave a car to a woman who kissed it for 50 hours.

The radio station in question, 96.7 Kiss FM, announced it would award a new Kia car to whoever could kiss it for longest. Participants were allowed to move around or lie on the ground, as long as they kept both lips on the car, and got a ten-minute break each hour. After 50 hours there were seven people still kissing the car, so the DJs picked a random winner from among them. (The contestants had been asked if they wanted to drop out in exchange for concert tickets, but declined.)

A write-up on *Vice* argued the competition was 'a metaphor for the contemporary human condition: humiliated, voiceless, competing for the largesse of corporations, and broadcast on social media for the world to see'. Most said it had been worth it 'for the experience'. One man who was disqualified for taking his lips off the car after he accidentally dropped his phone charger on to his face disagreed: 'I am really sad,' he said. 'I feel like I wasted a lot of time.'

KOREA, SOUTH ▶

South Korea's ex-president was caught having sheep injected into her face.

——— ▼ ———

A South Korean primary school decided to change its name after years of taunting. Daebyun Elementary School was named after a village, but the word also means 'faeces' in Korean. Over four thousand people signed a petition to have it changed.

Park Geun-hye, South Korea's president, was ousted in March after a scandal that rocked the entire country and saw her accused of corruption, influence-selling and being involved in shamanistic rituals. At her trial in May, four of President Park's doctors were convicted of perjury and of maintaining inadequate or fabricated medical records, after concealing the fact they had given the president Botox and shots of sheep embryo to keep her looking young. This wasn't the only problem Park faced – the charge sheet ran to 120,000 pages. And on top of all that, she got in trouble with animal rights groups for leaving her nine pet dogs behind when she moved out of the presidential home.

Also caught up in the scandal was Park's long-time confidant and so-called 'shaman adviser', Choi Soon-sil, who was jailed for conspiring to get her daughter into a good university and fixing her results. She also allegedly spent millions of extorted dollars setting up her daughter's horse-riding career, including spending $1 million on a horse called Vitana V.

When the new president of South Korea, Moon Jae-in, was asked what his worst attribute was, he said he was 'no fun', which sounds quite restful in comparison with his predecessor. Moon showed a softer attitude to North Korea than Park had done by suggesting the two Koreas launch a bid for the 2030 World Cup, even though the two nations have been in a state of war for the last 67 years.

In a year of political mayhem, there was one very bright spot for the country's sports fans. South Korea's women's hockey team won a game against Thailand. Not only was this the first time they'd ever beaten Thailand, it was the first game the team had won in their entire 19-year history. And even better, they won 20–0. Their goalkeeper said, 'My entire body was bruised from blocking pucks coming at an average speed of 100kph, but what hurts most is when others talk about our team in negative ways.'

KUSHNER, JARED

Before joining the Trump administration, Jared Kushner had to quit all 266 of his jobs.

Kushner had roles on 266 boards and businesses until he joined the US government in January this year, when conflict of interest and time constraints meant he had to step down from all his other positions. Since then, he's quickly picked up nearly as many new roles. In his new job as White House Innovations Director, Kushner became responsible for, among other things, improving relations with Mexico; overseeing relations with China; solving America's opioid epidemic; reforming veterans affairs; reforming the criminal justice system; modernising the government's data and technology infra-structure; revolutionising the way government works so that it operates more like a business; and bringing peace to the Middle East. He has no previous experience in government, but he has his father-in-law Donald Trump's vote of confidence: Trump has said to him, 'If you can't produce peace in the Middle East, nobody can.'

According to a survey, in the months immediately following the US election, the number of people who said they didn't know who Jared Kushner was decreased, while the number who disliked him increased by almost exactly the same figure.

KOREA, NORTH

Dan: North Korea has launched a new tourism website.

Andy: Is that the…most important North Korean news of the year?

Dan: Definitely. Can't think of anything more relevant. They offer a variety of themed vacations, including a surfing holiday, a taekwondo holiday, and a labour tour, where you can participate in rice planting, weeding and fruit picking.

Anna: That sounds like fun. They've also launched a new tourist ferry this year.

James: Can we stop saying 'launched'?

Dan: I bet they've done that to keep everyone on edge. In press conferences they probably say, 'We have launched…a ferry.'

Anna: They have actually launched a tourist ferry! It goes from the coast of North Korea to Vladivostok in Russia, and on nice days it slows down so that passengers can 'enjoy the smell of the sea'.

Andy: That is not the only overseas expansion they've had. Did you see that earlier this year North Korea posted an advert online, selling spare nuclear material?

James: Oh dear.

Andy: I know. The seller was listed as a North Korean diplomat living in Beijing, and the ad gave out his mobile number. They were effectively saying, 'We have so much nuclear material you can buy some off us.'

Dan: Did you know that Kim Jong-un has a copy of Donald Trump's book *The Art of the Deal*?

James: Has he?

Dan: Yeah, it was given to him by Dennis Rodman, the basketball player. Rodman has made several trips to North Korea and regularly hangs out with Kim Jong-un, who is a massive fan of his former team, the Chicago Bulls. Rodman is also a friend of Donald Trump – he was on *Celebrity Apprentice* – so as far as we know he is the only human being on Earth to be friends with both Trump and Kim Jong-un.

Anna: I also read that Rodman gave Kim Jong-un two autographed basketball jerseys, a soap set, a mermaid puzzle and a copy of *Where's Waldo?*

James: Lucky old Kim Jong-un. So, other people who went to North Korea this year include a group of Olympic corporate sponsors.

Andy: Really?

James: Yes – by mistake. The Winter Olympics next year is going to be in Pyeongchang in South Korea, but their pilot accidentally flew to Pyongyang in North Korea. They were marched off the plane and their bags were checked, and it was only when the North Koreans saw their Olympic badges that they knew there'd been a mix-up.

Andy: Bad day for that pilot.

When Ivanka Trump and Jared Kushner went on holiday to Whistler, Canada, the Secret Service agents who accompanied them had to spend $7,000 on ski passes for themselves, and $59,654 on hotel rooms.

Kushner is a property developer who took over his family business when his father was sent to jail. Charles Kushner was convicted on 16 counts of tax evasion, as well as witness tampering, after he hired a prostitute to seduce, film and blackmail one of the witnesses for the prosecution. Chris Christie, once tipped for Jared's role as Trump's most trusted adviser, was Attorney General at the time, and thus responsible for convicting Charles. In spite of this awkward history, Christie insists that he and Jared – with whom he works on the Opioid and Drug Abuse Commission – 'get along just great'.

Kushner's company's flagship, a 41-storey tower on Fifth Avenue, New York, was the most expensive property purchase in US history. It is building number 666. However, despite these demonic associations, some see the Kushners as heroes – specifically, residents of the Belorussian city of Novogrudok where, during the Second World War, the family led a daring escape from the Nazis. Jared's grandmother and her brother helped dig a tunnel out of the ghetto, and led 350 Jews to safety through it. It was the longest escape tunnel in Nazi-occupied Europe, and one of the war's most successful Jewish rescue operations.

In which we learn …
How disaster struck the British Kebab Awards, why
scientists are firing lasers at salmon, where to go for
terrorist LEGO, and what happened when
KFC met Mills & Boon.

La La Land *was involved in an extremely embarrassing awards mix-up. Twice.*

The *La La Land* team may not have taken a golden statuette home this year, but they did get a golden crayon. It came inside the goody-bags given to all nominees, along with treats that included a luxury T-shirt, an underarm patch to prevent sweating, and a 10-month supply of apples (as well as several holidays).

The world cringed as *La La Land* was mistakenly read out as the Best Film at the Oscars in January. (A post-mortem on the affair noted that one of the two officials giving out the magic envelopes had been taking a selfie with Emma Stone two minutes before.) A couple of days earlier, the *Huffington Post* had published an article entitled 'What Would Happen If a Presenter Announced the Wrong Winner at the Oscars?' Brian Cullinan, the man who was to hand over the wrong envelope on the night, was quoted as saying, 'It's so unlikely.'

It wasn't the only mistake made that night: in the course of paying tribute to Australian costume designer Janet Patterson in the 'In Memoriam' section, the Academy managed to put up a photo of the wrong person, producer Jan Chapman. She pointed out, 'I am alive and well and an active producer.'

Remarkably, *La La Land* was involved in *another* prizes mix-up. At Germany's prestigious Goldene Kamera awards, excitement that *La La Land* had triumphed again turned to embarrassment when the award was collected not by Ryan Gosling – as the organisers had expected – but by a Ryan Gosling impersonator, who turned out to be a cook from Munich called Ludwig. Two comedians had tricked the organisers into inviting the fake Gosling, and because the hosts were so excited to have such a massive celebrity they agreed not to host him on the red carpet and to leave him completely alone before the ceremony. It was only when he appeared onstage that everyone realised they'd been tricked.

This sort of thing happens quite a lot. The very night of the Academy Awards, the British Kebab Awards, 'the kebab equivalent of the Oscars', had its own *La La Land* moment. Staff from Koz, in Beckenham, took to the stage to collect their award for Customer Satisfaction, only to be told that the actual winner was Kosk, in Edmonton. And then, on UK general election night, the wrong candidate was named as the winner in Mansfield, until people pointed out to the returning officer that she'd got her numbers wrong.

LANGUAGES

Instead of their ABCs, Ethiopian children are now learning their LAGs.

The government of Ethiopia has changed the alphabet of the country's most commonly spoken language, Oromo. It used to go A, B, C, D, E, F... just like other Latin alphabets, but it now goes: L A G I M Aa* S. The government says that the new alphabet suits the language better, and so will help children to learn. But opponents say that it's a way of complicating the language so it eventually disappears, in favour of Amharic, which has four million fewer speakers but is the national tongue. It's been a long fight for the 25 million Oromo speakers in Ethiopia. It was illegal to write the language down in any alphabet until 1991.

Another language in danger this year is Icelandic: it's being killed by computers. According to the Multilingual Europe Technology Alliance (META), Icelandic was late to the language-technology party, and so is one of the least well-supported big languages. What this means in

* 'Aa' is the way that Oromo people write the 'long a' that you get in words like 'father' or 'water'.

163

France's slogan for its 2024 Olympic bid is in English, not French, even though French is one of the two official Olympic languages. French-language supporters campaigned for the phrase 'Made for Sharing' to be replaced with a French one, while the Académie Française pointed out it's been used in adverts for pizzas and sweets, which isn't in the spirit of the Olympics.

practice is that while you can speak to your smart fridge in English, French and probably Oromo, it won't understand you if you speak Icelandic.

And now computers are beginning to make their own languages. Facebook trained bots to trade with one another, and found that the programs started to communicate in a 'language' that humans couldn't understand. Here's an example:

Bob: i can i i everything else ...

Alice: balls have zero to me to me to me to me to me to me to me to me to

Bob: you i everything else ...

Alice: balls have a ball to me to me to me to me to me to me to me

Bob: i i can i i i everything else ...

Alice: balls have a ball to me to me to me to me to me to me to me

They turned the program off soon after this discovery.

Meanwhile, President Erdoğan of Turkey has launched a crackdown on Western-derived words. All sports grounds with the word 'arena' in their name, for instance, were ordered to replace it with '*stadyumu*'. In a speech in May, he said that borrowed words were not '*sik*', a Turkish word meaning 'stylish' which he may not have realised derives from the French word '*chic*'.

LASERS

Scientists have made a laser that can send a beam two million miles, one that can shine a billion times brighter than the sun, and one that can delouse a salmon.

The sharpest laser, which can transmit a beam two million miles without it going out of phase (i.e. before the light starts to look a bit fuzzy), was made by American and German researchers, and will be used to make clocks more accurate, and to test Einstein's theory of relativity. The brightest, made by scientists at the University of Nebraska–Lincoln, will help us to make better X-rays and smaller computer chips.

Either laser would be extreme overkill for a new smart underwater drone that's patrolling the fjords of Norway, checking salmon for lice and then, if it finds any, killing the lice with a laser blast. The laser doesn't injure the salmon because the salmon's scales reflect the light like a disco ball.

LAWSUITS, NON-TRUMP

Lawsuits this year included the following:

▶ *Warner Bros. vs The Paranormal.* The makers of the movie *The Conjuring* are facing a lawsuit of over $900 million from author Gerald Brittle, who says the film company took the story from his book *The Demonologist*. The production company has said that the movies were not based upon the book but instead based upon 'historical facts' – which would appear to involve proving that ghosts exist. Alternatively it could show that it was not aware of the book before starting work on the film. The second of these options, though, may be slightly undermined by a tweet sent in 2011 by the film's director which read: 'I watch/read a lot of scary stories. But f**k, THE DEMONOLOGIST... is the scariest book I've read.'

▶ *The Terracotta Army vs their substitutes.* China's Mausoleum of the First Qin Emperor announced it was preparing lawsuits against anyone who infringed copyright on its 2,000-year-old statues, after a Chinese theme park and a Belgian train station put on unofficial displays of replicas.

NASA announced that the Mars Curiosity Rover has had a successful year, driving around autonomously and firing lasers at rocks. The rover's software lets it select which rocks to blast, and then it vaporises them with a laser. This allows it to sniff out what chemicals the rocks are made of, revealing information about Mars's surface to scientists on earth.

▶ *The People vs The Spying Vibrator.* A Canadian vibrator firm agreed to pay up to £2.4 million in compensation after selling customers a 'smart vibrator' which tracked people's use without their knowledge. The We-Vibe 4 Plus can be activated remotely and collected data about 'temperature and vibration intensity'.

▶ *The Yellow Light Crusader vs Oregon State Board of Engineers.* Mats Järlström, an American who wanted to make traffic lights stay yellow for longer to improve traffic efficiency, filed a lawsuit against the Oregon State Board of Examiners for Engineering and Land Surveying after he was hit with a fine of $500 when he proposed his plans to the city council. He was fined for taking part in the 'practice of engineering' without a licence.

The board takes such claims by individuals very seriously. Last year it investigated a man standing to become Republican candidate for governor, whose political ads claimed: 'I'm an engineer and a problem solver.' The board concluded that he wasn't, as he was not registered in Oregon as a professional engineer.

LAWSUITS, TRUMP'S 134 ▶

Donald Trump was sued 134 times in his first 100 days.*

* The combined total of all the lawsuits levelled against Presidents Obama, Bush (W) and Clinton at the same point in their presidencies was just 48.

Fortunately, he's well used to lawsuits; in his life, he's been involved in more than 3,500 of them. This is probably why he has five lawyers, including his chief personal lawyer Michael Cohen, who this year hired a lawyer of his own to represent him during the investigation into the US government's links to Russia. Vice President Mike Pence, and the head of communications during the Republican presidential campaign, Michael Caputo, have also hired their own personal lawyers since becoming involved in the administration.

In 2013, Michael Cohen filed a lawsuit on Trump's behalf against American TV host Bill Maher. In response to Trump's demands that Obama publish his birth certificate, Maher had joked on *The Tonight Show* that he'd donate $5 million to charity if Trump could publish *his* birth certificate as evidence that he wasn't part orangutan. Trump took the challenge literally, revealed his birth certificate, which did indeed prove he wasn't fathered by an ape, and promptly sued Maher when he didn't pay up. The lawsuit was eventually withdrawn, but Cohen made it clear that they intended to re-file it at a later date.

Even Trump's golf clubs didn't escape lawsuits. One woman tried to sue Trump's Aberdeenshire course this year after she was photographed urinating on it. She had been relieving herself while on a walk near the course when she was spotted by golf-club employees, who took pictures on their phones and reported her to the police. It turned out she was acting perfectly legally, and she sued for damages over the distress caused by being photographed. She didn't win the case, although the club staff were heavily reprimanded by the court.

Trump's appetite for lawsuits probably explains why he bought up the URL iambeingsuedbythedonald.com before anyone else could. Other websites he has owned include donaldtrumpsucks.com, trumpscam.com and ihatetrumpvodka.com.

LEAKS, INFORMATION

The world learned the CIA has hacking programmes called Panda Poke, Panda Flight and Panda Sneeze.

In March, WikiLeaks published 8,761 documents that exposed the CIA's fondness for fun names. Other programme names included CrunchyLimeSkies, Elder-Piggy, BuzFuz, Magical Mutt, Secret Squirrel, DRBOOM and McNugget.

The leak also exposed multiple CIA hacking and surveillance techniques. For instance, TVs and phones can be set to 'fake off' mode, so that they can still be used for eavesdropping when users believe they're switched off. It was also revealed that the CIA understands that its employees might occasionally need some down time. Its advice to hackers when travelling with Lufthansa was: 'Booze is free, so enjoy (within reason)!'

Personal information about 60 per cent of the US population was accidentally leaked in June by a conservative data firm working for the Republican Party. The company, Deep Root Analytics, stored details of people's names, addresses, phone numbers, ethnicity and opinions on issues like gun ownership and stem-cell research, on a publicly accessible Amazon server. Anyone with the URL could access information on the 198 million people whose details were held there. It represented the largest leak of people's personal information in American history, and constituted enough data to fill 36,000 CDs.

LEAKS, WATER

A hotel called the Niagra had to close down because it was full of water.

In February, a budget hotel in Blackpool formerly known as the Vidella underwent an exciting name change. Proprietor Neil Marshall changed its name to the 'Viagra'. He also added a big sign on the front saying: 'We will keep you up all night!'*

Perhaps unsurprisingly, the council received complaints from the public and neighbouring businesses, who said that passing children were asking what the sign meant. The council promptly wrote to Mr Marshall, asking him to change the name to 'something less provocative and more in keeping with the nature of your business i.e. a hotel'. Not only that, but Pfizer – the firm which

* Despite the fact this is the opposite of what most people want from a hotel.

makes Viagra pills – said that 'Pfizer does not support nor condone the use of the Viagra trademark in this manner', adding that they would be 'taking appropriate action'.

Undaunted, Marshall crossed out the V and replaced it with an N, making the hotel the Niagra, and amended the sign to say: 'We will keep you wet all night!'* As he told the *Sun*, 'In this world there are some people who drink tea and coffee all day and don't have a sense of humour. There are others who drink lager and have a laugh – it's about opinions and people love it.'

* *Equally undesirable in a hotel, one would think.*

This new strategy backfired three months later, when a major pipe leak forced the newly christened Niagra to close for repairs.

LEFTIES

For an award-winning beard, *see* **Corbyn, Jeremy**; for a laughter-loving socialist *see* **Ecuador**; for an anti-capitalist hologram, *see* **French Presidential Election**; and for a left-wing leader who's running low on toilet paper, *see* **Venezuela**.

LEGO

In China, you can buy ISIS-themed knock-off LEGO.

The 'Military Figures Falcon Commandos Terrorist Assassination Charge Captain Medical Staff box' includes ISIS flags and decapitated heads (although, of course, many LEGO sets contain heads that are easy to remove). This is not real LEGO, though, and so isn't likely to be studied by Cambridge University's new 'LEGO professor'. This year, Paul Ramchandani, an expert in child mental health, was appointed the university's 'LEGO Professor of Play'. He will examine how children are encouraged to play at home and school.†

† *Cambridge University also hired its first 'Professor of Innovation'. The post was funded by the man who invented the switch that turns kettles off once they've boiled.*

Donald Trump's Treasury secretary had LEGO-related problems this year. Steven Mnuchin had to write to the Office of Government Ethics after suggestions that he had violated ethical rules by publicly plugging *The LEGO Batman Movie*, which his company had financed. When asked a question about his movie recommendations, he answered, 'I'm not allowed to promote anything that I'm involved in … but you should send all your kids to *LEGO Batman*.' It was, he said, an accident.

LICENCE PLATES ▶

Canada refused to renew a man's licence plate because his surname was too offensive.

Last year, a driver in China spent £113,000 on a personalised number plate which read '88888' (eight is a very lucky number in China), only to report later that it had made life a nightmare for him, as police kept pulling him over to check the plate wasn't a fake. He said, 'I ended up being stopped for longer periods than I was actually driving.'

Canadian Lorne Grabher's family have owned a personalised 'GRABHER' licence plate for 27 years. But when a member of the public saw it without realising it was a surname and made a complaint, Nova Scotia authorities revoked permission for the plate to be used. They argued that although Mr Lorne Grabher's surname is an old German one, the general public wouldn't know this and that the word 'GRABHER' could be misinterpreted as a 'socially unacceptable slogan'.

Mr Grabher didn't give up, saying, 'Where does the Province of Nova Scotia and this government have a person with that kind of power to discriminate against my name?' His lawyers stated that Grabher and his family are 'deeply offended and humiliated' by the authorities' decision, that it qualifies as an 'ongoing insult to their heritage', and said it was 'censoring of expression' for good measure. In early 2018, the case will arrive at Nova Scotia's Supreme Court. To raise money, Mr Grabher's legal team are selling 'GRABHER' bumper stickers.

Canada is not the only country to have experienced problematic number plates. In Wales this year, licence plate

'JH11 HAD' was withdrawn at the behest of the DVLA for looking a bit too much like 'Jihad'. In Sweden, a man who last year failed to get '3JOH22A' registered (it looks like ASSHOLE in a mirror) tried again, this time attempting to register a plate reading '8UTT5EX'. He failed for a second time, and so reversed it to 'X32TTU8', before failing for a third time. As a member of staff from the Swedish Transport Agency said, 'We get a lot of requests and some of them are very subtle…This one was quite easy to reject.'

LITERATURE

KFC released a romance novel called **Tender Wings of Desire.**

The novel, supposedly written by Colonel Sanders, and starring him as the main character, was part of a promotion for Mother's Day, which the company claims is their best sales day of the year. It is the first book by the Colonel since his 1974 autobiography, *Life as I Have Known It Has Been 'Finger Lickin' Good'.**

Tender Wings of Desire met with a mixed response on Amazon. While many enjoyed the 96-page love story, some readers were frustrated by the lack of KFC references. 'There were no chicken wings,' wrote one reader in their one-star review. 'The only thing that vaguely links the story to the restaurant is frequent and copious references to salt,' wrote another. Many complained there weren't enough steamy scenes in the book.

Elsewhere, erotic author Chuck Tingle, whose book titles include *Pounded by the Pound: Turned Gay by the Socioeconomic Implications of Britain Leaving the European Union, Fake News, Real Boners, Pounded in the Butt by Covfefe* and *Slammed by My Handsome Fidget Spinner,* has released a colouring book.

Tory politician Gavin Barwell, who wrote a book called *How to Win a Marginal Seat,* lost his marginal seat in the 2017 general election.

* *The real Colonel Sanders died in 1980. The new book is by the fictional character on the side of the bucket.*

Objects lost and found this year included:

The Welsh coastguard called off the search for a man lost at sea when it turned out he was in the pub. A helicopter and lifeboat both looked for him, only for a Holyhead Coastguard spokeswoman to announce the man had 'rescued himself', and had then retired to the appropriately named local pub, the Ship Aground.

Lost: *A controversial monk.* Phra Dhammachayo is a Thai monk, wanted on charges of massive embezzlement. But when the Thai government finally got access to his huge religious complex in Bangkok, in a massive police raid involving 3,600 officers, it found only an empty bed stuffed with pillows. One local website called it 'a trick straight out of *Scooby Doo*'.

Found: *Napoleon's horse's hoof.* The hoof of Marengo, the horse Napoleon rode at Waterloo, was found in a plastic bag in a kitchen in Somerset. The two front hooves of the horse had been removed after its death and turned into silver snuff mills.

Found: *A Nazi bomb.* It was found under a petrol station in Greece. Seventy-two thousand people had to be evacuated – the largest peacetime evacuation in Greek history. The bomb had been there since at least 1944.

Lost Then Found: *A beach in Ireland.* The 300-metre beach, which had been washed away by freakish waves 33 years earlier, reappeared after 10 days of high tides in May as sand washed in to cover the rocks. When the beach went missing, local cafes and hotels shut down – hopefully they can now open up again.

Lost Then Found: *Two teenage boys.* They got lost in the Paris catacombs, a 200-mile maze of tunnels and bones under the city, after getting separated from their tour group. They wandered about for three days among six million skeletons until they were found by search dogs.

Found, Lost, Then Found Again: *The Millennium Time Capsule.* Builders working on the O2 arena in London accidentally dug up the time capsule buried there by the presenters of *Blue Peter* in 1998, which was meant to be left until 2050. Unfortunately the workers crushed it and threw it in a skip without realising what it was. It was eventually retrieved, meaning that the nation still has a vital record of life in 1998, including a Tamagotchi, a Spice Girls CD, some rollerblades, some felt from the Millennium Dome roof and a picture of Tony Blair in a high-vis vest.

LOTTERIES

Daylight saving time helped Romanians win the lottery.

A group of gamblers took advantage of the clocks going forward by one hour in Romania, but not in Greece, and bet on the Greek lottery after the results had been announced online, but before they were logged in Romanian computers. The scam was only uncovered when the bookmakers ran out of money, and the gamblers called the police. Once the police were involved, the bookies realised their mistake and cancelled all the bets. Generously, given the fact that they were thousands of pounds out of pocket, they agreed to refund all the stakes.

In other gambling news: a woman in New York is suing a casino because when a slot machine displayed a win of nearly $43 million, staff refused to pay out and claimed it was faulty. Had she won, it would have been the biggest slot-machine win in US history. Instead she was offered $2.25 and a steak dinner. She declined.

In which we learn …
What's the best kitchen appliance to carry for 26 miles,
why Japan is running out of ninjas, what happened
when the prime minister met the glamour model,
and WTF happened to the WTF.

MAFIA

For a don's dong, *see* **Arrests, Human**; for Archbishop Pennisi's intervention, *see* **Godfather**; for gangsters in pizza parlours, *see* **Godfather: Part II**; for a monkey mafia, *see* **Godfather: Part III**; and for an Indian beach cartel, *see* **Sand**.

MAGA

The phrase 'Make America Great Again' adorned half a million hats and one anus.

LGBTQ performance artist Abel Azcona crouched naked for two hours at the Defibrillator Gallery in Chicago while the words were stenciled around his bottom, before announcing that 'The anus is a land of pleasure and a terrarium of empowerment for many … writing a fascist political motto like that in my anus is a clearly critical and subversive action.' He seems happy with the decision, unlike Joshua Hughes, the Bernie Sanders fan who in 2016 admitted he regretted getting a tattoo on his penis that read 'Feel the Bern'.

Of course, the slogan is more commonly seen on heads than on arses. The Trump campaign has now sold more than half a million caps with the 'Make America Great Again' motto. They were particularly popular at his inauguration, during the course of which Trump announced that he would 'buy American and hire American'. Those of his supporters who bought their caps from street vendors in Washington – as opposed to purchasing them from Trump's official website – were probably not aware that they were made in China, Vietnam and Bangladesh.

MAR-A-LAGO

See **White House, Winter**.

EastEnders **star Adam Woodyatt was beaten in the London Marathon by a man in a sleeping bag, a woman in a full-body dinosaur suit and a man carrying a tumble dryer.**

TIMES:

2:05:48 – Daniel Wanjiru – Men's London Marathon winner

2:14:49 – Josh Griffiths – Previously unknown top British runner

2:17:01 – Mary Keitany – Women's London Marathon winner

3:13:18 – Simon Couchman – Fastest marathon dressed as a crustacean

3:26:13 – Nicola Nuttall – Fastest marathon dressed as a witch

3:44:01 – David Smith – Fastest marathon in a sleeping bag

4:07:57 – Warren Edwicker – Fastest marathon dressed as a telephone box

5:58:37 – Ben Blowes – Fastest marathon carrying a household appliance

7:04:34 – Adam Woodyatt – Soap star

6.5 days – Mr Gorilla – Man dressed as a gorilla

A total of 73 world records were attempted in this year's London Marathon and 39 were broken, including the fastest marathon run in a sleeping bag, and the fastest dressed as a swimmer, a star, a crustacean, an elf, a fast-food item, a toilet roll, a telephone box, and a witch. Nicola Nuttall from Pendle, Lancashire, who broke the witch record, finished five minutes quicker than last year, when her record attempt was annulled because her skirt was deemed to be too short. Nuttall ran the race in three hours and 26 minutes; less than half the time it took *EastEnders'* Adam Woodyatt to complete the course. Woodyatt's time of seven hours and four minutes may have been slow, but it wasn't entirely his fault – it was at least partly due to the fact that he stopped for so many selfies on the way.

Arguably the most impressive world record was set by roofer Ben Blowes, who ran the race carrying a tumble dryer. He heaved the 25-kilo kitchen appliance along the course in five hours and 58 minutes after months of training in his home town of Newmarket, where he was occasionally stopped by police who thought he was the world's most brazen burglar. He initially trained with a fridge but came to the conclusion that this was stupid and that it would make much more sense to race with a tumble dryer on his back.

The star of the London Marathon was undoubtedly Mr Gorilla, aka policeman Tom Harrison, who completed the course 'gorilla-style', originally on his hands and knees and then walking on his knuckles, in order to raise money for a gorilla conservation charity. (He was also wearing a gorilla costume.) When stopped and asked to give advice to future gorilla runners, he said, 'Get a bit more training in. We only did about four crawling sessions beforehand. I'd also recommend painkillers and bloody-mindedness. Anyway, I better get crawling…' He completed the race in six and a half days. Had he managed to do it just six days and four hours quicker, he would have qualified for a medal.

The fastest British contender was Josh Griffiths. Completely unknown before the race, his success allowed him to represent Britain at the subsequent World Championships. What made his feat at the London Marathon particularly remarkable was that, unlike the top runners, who had to cover 26 miles, 385 yards, he had to cover 26 miles, 400 yards: as someone who was thought to have no chance of winning, he had to start 15 yards behind the main contenders.

MARATHONS, NON-LONDON

The fastest marathon of all time took place on a Formula One racing track.

Reigning Olympic marathon champion Eliud Kipchoge raced around the Monza racing track in Italy, with the intention of achieving the holy grail of long-distance running – a sub-two-hour marathon. It was not an official record attempt, however, as he had some help along the way:

◆

Gary Robbins of Vancouver attempted to become one of only 15 people ever to run a 100-mile marathon in under 60 hours. However, he took a wrong turn with two miles to go and ended up at a deep, fast-flowing river, which he swam across before struggling to the finish line from the wrong direction. He finished the race six seconds later than the 60-hour target, acknowledging the time wouldn't have been recognised anyway, given the unorthodox route he had taken.

- Pacemakers ran alongside him, coming in and out of the race at various times (something that is absolutely not allowed in official races).

- They ran in a diamond shape with Kipchoge always in the middle – so that he could hide in their slipstream.

- There was a car driving in front of the group that beamed a green line on the road to show them the required speed for their two-hour target. If he kept up with the green line he'd make the time.

- The car also held a very tall screen that showed the current time – tall enough to ensure not only that they could all see it, but that it would cause an even bigger slipstream.

- Kipchoge wore special shoes, made by Nike, that had carbon-fibre insoles to minimise energy loss (the calculation was that these would give him a 4 per cent energy saving). Nike presumably hoped the shoes would fare better than they did in Berlin the year before when the insoles slipped out, causing serious blistering and even some bleeding to Kipchoge's feet.

In the event, Kipchoge missed out on his aim of a sub-two-hour marathon by just 26 seconds: he was around 200 metres away from the finishing line when the second hour clicked by.

One way he could have beaten the record would have been to run the Brighton Half Marathon course twice. Hundreds of runners who thought they had beaten their personal best this year were gutted when they found out that the race was 146 metres shorter than it should have been. It was not the first time Brighton experienced measurement problems. Five years ago, the course turned out to be nearly a third of a mile longer than expected.

A group of 'lavanauts' spent eight months in a plastic bubble on a volcano, pretending they were on Mars.

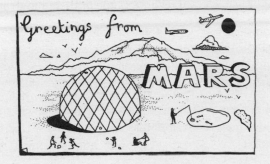

As part of a NASA study, a crew of six – four men and two women – moved into an airtight vinyl dome the size of a two-bedroom house on the slopes of the Hawaiian volcano Mauna Loa. Because they were on a volcano, they were called 'lavanauts'. NASA funded the study to examine the psychological problems that emerge when people live in cramped conditions for a long period of time, in preparation for manned missions to Mars (for more inhospitable living conditions, *see* **IKEA**).

Because it would take 20 minutes for an email to get from Earth to Mars, the crew had a 20-minute delay on their emails too. They weren't allowed to leave and walk around the featureless landscape unless they were wearing a spacesuit. To preserve the sense of isolation, their food was dropped off outside the dome, and the team had to send a robot to pick it up. According to one of the people running the experiment, 'Spam gets quite popular.'*

In a similar exercise, France's Institute for Space Medicine and Physiology announced they were recruiting subjects who would be paid 16,000 euros to spend 60 days lying down, in order to recreate the weightlessness of

A similar experiment took place this year in Poland. Volunteers lived underground in pods meant to simulate life on the Red Planet, bathing in water mist and eating pancakes made from crushed insects. The project is known as the Modular Analog Research Station (MARS).

* When they emerged in September, the lavanauts gave advice to future Mars adventurers: 'remember the toilets…are a living system…let them talk to you, if they smell a certain way or act a certain way they're trying to tell you something, so listen.'

the International Space Station. Applicants had to be non-smoking 20- to 45-year-old men in 'perfect' physical health. They also had to be prepared to eat, wash, and go to the toilet while lying in bed. 'The rule,' organiser Dr Arnaud Beck said, 'is to keep at least one shoulder in contact with the bed or its frame.' (For other body parts constantly in contact with a surface, *see* **Kissing**.)

MARTIAL ARTS

A t'ai chi 'thunder master' who claimed to possess supernatural powers was defeated by a boxer in 10 seconds.

The new president of Mongolia is a former martial arts champion. Khaltmaa Battulga, once world champion of the Soviet martial art Sambo, is also a real estate tycoon who owns a hotel, food firms, and a Genghis Khan-themed amusement park.

Mixed martial arts boxer Xu Xiaodong challenged one of China's t'ai chi masters, Wei Lei, to a fight in Sichuan. Wei Lei, who practises the 'thunder' style of t'ai chi, had for years maintained that he had supernatural powers, declaring in a documentary, for example, that he could smash the inside of a watermelon without harming its skin, and that he could create a force field using 'chi' to stop a pigeon perched on his hand from flying away (sceptics claimed it was duct-taped to him).

After a lot of online slanging, the two men agreed to a fight. It didn't last long. After just 10 seconds, the t'ai chi 'thunder master' was lying curled up on the floor, being repeatedly punched by Xu.

Afterwards, people criticised Xu for presuming to attack traditional martial arts, and he released a video apologising for his arrogance. As for Wei, he explained his defeat by pointing out that he had been wearing the wrong sort of shoes (causing him to lose his balance), adding, moreover, that winning would have caused 'disharmony' in his life, and that he had held back so he didn't kill his opponent. 'He never touched me when I was standing up,' he said, '…I only got hit when I fell on the floor. Do I need to explain any more?'

In other martial arts news:

▸ A pair of kung fu fighters in China both displayed their genital strength. Wei Yaobin, known as the Iron Crotch Kung-Fu Master, used his genitals to pull a bus 6 feet down a road, while Ye Hongwei went one better – beating the world record for pulling a military helicopter with his private parts. His goal was 26 feet; he actually achieved 33.

▸ Japan suffered from a shortage of ninjas. They are needed for the traditional shows loved by tourists, but although they don't have to be able to make themselves invisible or walk on water any more, they do need to be proficient in martial arts – and organisers complained that new applicants tend not to be.

▸ The World Taekwondo Federation* (WTF) changed its name, and is now known simply as World Taekwondo. President Chungwon Choue said, 'In the digital age, the acronym of our federation has developed negative connotations unrelated to our organisation and so it was important that we rebranded to better engage with our fans.'

*Egypt's President Abdel Fattah al-Sisi has been awarded a black belt in Taekwondo even though he's never set foot in the ring.

MAYORS

A pitbull called Brynneth Pawltro was elected mayor of Rabbit Hash for the fourth year in a row.

The Kentucky town began electing dogs as mayors in 1998, and to date three of them have served in office. This time around, other animals tried to challenge the canine dominance, with Brynneth facing competition from a donkey, a cat and a chicken.

Meanwhile, the human mayor of Nashville, Tennessee, publicly excused the city's ice hockey fans for turning up late to work the day after a big match. Following the Nashville Predators' 4–1 victory over the Pittsburgh

Penguins, Mayor Megan Barry shared a signed template letter online. It read:

> It is with all the powers invested in me that I hereby excuse _____ for showing up to work an hour or two late this morning. _____ was merely performing their civic duty last night by staying up late to watch our Nashville Predators take on the Pittsburgh Penguins. In fact, I would be disappointed if you were not doing the same.

Over in Italy, a human mayor was overwhelmed with calls after rumours spread that he'd pay 2,000 euros to anyone willing to move to his village. He proposed the idea in a Facebook post as a way of boosting the village of Bormida's dwindling population, but the story got exaggerated along the way and newspapers were soon reporting that new arrivals were guaranteed 2,000 euros. Over 17,000 people called the council in four days, wanting to move to a village that has a current population of 394. The mayor, Daniele Galliano, made it clear that he couldn't possibly take all those people and asked them to stop calling – please.

MAYWEATHER VS MCGREGOR

The Mayweather–McGregor fight was the ninth highest-grossing 'movie' in the US weekend box-office charts.

In what was said to be the biggest boxing match of the century, undefeated American boxer Floyd Mayweather Jr took on Irish Ultimate Fighting Championship (UFC) fighter-turned-boxer Conor McGregor, in a fight that was screened in 532 cinemas across America. It grossed $2.6 million in ticket sales, beating *The Emoji Movie*, which charted at 10 that weekend. :(

Media coverage of the fight, which took place in Las Vegas, was obsessed with the numbers – from how much the fighters stood to take home (reportedly $100 million for McGregor and $300 million for Mayweather) to the number of people who paid to watch it (6.5 million), and the number of people who watched it illegally (estimates went as high as 100 million). Boxing history was made when the victorious Mayweather became the only boxer with a record of 50 wins and no defeats.

The less well-reported figures include:

▶ **$30,000:** The sum of money Mayweather was offered by one club in Las Vegas if he walked through it for 10 minutes after the fight.

▶ **$400,000:** The amount Floyd Mayweather tried to bet on himself hours before the match. His bet was denied because the casino recognised who he was, so he sent a friend to bet for him. Unfortunately, the friend was only allowed to bet $87,000.

▶ **14,623:** The total number of ticket holders in attendance, according to ESPN. Despite the hype, the event didn't manage to sell-out the 20,000 capacity arena.

▶ **$500:** The amount it cost to attend Mayweather's post-fight party, which was held in his own strip club, Girl Collection. Mayweather spent the nights leading up to the fight in the venue so that he could meet fans and answer their questions. Though he would have had to pay, McGregor was welcome to join Mayweather at the strip club, according to Mayweather's bodyguard, Jizzy.

MEXICO ▶

For a wall of mirrors, *see* **Border Wall**; for 34,764 balls of marijuana, *see* **Cannabis**; for the worst place to be struck by an asteroid, *see* **Extinctions**; for a museum full of fakes, *see* **Failures**; for a cloud that rains tequila, *see* **Food and Drink**; and for a phallic seat, *see* **Railways**.

MAY, THERESA

James: So, Donald Trump met Theresa May this year, and she was the first foreign leader he met. But in the official schedule they spelled her name wrong three times, accidentally putting in the name of a glamour model. The model is also called Teresa May, but without the 'H'.

Anna: And are we absolutely sure that this wasn't the person that Donald Trump wanted to see? Because it's not implausible that he googled it, saw the pictures of her, and thought to himself, 'This is the first world leader I want to meet.'

Andy: May-the-model's previous work, just so you know, includes the movies *Petticoat Passions Volume 1*, *Lesbian Student Nurses* and *Nude and Naughty*.

Dan: How do you know that?

Andy: Extremely cautious googling. But May-the-model is well aware of the problem. On her Twitter profile, she says, 'I'm a UK model, not Theresa May the prime minister.'

James: Sensible precaution. Actually, Theresa and Teresa have met. In 2000, the Tory press office organised for them both to be on the TV show *GMTV* in order to make May-the-MP seem more fun.

Anna: Did it…work?

James: Surprisingly well. The Tory Party claim that it was one of their most successful PR stunts ever. And the two Mays got on quite well and apparently went out for coffee afterwards.

Dan: In slightly less big Theresa May news, she called a general election this year.

James: How did that go for her? Was it another PR triumph?

Dan: Not so much. But did you know there's a theory that the reason the 2017 UK general election was called was because of a Welsh hiking book? May went for a walk in the Welsh hills, and bought this book called *Walks in and around Dolgellau Town*, by Michael Burnett, which contains a passage that says, 'During the walk, there are a series of revelations. They focus you and give you the moment of clarity you need to make those big decisions.'

Anna: Yeah, I read that – and the man who sold her the book said that you wouldn't have recognised her because she was wearing walking gear. How heavy a disguise is walking gear?

Andy: Good point. Although there are loads of stories about her clothing. She got into trouble recently for wearing some £1,000 leather trousers for a photo shoot, I think.

James: Yeah, but not proper trouble; it's not like she ran through a field of wheat or anything.

Anna: It is amazing how much the press obsess over her outfits. The first time she attempted to be selected as a candidate, In 1989, she supposedly failed because she was wearing too short a skirt.

James: It did take a couple of attempts to become an MP. When she first ran, in North-West Durham, she lost by nearly 14,000 votes to Labour.

Andy: But at that election she did at least beat the Lib Dem candidate, Tim Farron, who at the time was president of the University of Newcastle Student Union.

Anna: And what became of Tim Farron?

Dan: Nobody knows.

MICE, SPACE

Ten brave mousetronauts parachuted back to Earth.

America sent a squadron of 40 mice to the International Space Station (ISS) in June to test a new therapy designed to rebuild bone – part of a study into osteoporosis. The therapy could help sufferers on Earth and also astronauts, who suffer rapid bone loss due to the microgravity environment. Ten of the mice came back, parachuting into the Pacific. The good news was that they were the first mice NASA has ever sent up that made it back alive; the bad news was that, as part of the experiment, they were euthanised immediately on landing.

In Japan, researchers published a scientific paper describing their experiment that sent freeze-dried mouse sperm into space. They wanted to see how the higher levels of radiation affected it. As it turned out, it was fine – after nine months floating in a freezer on the ISS in 2013, the sperm was brought back and defrosted, and now over 70 mice have been bred from it.

Human DNA is slightly damaged in space by the sun's radiation. The mouse DNA was slightly damaged too, but it still produced healthy 'space pups', which then had healthy babies themselves. It's possible that the damaged DNA in the mouse sperm repairs itself when it meets the egg. Other mice sent up in 2011 showed early signs of liver disease, but scientists believed this could have been due to the stress of being sent into orbit.

* Micronation (n): An area or territory that claims national sovereignty despite not being recognised by most or all other nation states.

MICRONATIONS

Thousands of Brits tried to escape Brexit by becoming citizens of an offshore military platform.

Sealand is a rusty naval platform off the Suffolk coast that its occupiers claim is an independent micronation.*

Its leader, Prince Michael, who makes a living selling Sealandic aristocratic titles, mugs, stamps and coins, said he'd been inundated with hundreds of applications per day to settle there, after Britain voted to leave the EU. However, he explained that they're not issuing any passports or visas at the moment due to 'the current international situation'. And possibly because Sealand's surface area is about the size of two tennis courts and accommodates a maximum of 150 people.

Regardless of size, micronations aren't officially recognised as sovereign states, so are subject to the laws of the nation that claims their territory. Australia's oldest micronation felt the effects of this recently. The Principality of Hutt River has for some time justified tax evasion by arguing that the tax system is a form of torture (referred to by the region's self-proclaimed leader as 'Old Hags Nagging'). But a judge took an unsympathetic view, dismissing its claim of sovereignty as 'gobbledygook' and handing it a £1.8 million tax bill. Hutt River had already suffered one upset this year when its ruler abdicated and handed the leadership to his son, Prince Graeme.

Another royal family with a dubious claim to power made the news when a Russian politician began trying to restore the Romanov dynasty by creating a micronation. Former MP Anton Bakov offered £280 million to the government of Kiribati, a Pacific island nation, in exchange for sovereign rights to its uninhabited Malden, Starbuck and Millennium Islands. He planned to use them as a base from which to bring back the tsars, starting with the German Prince Karl Emich of Leiningen, who has been declared heir to the Russian throne and adopted the name Nicholas III. Kiribati rejected the offer.

It wasn't all bad news for aspiring nations, at least according to the founder of Liberland, a 7km-square micronation between Croatia and Serbia. Vit Jedlička expressed the hope that because Mr Trump had phoned Taiwan when he took office, implying (as Jedlička saw it)

In June, the leaders of 26 micronations met in Atlanta for their conference, MicroCon 2017. They included representatives from the Kingdom of Jupiter, the Republic of West Who and the Kaotic Ambulatory Free States of Obsidia.

that the president recognised it as a nation independent of China, he might do the same for Liberland as well. As yet, there has been no word from Mr Trump.

MIX-UPS

The White House mistook China for its sworn enemy.

The US government managed three political faux pas about Asia in a single day at the G20 summit in July. Firstly, Donald Trump's Instagram account mislabelled the prime minister of Singapore as the Indonesian president. The same day, a press release misidentified Shinzō Abe – the prime minister of Japan – as the country's president (Japan doesn't have a president). And to cap it off, the White House then published *another* press release stating that China's president, Xi Jinping, was president of 'the Republic of China'. China is actually called the People's Republic of China. 'The Republic of China' is the official name for Taiwan, a state with whom China is technically at war.

Donald Trump was himself the victim of an unfortunate mix-up in February. A Dominican newspaper, *El Nacional*, had to apologise to its readers after it mistakenly ran a photo of Alec Baldwin doing his impersonation of Mr Trump from *Saturday Night Live*, claiming the absurd caricature was the actual president.

When Trump took office, the White House set up an official Twitter 'group' of administration officials' accounts. Added to the group, along with Jared Kushner, Mike Pence and Reince Priebus, was a Scottish man called Steve Bannon, who unfortunately has the Twitter handle @SteveBannon, and whose profile picture featured him with a big teddy bear. He now spends a lot of time telling people they've got the wrong Steve Bannon, and his profile reads, 'Nothing to do with US politics or running the White House etc.'*

* This, of course, is now also true of the other Steve Bannon.

MOAB

The US military dropped the MOAB but didn't drop the MOP.

The American military's most powerful non-nuclear bomb is the MOAB, which stands for Massive Ordnance Air Blast, but is more commonly known by its nickname, the Mother of All Bombs. It had never been used outside testing facilities until Trump gave the order to drop it on a network of ISIS tunnels in Afghanistan in April. The bomb operates partly by sucking all the oxygen from the surrounding air as it explodes, which suffocates anyone nearby or underground, rather than directly blowing them up. It killed 94 ISIS militants, but avoided causing any civilian casualties.

MOAB isn't the heaviest bomb in America's arsenal; that's the MOP – Massive Ordnance Penetrator – which has never been used but has the capacity to smash through 200 feet of earth or 60 feet of concrete before exploding.

Russia has a bomb four times more powerful than the MOAB, which, predictably, is nicknamed FOAB – the Father of All Bombs.

The MOAB is so big and heavy that it can't be dropped like a normal bomb – it has to be dragged out of the plane on a wooden pallet, which is then pulled out by a parachute.

MOUSTACHES

Twenty-eight years after his death, Salvador Dalí's moustache remains perfectly intact in the '10 past 10' position.

This discovery was made in July when the artist's body was exhumed to settle a paternity case. Narcís Bardalet, who had embalmed him 28 years previously, and who was invited back to open his crypt, said that his body looked exactly as it did when he was buried. The artist's moustache was still arranged as Dalí had requested, in the ten and two positions on a clock face. 'It's a miracle,' Bardalet said.

* This wasn't Martinez's first attempt to prove Dalí is her father. In 2007 she collected hair and skin from his death mask and had that tested, but the results were inconclusive.

Dalí was dug up because fortune-teller Maria Martinez, whose mother worked as his cleaner, claimed she was the artist's daughter. To uncover the truth, DNA was extracted from his nails, teeth, and shinbones and sent off to be tested.* A crane was used to lift up the 1.5-tonne tombstone in the museum where he's buried and the operation was done at night with no media, phones or cameras allowed, with a tarpaulin draped over the museum so drones couldn't see in. Despite being a fortune-teller, Martinez failed to predict the outcome: Dalí was not her father.

MOVIES

The film Man Down *made £7 in the first week of its UK release, despite the average price of a cinema ticket being £7.21.*

Professional clowns complained that they were losing business due to the reboot of Stephen King's *It*. 'It's a science-fiction character. It's not a clown and has nothing to do with pro clowning,' said Pam Moody of the World Clown Association.

The film starred Shia LeBeouf as an army veteran suffering from PTSD. It was released in one cinema only, the Reel in Burnley, Lancashire, and tempted only one person into buying a ticket in its first week. By the following week four more tickets had been sold. *Man Down* was variously reviewed as an 'insult to the intelligence', a 'post-apocalyptic shambles' and 'misjudged on almost every level'.

It wasn't the only 2017 film to experience a tricky launch. *Beauty and the Beast* was banned from Kuwait and pulled from a drive-in in Alabama due to the fact that one of its characters is gay; *Wonder Woman* was banned in Lebanon and Tunisia because the film's lead actor, Gal Gadot, is Israeli (*see* **Wonder Woman**); and a feminist Indian film called *Lipstick Under My Burkha* was denied a certificate by censors because the story was deemed to be 'lady oriented'. In Uzbekistan, courts banned a film from being shown because it *didn't* star Morgan Freeman. The film, called *Daydi*, used Freeman's images in promotion, but he was nowhere to be seen in the movie.

MUSEUMS

For a man pretending to be a chicken, *see* **Art**; for dino-saurs on Noah's Ark, *see* **Body Slams**; for the priceless collection that got incinerated by immigration, *see* **Cock-Ups**; for a coal museum that runs on renewables, *see* **Energy**; for a success story, *see* **Failures**; for kimchi, *see* **Kimchi**; for an Ice Age cold case, *see* **Ötzi**; for half a wax Hillary, *see* **Waxworks**.

MUSIC

A musician broke a world record by hitting one piano key 824 times in a minute.

Domingos-Antonio Gomes practised for four months and beat the previous world record of 765 hits in 60 seconds. The trick to it, he explained, is to alternate between two fingers.

Nigerian musician Femi Kuti attempted to break a different musical world record. He sustained a single note on his saxophone for 46 minutes and 38 seconds, beating the record set by Kenny G in 1997 for the longest note played on a wind instrument. Unfortunately, after spending the weekend celebrating, he discovered that another musician had held a note for 47 minutes and 6 seconds in 2000. Undaunted, Femi made a second attempt a few days later and successfully broke the record by holding the note for 51 minutes and 35 seconds, only to be told that Guinness no longer recognises the breathing technique he used.

Meanwhile, in Sweden, a local councillor is campaigning for music to be played in school bathrooms to hide the sound of students defecating. Cecilia Cato, who represents the Swedish Centre Party in the Tingsryd municipality, argues that many pupils are too embar-rassed to poo in public toilets for fear of being overheard,

Donald Trump lost a legal battle against a 40-year-old amateur musician who made an iPhone app designed to teach people to play the trumpet. It was called iTrump. After a six-year battle, Tom Scharfeld won his case, despite not even having a lawyer. His other app is a trom-bone app called iBone.

In February, Bulgaria's public radio broadcaster was permitted to play modern music for the first time in two months. Since December, a copyright dispute had limited it to playing music that was at least 70 years old. During that time it broadcast almost exclusively classical and traditional folk music, and its audience figures increased by 20 per cent.

and that playing music in the bathrooms would solve this problem. She's not the only politician who favours musical accompaniment: in July, India's Prime Minister Narendra Modi had a well-known tune played over the end of his speech on a new goods and services tax. The piece of music he chose to broadcast to the crowd gathered at the Institute of Chartered Accountants was 'The Imperial March' from *Star Wars*, aka Darth Vader's theme tune.

Someone else who made a surprising musical choice was Tony Iommi, lead guitarist and songwriter for Black Sabbath. Having helped invent the genre of heavy metal, he took a slightly different direction this year and wrote a choral piece inspired by Psalm 133. And in other metal news, the band Korn replaced their 47-year-old bassist with a 12-year-old one (the son of Metallica bassist Robert Trujillo) for a series of live dates in South America.

In which we learn ...
Whose name beats Eliza Fox Teats, which rapper sued the
Kiwis, why you shouldn't lick computer games, which dictator
loved his teddy bears, and what the Prince of Wales wants
to do with a squirrel and a jar of Nutella.

NAMES

According to the Internet, the Name of the Year is Boats Botes.

President Macron got a 'First Dog' this year. The French Canine Society demands that pedigree dogs have to be named alphabetically by year, and since this year is 'N' he named it Nemo, after Captain Nemo.

One of the people on the FBI's 'most wanted' list this year was a man called Joe McCool. McCool was wanted for allegedly running a $10 million Ponzi scheme.

Mr Botes, a South African mining executive, defeated Eliza Fox Teats, Bird Lovegod, Aphrodite Bodycomb, Quindarious Monday and Andy Brandy Casagrande IV on his way to the final of the online poll, where he beat Chicago resident YourMajesty Lumpkins.

It was a good year for people with appropriate names. Lauren Child became the new Children's Laureate; Hubert Legal was given responsibility for heading the EU's legal taskforce in Brexit negotiations; the asset management firm Walker Crips hired a man called Crispin Cripwell; and in Oregon, a convicted felon called Fellony was charged with three more felonies. Somewhat less fittingly, an amateur football manager called Aaron Pride was fined for shouting homophobic abuse at a referee.

Meanwhile, an Indian restaurant owner in San Francisco found that he sold more curries when Golden State Warriors basketball team played, as they have a player called Steph Curry. And in the science arena, a paper explaining why horses evolved to have only one toe on each hoof was coauthored by Brianna McHorse. The year 2017 featured many other brilliantly named people (and animals) who were absent from the Name of the Year poll, but do appear in this book:

For Professor Cock van Oosterhout, *see* **Fish**; for Seedy Baldeh, *see* **Gambia**; for Archbishop Pennisi, *see* **Godfather**; for Fany Brotcorne, *see* **Godfather: Part III**; for Alfie Plant and Daisy Meadows, *see* **Golf**; for Cluck Norris, *see* **Kangaroos**; for Officer Hyman, *see* **Kinky**; for Lorne Grabher, *see* **Licence Plates**; for Chuck Tingle, *see* **Literature**; for Brynneth Pawltro, *see* **Mayors**; for Terry Peck aka 2pec, *see* **Runner, Doing a**; and for Randy Dickensheets, *see* **Waxworks**.

NASA

For a flying machine that could fit four *Titanic*s in it, *see* **Balloons**; for a photograph of the end of the world, *see* **Extinctions**; for flat-packs on Mars, *see* **IKEA**; for advances in baking, *see* **International Space Station**; for astronauts living on a volcano, *see* **Mars**; for space mice, *see* **Mice, Space**; for a super spud, *see* **Potatoes**; for something that smells of farts, *see* **Uranus**.

NATIONAL ANTHEMS

Chinese people can now be sent to jail for 15 days if they don't sing the national anthem properly.

The legislation was passed in response to concerns that the song, 'March of the Volunteers', is not sufficiently respected, following reports that people were singing it without due solemnity, or were laughing or being disruptive while the tune was played. It was already the case that the national anthem couldn't be performed at private celebrations, only at major sporting events and on diplomatic occasions. In September a new law ruled that singers also had to perform it in a prescribed way, with appropriate dignity, and while standing in an upright posture. One politician also proposed banning people from putting their hands on their hearts while singing the anthem, because the gesture is 'too American'.

In other national anthem news:

▶ **Philippines:** A bill was proposed ruling that citizens must sing the national anthem when it's being played in public, and with fervour. Failure to do so could result in a large fine and up to a year in prison.

▶ **India:** Before a film showing, not only do cinemas now have to play the national anthem, but audiences have to stand up while it is being performed (people have been arrested for failing to do this). The government

A Malaysian man called Thean See Xien has memorised 112 national anthems, despite speaking only two languages. He's been learning them for 15 years, and says he intends to master the national anthems of all the countries from every continent, barring Antarctica. He said, 'It's too bad about Antarctica, but if penguins taught me a national anthem, I'd do my best to learn it.'

* Some readers may
remember that 'God
Save the Queen' was
played at the end of
films in UK cinemas
until the 1960s, and
that audiences were
expected to stand and
wait for it to finish
before leaving.

also said that those who are unable to stand due to
injury or disability should still 'maintain the maximum
possible alertness physically'.* The law led to confusion when a film included the national anthem in one
of its scenes, and viewers didn't know whether they
were supposed to rise to their feet. The Supreme
Court subsequently clarified that if it's played as part
of the film, you don't have to stand up.

▶ **Slovenia:** The Slovenian national anthem was played
instead of the Slovakian anthem at the world hockey
championships.

▶ **Australia:** A petition demanding that the Australian
national anthem be changed to the Outkast song
'Hey Ya!' was signed by four people. Prime Minister
Malcolm Turnbull formally responded, declaring that
the government had no plans to abandon 'Advance
Australia Fair' just yet.

-NAUTS

For astronauts, *see* **International Space Station**; for lavanauts, *see* **Mars**; for mousetronauts, *see* **Mice, Space**; and
for larvaenauts, *see* **Potatoes**.

NEW ZEALAND

*Eminem sued New Zealand's ruling National Party for
using one of his songs.*

The National Party insists that its advert didn't actually
use the song 'Lose Yourself' in its 2014 campaign advert.
It was, the party says, another song loosely based on
it. The National Party set up a company called Stan 3
to manage that campaign. Coincidentally, 'Stan' is the
name of another Eminem song, although the party says it
named the company that because it's 'Nats' (the party's
nickname) spelled backwards.

196

When not fighting rap battles, the Nats have been confronting the country's pests. The government has set itself the target of ridding the country of every single rat, possum and stoat by 2050. The aim is to protect the country's native bird population, and the government has invested an extra $20 million in the project over the past year, on top of its standard conservation budget.

As well as invasive species, Kiwis are worried about invasive breakfast cereals. In June, 300 boxes of Weetabix were held at New Zealand customs because officials were concerned that customers would confuse them with the indigenous equivalent, Weet-Bix.

In order to combat continuing revenue loss, a New Zealand postal service in the city of Tauranga has started delivering KFC.

NICKNAMES

The electoral chief of Papua New Guinea won a court order to stop people calling him 'Mr Tomato'.

Electoral commissioner Patilias Gamato insisted blogger Martyn Namorong had named him wrong, and had posted a picture of him with a tomato for a head (Namorong denied the latter accusation). According to Gamato: 'He made some defamatory statements and also called my surname "tomato". I don't look like a tomato, I'm a human being. He put a big tomato on my head, what if he did that to you?' One of the country's former prime ministers asked, 'Is Mr Gamato so thin skinned?' Gamato's legal statement insisted he was 'not a vegetable'.*

This wasn't the only nickname to make the headlines this year. Camilla, Duchess of Cornwall, revealed she was known as 'The Growler' at school because she was so bad at singing;† White House aides leaked to the press that their private nickname for Ivanka Trump is 'Princess Royal'; and newspapers discovered Trump's press secretary Sean Spicer's university nickname was 'Sean Sphincter'. In 1993, Spicer furiously demanded a retraction and apology after his college paper printed

* Tomatoes, of course, are not vegetables either.

† Kate Middleton revealed this year that at school her nickname was 'Squeak' because her sister, Philippa, was known as 'Pip'. We also discovered that when he was a toddler, Prince William couldn't pronounce 'Granny' and so would call the Queen 'Gary'.

the insulting name. The newspaper apologised, insisting it had been a perfectly innocent error due to their auto-correction software, but Spicer insisted it was a 'malicious and intentional attack'.

NINTENDO

Nintendo made the games for their new console taste disgusting.

———— ▼ ————

Nintendo confirmed that Mario, their most famous character ever, is no longer a plumber. The website now says Mario 'seems to have worked as a plumber a long time ago'.

When the Nintendo Switch was released in March, journalists started licking the games after hearing they tasted absolutely foul. *Guardian* correspondent Alex Hern took a 'fairly meaty lick' of the game *The Legend of Zelda: Breath of the Wild* and reported that the cartridge provided a 'pure, concentrated dose of unpleasantness'. Tech writer Jeff Gerstmann said it tasted 'like someone poured a bottle of concentrated [new car scent] into my mouth', and Mike Murphy wrote, 'It took over an hour for the taste from the cartridge to start receding.'

Nintendo confirmed that this was deliberate. They made the games cartridges taste disgustingly bitter by coating them in a chemical substance, to stop small children putting them in their mouths and accidentally swallowing them. Paradoxically, this led to far more grown-ups licking the cartridges than would ever have been the case otherwise.

This 'bittering agent', a chemical called denatonium benzoate, is officially listed by the *Guinness Book of Records* as the most bitter chemical compound known to mankind. It's non-toxic, but its foul taste has led to its being used in anti-nail-biting treatments, paints, shampoos, antifreeze and animal repellents. Only a few parts per million will do the trick: Bitrex, the company that sells it, says that if you dropped a thimbleful of it into a swimming pool, the whole pool would taste bitter.

The world lost the only military dictator known to have dressed his teddy bears up as soldiers.

Manuel Noriega (1934–2017), who ruled Panama for six years from 1983 to 1989, and who spent the last 28 years of his life in prison before his death in May, liked to dress his teddy bears up as paratroopers and then installed them on a shelf in his office. They were stationed between his graduation photograph and a bust of Napoleon.*

Noriega always wore red underwear to ward off the 'evil eye', according to one of his friends.

Initially a US ally and CIA informant, Noriega was ultimately deemed too erratic to be trustworthy, especially following the assassination of his arch-rival, the famously charismatic, revolutionary doctor Hugo Spadafora. Spadafora's headless body turned up in a US mailbag in Costa Rica in September 1985.

Deciding that enough was enough, the US invaded Panama in 1989, but Noriega avoided capture at first by hiding out in an apostolic nunciature, the Vatican's equivalent of an embassy. The American military responded with Operation Nifty Package, which involved erecting huge loudspeakers outside the building and blasting rock and roll music at it. They even opened a phone line to the public, who called to request tracks like Springsteen's 'Born to Run', Bon Jovi's 'Wanted Dead or Alive' and, of course, Rick Astley's 'Never Gonna Give You Up'. Noriega got the not-so-hidden message and surrendered after 10 days.

* For other much-loved political figures with Napoleonic art, see Paintings.

In prison, Noriega remained combative. In 2014 he tried to sue the makers of *Call of Duty* after his grandchildren played it and informed him that he featured as a character. The court ruled against him, so Noriega lives on in *Call of Duty* at least, where his real-life nickname is also listed: because of his acne scars, he was often referred to as Pineapple Face.

NORTHERN IRELAND

DUP politician Alan Graham once kicked Rihanna off his land when he caught her running through a field of crops.

This 2011 story became particularly relevant this year as Theresa May – who, during the election campaign, revealed that running through a field of wheat was the naughtiest thing she had ever done – was forced to prop up her government by doing a deal with MPs from Graham's very own Democratic Unionist Party. Rihanna's transgression differed from May's in two ways: first, the singer ran through a field of barley, not wheat; and second, she was topless when she did so. Graham shooed her off his land, and told her to 'find a greater God'.*

As DUP politicians were becoming more politically visible across the UK, other comments that they had previously made started to surface. Ian Paisley Jr, for instance, once described himself as being 'pretty repulsed' by homosexuality, though he defended himself afterwards on *Newsnight* by saying he was 'repulsed by many things'. Trevor Clarke, who lost his seat in the Northern Ireland Assembly at this year's election, admitted in 2016 that he hadn't realised HIV could affect heterosexuals until a charity explained it to him. And David Simpson, who retained his seat, famously referred to the phrase 'It was Adam and Eve, not Adam and Steve' when speaking out against gay marriage in 2013, although he got the phrase wrong and accidentally said, 'In the Garden of Eden, it was Adam and Steve'.

After the Rihanna incident, Graham went on to present a documentary for the BBC about the overly sexualised state of pop, saying, 'Some of these videos are simply porn to music.' Celebrities including Barbara Windsor expressed support for him and he began receiving fan mail that managed to reach him despite being addressed simply to 'Rihanna's Farmer, Northern Ireland'.

200

While the DUP was pulling out the stops in Westminster to give Theresa May a viable government, it was unable to form its own in Northern Ireland. The country was entirely without a government for most of the year, after Deputy First Minister Martin McGuinness retired (dying shortly afterwards), meaning his political opponent and coalition partner, the DUP First Minister Arlene Foster, also had to step down. All power-sharing talks failed and it was left to the Secretary of State for Northern Ireland to fix things – the ironically named James Brokenshire.*

A more appropriately named political figure is David Sterling, the civil servant who was given the responsibility of sorting out Northern Ireland's budget in March.

NORTHERN LIGHTS

A purple atmospheric phenomenon was discovered. Unfortunately, it was named by the public, so it's now called Steve.

Steve was discovered on Facebook, in a photo shared among the Alberta Aurora Chasers, a group of amateur astronomers dedicated to posting shots of the aurora borealis. The phenomenon, originally thought to be a part of the Northern Lights, is not new – it's just scientists haven't noticed it until now.

They're still not quite sure what it is. Since its discovery last year, the European Space Agency has sent electric field instruments 300 kilometres above the Earth's surface to test for what it might be. All they do know is that it is definitely not an aurora.

Scientists suggest that Steve might stand for Strong Thermal Emission Velocity Enhancement. It's a rather desperate back-to-front justification. The people who named it were actually inspired by a cartoon called *Over the Hedge* in which a talking squirrel names a hedge Steve.

In Iceland, police have warned tourists to stop looking at the aurora borealis while driving. Officers reported that they've been pulling cars over, suspecting the drivers are

The auroras visible over the UK in mid-September were due to a solar flare ejected from the sun with the power of a billion hydrogen bombs.

drunk, only to find they're moving erratically because they're looking at the sky. This behaviour has been dubbed 'driving under the influence of the aurora'.

NOSE, PICKING YOUR

Eating bogeys is good for you.

A study by researchers at universities including MIT and Harvard revealed that ingesting bogeys is good, both for your teeth and your general health.
As for snot (the bogey's more liquidy cousin), this can prevent bacteria from sticking to teeth, as well as boosting the immune system.
As a result of the studies, the researchers are working on a synthetic mucus toothpaste and a chewing gum.

NUCLEAR POWER PLANTS

The owners of a Czech nuclear power plant apologised for trying to hire interns with a bikini competition.

The company, CEZ, claimed it wanted to 'promote technical education' by posting pictures of ten high-school graduates wearing bikinis and hard hats on their Facebook page and asking the public to vote on them. Whoever had the greatest number of likes on her photo would be crowned 'Miss Energy 2017' and given a two-week internship. Following a backlash, the company offered all applicants an internship.

Conversely, this year's 'Miss USA 2017' competition was won by a chemist whose job is to regulate nuclear power plants.

NUTELLA

Prince Charles supported a plan to sterilise squirrels with contraceptive Nutella.

The government announced plans to save Britain's native red squirrels – which have suffered a disastrous population collapse after the introduction of grey squirrels – by stealthily sterilising the greys. The chosen method for controlling them, at the moment, is to feed them contraceptive-laced chocolate spread.

There are currently 3.5 million grey squirrels in the UK, but if they eat the specially treated Nutella deposited around the country, their numbers could be reduced to fewer than 300,000, giving the red squirrel a chance to make a recovery. Prince Charles likes the plan because it doesn't involve actually slaughtering squirrels, and the UK Squirrel Accord, a pro-red-squirrel pressure group, has been raising money to fund further trials. It's more media-friendly than the alternative proposed by conservation charity The Wildlife Trusts: recruiting an army of 5,000 people and training them to kill trapped grey squirrels by hitting them on the head.

America got its first ever Nutella Cafe, which is entered through a door shaped like a Nutella jar. All the dishes are supposedly inspired by Nutella in some way.

NUTTALL, PAUL

In the General Election, Paul Nuttall found he couldn't even vote for himself.

The UKIP leader realised he hadn't registered to vote in the Boston and Skegness constituency where he was standing. It wasn't the only trouble he got into: during a by-election campaign in Stoke earlier in the year, *Channel 4 News* revealed Nuttall didn't live at the house listed as his 'permanent address' on his nomination papers.

There were policy difficulties, too. When the party announced their proposal to ban full-face veils (in a move aimed at Islamic face coverings), the British Beekeepers' Association expressed concern, saying beekeepers would clearly need to be exempted. UKIP said the idea they would ban beekeepers' veils was 'ridiculous', and Nuttall was forced to clarify that he wouldn't ban 'big hats' either.

One poll found that 2 per cent of Christians thought he was the leader most like Jesus Christ (*see* **Surveys**). But Nuttall told the *Express & Star* newspaper his integration policy was more like that of another historical figure: 'It is a bit like the Gandhi thing – first they laugh at you, then they attack you, and then you win. Unfortunately on this issue we seem to be on the laughing or the mocking phase'.

Soon after the election, Nuttall resigned, and when asked what was next, said, 'Holiday. Or if that bar is open, a pint.'

In which we learn ...
What's shaped like a penis and shrinks when
threatened, what happens when a parrot goes cold
turkey, how drinking espresso can save the planet
and what Obama did next.

OBAMA, BARACK

Tuscan authorities banned boar hunting within 3 miles of Barack Obama.

During the last days of his presidency, as well as commuting the sentence of Chelsea Manning for leaking classified intelligence, Barack Obama also pardoned or commuted the sentences of (among others) John E. Stewart and Jonnie Stewart; Rod Love and Daryll Loveless; and Kunta Redd.

When Obama went to Tuscany in May, Italian officials prohibited hunting within 3 miles of where he was staying to avoid him being accidentally shot. This wasn't the only treat that was laid on for him. As he landed in the country, six Eurofighter jets escorted his plane into the airport before he headed to a Tuscan retreat with a 13-car motorcade.

Since stepping down, Obama's been making up for holidays he missed out on during his presidency. He started by visiting Richard Branson's Necker Island in the British Virgin Islands within two weeks of leaving the White House.* He and Branson competed to see whether Obama could learn to kitesurf before Branson learned to foilboard (foilboarding is similar to kitesurfing, except the rider is suspended above the water on a foil – *see* **Yachting**). The former president won the competition, successfully travelling 100 metres on his board before his host could do the same.

Branson bought Necker Island in 1978 to impress a girl he'd just met. It did the trick: they're still married.

He also got to surf at Necker Island – something he hadn't been allowed to do for eight years. He'd last indulged just a few weeks before taking office, but security guards had then informed him that, for safety reasons, he'd have to take a break until he'd finished governing America.

Another island that Obama visited was Tetiaroa, an atoll in French Polynesia that was once owned by Marlon Brando. According to the *Washington Post*, Obama started writing his White House memoir while there. By an odd coincidence, Obama's first memoir was called *Dreams from My Father*, while Brando's was called *Songs My Mother Taught Me*.

OBESITY

Instant noodles led to the first obese Siberians.

The Western lifestyle appears to be permeating the whole world. Even in the far north of Russia, the nomadic herders of the Yamalo-Nenets region now prefer to stay in and have noodles for dinner rather than head out to catch the fish that they used to subsist on. They walk a lot less, too; owing to oil and gas companies encroaching on their land, they herd their reindeer over a much smaller area. All of this has led to the first cases of obesity in this area of the Arctic being documented by researchers.

Further west, a researcher in Latvia came up with an innovative way to fight obesity. Nauris Cinovics from the Art Academy of Latvia has invented a plate that has crinkles, as well as bulging upwards in the centre, making a relatively thin layer of food look like a large pile. Cinovics suggests people should eat from it with his special cutlery: a knife, fork and spoon that weigh 1.3 kilos each, forcing diners to slow down, and making a meal that usually takes seven minutes last for eleven. Eating slowly is a useful tactic because the brain takes at least 20 minutes to receive the message that we feel full.

Given that there are now 2.2 billion overweight people on Earth, and that one in ten people on Earth is clinically obese, Cinovics's innovation seems timely. Obesity is

House dust was linked to obesity in a study this year – but only in mice, as far as we know. Mouse cells which were exposed to household dust were more likely to become fat cells, and accumulate more fat. Another study found that rats were likelier to become fat after having fizzy water.

killing more people than traffic accidents, Alzheimer's and terrorism combined. And it's not just humans: one in three American pet cats and dogs is overweight. In Thailand, an obese monkey called Uncle Fat hit the headlines when he was caught and put on a diet. He might as well have been called Uncle Lazy, as he didn't even bother getting food himself, instead persuading minion monkeys to collect it for him.

OCEANS

Deep-diving scientists found a penis-shaped worm that shrinks when threatened.

Australian researchers looked into the abyssal area of the ocean (between 3,000 and 6,000 metres below sea level), searching for new creatures. As well as the worm, they found more than 300 species never before seen, including a faceless fish (which does have a face, it's just not where you'd expect it to be) and giant anemone-sucking sea spiders. They also came across a herd of sea pigs, a shark whose teeth look like a steak knife, and a shortarse feelerfish (the unflattering name derives from its short anal fin). Their scariest discovery, however, was trash: 200 years' worth of bottles, PVC pipes, tins of paints and discarded beer cans. (For more rubbish in the ocean, *see* **Plastics**.)

* In fact, there are three identical submarines called Boaty McBoatface. They all have a fax number written on them in case they get lost and someone finds them, as well as a big label saying 'HARMLESS SCIENTIFIC INSTRUMENT'.

Boaty McBoatface

Also to be found in the abyss this year was one of the stars of 2016, *Boaty McBoatface*.* The remote-controlled

underwater vehicle, which lives aboard the altogether
less interestingly named RRS *Sir David Attenborough*
research vessel, went on its first ever mission. It dived
into the abyssal zone of the Antarctic, testing the
currents found in the area known as the Antarctic
Bottom Water.

OLD AGE

*Scientists can now predict that an elderly person is going
to fall over three weeks before it happens.*

Scientists at the University of Missouri have discovered
that by monitoring an elderly person's gait, they are able
to prevent dangerous falls. It's all to do with walking
speeds. When someone starts walking, or getting up from
the sofa, more slowly than normal, it indicates something
is wrong with them and that the chance of them falling
over has increased. If someone slows down by as little
as 5.1 centimetres a second, the chances of a fall within
three weeks are 86 per cent higher. So the Missouri team
came up with a camera sensor system that can be fitted
in the homes of the elderly. When the system detects any
change in walking patterns it texts relatives and support
workers, allowing them to intervene before any mishaps
occur.

If the idea of fitting an elderly person's house with
cameras seems a bit creepy, researchers in Switzerland
and Italy have been working on an alternative option –
fitting your loved one with a robotic exoskeleton. The
prototype device, called the Active Pelvis Orthosis,
increases older people's leg force by 20 to 30 per cent.
The device straps on around the waist and thighs, and is
designed to measure the wearer's gait. By doing so it can
detect an oncoming fall, and use a motor to adjust their
leg position to a non-slip stance. The devices may be in
use in nursing homes within 10 years.

A new French service
called Lou Papé has
been launched that
sends a grandmother to
your home to cook you
a meal. She will also do
the washing-up. All the
grandmothers are guar-
anteed to be at least 58
years old.

A centenarian from
Manchester, Arthur
Johnson, has been
awarded free beer for
life after the landlord of
his local pub promised
it to him at the age of
93, if he made it to 100.
He is now making the
most of it.

The last person to have been born in the 19th century died this year in northern Italy. She lived through 90 Italian governments.

The world also got a new oldest man, 112-year-old Francisco Olivera of Spain, but his title could not be immediately verified because his birth certificate was lost during the Spanish Civil War. Dental records couldn't help either as he lost his teeth four decades ago.

Emma Morano, the world's oldest person, died aged 117. The secret of her long life seems to have been 'routine': she spent 42 years of her life sewing potato sacks. For almost 100 years she ate two raw eggs a day, had pasta and raw meat for lunch, and had a glass of milk for her dinner. She said her longevity was due to two things: firstly, the raw eggs, and secondly, staying single after kicking out her abusive husband in 1938.

She was replaced as the world's oldest person by Jamaica's Violet Brown, who turned 117 in March. A former cemetery record-keeper, she is the last surviving person to have been a subject of Queen Victoria. Her son, Harold Fairweather, 97, was the oldest child in the world who had a parent still alive, but sadly died just a couple of days after his mother was declared the world's oldest person. Brown died in September and was replaced as the world's oldest person by Nabi Tajima of Japan, who is also 117.

Meanwhile, in Indonesia, a man who claimed – slightly implausibly – to have been the world's oldest human died, 'aged' 146. Supposedly born in 1870, Mbah Ghoto was regrettably unable to confirm his age as Indonesia only started recording births in 1900, just as he was hitting his thirties. He claimed to have been 70 at the start of the Second World War.

According to an interview Ghoto gave last year, he had been expecting his death for some time: 25 years, in fact, having had his gravestone made in 1992. When interviewed about his life in 2016, he told the reporter, 'What I want is to die.'

Olive oil supplies are decreasing on Earth and increasing in space.

In Italy, a million olive trees have been killed by a disease called 'olive quick decline syndrome'. It's caused by a bacterium, *Xylella fastidiosa*, that insects carry on to the trees. It led to a 30 per cent fall in olive oil production this year and the highest prices for a decade. And worse is to come. Spanish officials confirmed that the disease, dubbed 'the ebola of olive trees', had arrived in Spain – and Spain makes more than half of the world's olive oil. In August, an EU report suggested that the island of Mallorca chop down all its olive trees, and all plants within a 100-metre radius of infected plants, to combat the disease. Opponents say that if they do that, there will be virtually no vegetation at all on the entire island.

Meanwhile, Amazon.com founder Jeff Bezos (*see* **Amazon**) announced that his Blue Origin space-flight start-up would be sending olive oil into space 'to examine if olive oil will maintain its liquid shape once it has left the Earth'. *Olive Oil Times* reported that the experiment would help the Mediterranean diet become the 'food for astronauts for many years to come' – provided, of course, there's any left on Earth.

ON TOUR

For a diplodocus *see* **Dinosaurs**; for a block of ice, *see* **Icebergs**; for Santa, *see* **Saints**; for a troupe of Zulu dancers with terrible GPS, *see* **Sat Nav**; for a giant crayon, *see* **Yellow**; and for a Facebook founder, *see* **Zuckerberg, Mark**.

Heroin-addicted parrots threatened Indian farmers' livelihoods.

In North Carolina, a $500 million opium-growing operation was busted when an investigator visiting on a completely unrelated matter knocked on the farmer's door only to hear him say, 'I guess you're here about the opium.'

In India, the farming of opium is legal so long as the end product is sold to the government (which regulates its use in medicine). Parrots, however, have started consuming it recreationally. One farmer estimates that they've stolen 10 per cent of his crop. To avoid capture, the parrots have learned not to squawk as they steal the opium. Attempts to deter them by beating drums and exploding firecrackers have proved fruitless.

If it's bad news for humans, it's not that great for the birds either. Parrots swoop when the pods are ripe, chew on the morphine-rich stalks and return to their branches in an opium-addled stupor. They then fall into a deep sleep, which means they sometimes fall off their perches and die. Worse still, when the opium season is over they suffer from extreme withdrawal, losing their appetites and energy, and many of them die as a result.

Farmers in Afghanistan, meanwhile, are replacing opium with pomegranates and mulberries. The project was started by a former heroin addict from Swindon who, on a visit to the country, worked out that mulberries could be more profitable per hectare than opium. He campaigned to replace one with the other, erecting placards across the countryside, appearing on Afghan TV and holding meetings for farmers, one of which was attended by 14,000 people. He's persuaded 22,000 growers to swap poppies for mulberries, and the resulting Plant For Peace fruit bars went on sale in the UK in June.

Parrots aren't the only ones stealing opium. In Australia, poppy theft increased 24-fold within a year in Tasmania, which supplies half the world's legal opium. Five hundred and sixteen poppy heads were stolen from its fields in the 2015–16 financial year, rising to 12,239 in 2016–17.

ORANGE IS THE NEW BLACK

Scottish prisoners beat the system with a trick stolen from Netflix.

More than 100 inmates at Saughton Prison in Edinburgh successfully got better food by claiming to be Jewish, after seeing the same trick performed on *Orange Is the New Black*. Officials were not happy, as a kosher diet is four times as expensive as the regular one on offer in the prison. If all those prisoners had actually converted to Judaism, the Jewish population of Edinburgh would have increased by approximately 12 per cent.

Fittingly for a drama about a bunch of criminals, episodes of *Orange Is the New Black* were stolen. A group of hackers called The Dark Overlord stole and leaked episodes and threatened to release other stolen episodes unless they were paid £57,000 in bitcoin.

The hack came just days after the papers reported an even more ironic case of hacking: the pirating of *Pirates of the Caribbean*. As it turned out, this was a hoax, but weeks later The Dark Overlord struck again, leaking eight episodes of a TV show called *Funderdome* online. It was widely viewed as The Dark Overlord's 'difficult second leak', as very few people had heard of, or were interested in, *Funderdome*.

ORANGUTANS

The Indianapolis Colts announced their pick in the NFL draft using a trained orangutan.

The publicity stunt, in which Rocky the orangutan pressed a touch-screen that named offensive lineman* Zach Banner as the American football team's newest player, was widely enjoyed by fans, but commentator Mike Mayock thought that it made a monkey of the whole thing, and threatened to walk off set.

* *An offensive lineman is a player who blocks the opposition from tackling the guy with the ball. They're not (necessarily) offensive in character.*

It wasn't the only time orangutans and touch-screens came together this year. A Dutch animal sanctuary introduced what they called 'Tinder for orangutans', whereby their orangs were shown pictures of other apes, and researchers evaluated their responses. The plan was to discover whether females can show a preference for potential mates by looking at pictures on a tablet, before the suitors are flown all the way from South East Asia to the Netherlands.

Back in the apes' native home, the Borneo Orangutan Survival Foundation rescued a rare albino orangutan – the first albino encountered by the foundation in its 25 years of existence. Taking something of a risk, they asked the Internet to name the white-furred animal, but for once the public came up with a decent name: Alba, meaning white. The foundation sensibly ignored other suggestions such as Meringue-utan, White Walker and Orang No-tan.

OSBORNE, GEORGE

The new editor of the Evening Standard *managed to miss a scoop even though he was the sole source for it.*

After being sacked in the aftermath of the Brexit referendum, George Osborne – the former chancellor and architect of 'Austerity Britain' – did his bit for employment statistics by taking on six new jobs.

The biggest surprise was the announcement that he'd be the new editor of London newspaper the *Evening Standard*. He explained he could edit the newspaper in the morning and pop over to the House of Commons for parliamentary votes in the afternoon. Some people said he lacked journalistic experience, which is unfair – as a student at Oxford he edited the now unfortunately named student magazine, the *ISIS*, and even printed an edition about cannabis on hemp paper. His further experience is limited to being rejected for graduate traineeship at

The Times and the *Economist*, although as a freelancer he briefly worked on the *Telegraph*'s diary column and managed to get two articles published in *The Times*.

Osborne racked up more post-chancellorship jobs thick and fast. They included a fellowship at a US think tank (for an estimated £120,000 a year), a one-day-a-week job advising US fund management firm Blackrock (£650,000 a year), a role at the Washington Speakers Bureau (earning £786,000 in about nine months), an unpaid position as chairman of the Northern Powerhouse Partnership, and, of course, he kept his minor role as MP for Tatton (£76,000 a year).

The strain of juggling all these jobs may have proved too much, and eventually Osborne decided to stand down as an MP. This was a big news story, which naturally he wanted to give to his own newspaper. Unfortunately, he told the *Evening Standard* too late for that afternoon's deadline, with the result that it didn't make the first edition and was all over the Internet before anyone read it in the *Standard*. Soon, however, he tired of having only five jobs, and announced that he would be taking an extra, unpaid sixth gig as an honorary professor of economics at the University of Manchester. The students' union described the news as 'distasteful' and 'upsetting'.

ÖTZI

A private detective was hired to solve a 5,300-year-old murder.

Ötzi the Iceman is the oldest intact human ever found. He died 5,300 years ago, after being shot in the back with an arrow, and was found in 1991 by hikers in a high mountain pass in the Northern Alps.

This year the museum where Ötzi is on display hired a professional detective – Chief Inspector Alexander Horn of the Munich Police Department – to solve the mystery

* Dating back rather
further than that: this
year scientists in the
Antarctic confirmed
they'd found the oldest
known ice – a core (a
cylinder drilled out of
a glacier or ice sheet)
that's 2.7 million years
old. This easily beat
the record, which was
previously held by
ice that was a mere
800,000 years old.

of his death. 'The usual cold case that we have is 20 or maybe 30 years old,' Horn said, 'and now I was asked to work on a case 5,300 years old.'* He determined that 'it looks a lot like a murder', that Ötzi had been shot from 30 metres away, and that he was taken by surprise, as his own bow wasn't strung.

Horn said the body was in better condition than some he has had to work on, but, disappointingly, failed to pin down the killer's motive. He said it was probably caused by 'some strong personal emotion', but also conceded, 'I don't think there is a high likelihood we will ever be able to solve that case … I don't like the fact that we have an unsolved homicide here.'

Recent examination of Ötzi's stomach contents revealed that among the final things he ate was goat bacon. It's a discovery that has rocked the bacon world, since it shows that bacon is twice as old as was previously thought.

OZONE

Decaf drinkers discovered they are killing the planet.

The ozone layer had a good year – there's now strong evidence that the hole in it is shrinking, thanks to the 1987 ban on dangerous CFC chemicals. But there's bad news, too. It turns out that a previously obscure chemical called dichloromethane (DCM), used to extract caffeine from coffee and tea, is very bad for the ozone layer. In fairness, it should be noted that it's not only used for decaffeination – it's also used in paint strippers, hairspray and deodorant, so coffee drinkers aren't solely to blame. There's currently twice as much DCM in the atmosphere as there was in 2000. If current trends continue, the recovery of the ozone layer will take 30 years longer than it otherwise would have.

Ozone gas caused a brief hoo-ha this year when it emerged that some medical centres are now offering women the chance to pump it into their vaginas to induce 'wellness'. There are various problems with the procedure: for one, ozone gas is toxic to humans. Consequently, not only could the treatment easily kill a patient if a gas bubble got into her bloodstream, but it could even harm patients accidentally inhaling it while in the treatment room. As expert Dr Jen Gunter put it, ozone gas may be 'natural', but only 'in the way that cyanide is natural. It has some uses in nature but it's really, really bad for people.' There is, also, no evidence that it promotes 'wellness'.

In which we learn …
Who Mike Pence refuses to have dinner with, how to tell a penguin from a rock, why the Pope is gluten-intolerance-intolerant, the perfect name for a large boring machine, and which crime is punishable by six months of hairdressing.

*Michael Jackson's chimpanzee Bubbles sold five
paintings. The gallery owner described them as 'abstract'.*

Bubbles's pictures featured in an exhibition called 'Apes
That Paint', in which artworks created by chimpanzees and orangutans were displayed. He made $3,750
altogether from the sales, which will be donated to the
Center for Great Apes, in Florida, where he lives. All
the artists whose work was on show are retired, after
careers in entertainment or medical research, and live
at the Center. Other famous apes there include Jonah,
who starred in the 2001 remake of *Planet of the Apes*, and
BamBam, who played a character called Nurse Precious
in the soap opera *Passions*. Bubbles took up painting
after Jackson's death, and according to the Center he also
enjoys listening to flute music, but his favourite activity is
'playing in tubs of water'.

Elsewhere in art news:

▶ The world learned of a painting that's been hidden in
the Antarctic for 118 years. It's a watercolour of a dead
bird painted by one of Captain Scott's companions,
Dr Edward Wilson, who died along with Scott in 1912.
It was found in a pile of papers in one of their huts,
covered in mould and penguin excrement.

▶ The oldest known Australian oil paintings were found
at London's Royal College of Surgeons. The paintings,

It was revealed this year
that former White House
adviser Steve Bannon
owns a huge painting
of himself dressed as
Napoleon. It was a gift
from Nigel Farage.

produced between 1800 and 1807, are – predictably – of kangaroos.

▶ In Georgia, a painting longer than a football pitch moved to a new home. The 374-foot-long, 40-foot-high structure was successfully relocated from the Atlanta Cyclorama & Civil War Museum (to make way for a zoo) to the Atlanta History Center, 12 miles away. Two huge holes were cut into the roof of the 100-year-old Cyclorama building, and the 131-year-old oil painting *The Battle of Atlanta* was split in two, rolled up and lifted out by a crane. It was transported on the back of a truck to its new home, where it was lowered through the roof, unrolled and reassembled.

▶ A painting by Kandinsky became the most expensive painting by the artist ever to be sold, going for a record £21 million. Twenty-two minutes later, the record was broken again by a different Kandinsky work, which sold for £33 million.

PARLIAMENTS

The Houses of Parliament spent £8,900 on killing moths.

The total amount spent on pest control during the course of the last year was around £130,000, including £16,000 to hire a hawk to keep pigeons at bay. More than 1,700 traps were set – not surprising given that there were 411 recorded mouse-sightings (up from 313 the year before).

And it's not just vermin that are a problem. Parliament is in a state of terrible disrepair: it's draughty, full of asbestos and is prone to flooding (in 2012, MP Ben Bradshaw discovered that urine from the lavatories on the floor above him was leaking through the ceiling and on to his desk). What's more, the Palace of Westminster is a huge fire risk and had to be made subject to a fire safety order in 2005. This means that it can only continue to

Drivers in Sussex, Wisconsin, were shocked when they drove past a water tower bearing the huge letters 'SEX' after the letter painters took a break in the middle of painting the word 'SUSSEX'.

220

be used if fire safety officers, working in shifts, patrol it 24 hours a day.

Perhaps China might be prepared to help. This year the Chinese government announced that it would spend $58 million building a new parliament for the Republic of Congo as a gift. In recent years, China has generously constructed a new parliament for Zimbabwe, refurbished Sierra Leone's parliament and foreign ministry, renovated Zambia's government buildings, erected a new presidential palace in Mozambique, donated security facilities to Ghana's parliament, and given $25 million to help build residences for the Ugandan president and prime minister.

China wasn't the only country to build a new parliament this year: the Russian defence ministry built a miniature model of Germany's Reichstag parliament building, so the country's youth soldiers could practise storming it. It was built in Russia's 'Patriot Park', nicknamed 'Military Disneyland', for Russia's Youth Army – a network of children being taught military skills by the real army. In April, 2,000 people re-enacted the storming of the Reichstag in 1945 – although observers noticed that the replica building appeared to have been modelled on the contemporary Reichstag. A German foreign ministry spokesman reacted with surprise, saying 'We wouldn't build something like that for the education of German youth.'

▼

After electing a solitary woman MP, the Tongan parliament found that it no longer had a word that accurately described all its members. 'Matu'a', which was used while the parliament was all-male, means 'a group of old men', and, as someone rightly pointed out, the Tongan version of 'a group of old men and one old woman' wouldn't sound that great. Eventually they just used the word 'mau', which means 'we'.

PASSPORTS

Brexiteers looked forward to new blue passports, but blue travel documents are already used in the UK: by refugees.

The 'traditional' blue design was actually used on British passports for only 68 of the 477 years that they have existed, but it seems certain to return when Britain reveals its post-Brexit design. If that happens, Britain will join the list of blue-passport countries, which currently includes the USA, Australia, El Salvador, Venezuela, Israel, Iraq, Syria and North Korea. It may at least save money, since the main reason they were blue in the first place was that it was an extremely cheap ink to make.

Britain's passports ceased to be the world's most powerful this year, losing that position to Germany. Germans can visit 176 countries around the world without needing a visa, while Britons can visit only 173. At the bottom of the table is Afghanistan, whose passport gets holders into just 24 countries without a visa being necessary.

Pakistan features just a couple of places higher than Afghanistan. It's not usually seen as an LGBTQ friendly country because homosexuality is still illegal there, but this year it did introduce gender-neutral passports, joining India, Germany, New Zealand and Nepal in offering a third sex option.

A pet passport photo booth has opened up in London, with an adjoining dog-grooming centre so that dogs can look their best in passport photos. Raw meat is placed behind the camera to make sure the dog focuses on it.

PENCE, MR AND MRS

The US vice president refuses to dine alone with any woman he's not married to.

While writing a profile of Mike Pence's wife, Karen, the *Washington Post* found some comments from an old interview in which Pence had said he refused to eat alone with any woman but Karen. Pence also revealed that he declined to attend events that involved alcohol unless Karen was with him, saying, 'If there's alcohol being served and people are being loose, I want to have the best-looking brunette in the room next to me.' In another profile this year, *Rolling Stone* revealed that Pence calls his wife 'Mother' when they're dining together.

It turned out that a lot of Americans agree with the Pences' dining arrangements: a *New York Times* poll found 53 per cent of women and 45 per cent of men thought it inappropriate for someone to have dinner with someone of the opposite sex unless they were married to them.

The story of the Pences' engagement is extremely romantic: nine months into their relationship, the two went to feed some ducks at a canal, only for Karen to discover that Mike had hollowed out two loaves of bread, with a small bottle of champagne in one and a ring in the other. She had her answer prepared – for a month she had been carrying around a small gold cross engraved with the word 'Yes', just in case Mike proposed. They later had the bread shellacked as a keepsake.

Karen Pence used to run a company that sold 'towel charms' – little metal tags that can be attached to towels to tell them apart (as she put it, 'The goal is to eliminate having to wash towels every day because no one knows which towel is theirs'). But it's not all just about work. Religion, too, plays a big part in the Pences' lives: Mike's colleagues nicknamed him 'the Choirboy' and Karen occasionally prays for an ill friend's haemoglobin count.

Pence is generally seen as more popular than Trump, but not by much: one September poll found that 44 per cent of voters were favourable towards him compared with 43 per cent for Trump. The bad news was that the same poll found that 17 per cent of Americans had no idea who Pence was.

PENGUINS

A male penguin looked for a mate on Plenty of Fish.

A penguin specialist at a Dorset sea-life centre uploaded a dating (or, more precisely, mating) profile for a Humboldt penguin called Spruce after all the other penguins in his

In giant penguin news:

A fossil of a human-sized penguin has been discovered in New Zealand. At 150 centimetres tall, it dates back 61 million years. We know from other fossils that penguins even taller than that roamed the Earth 33 million years ago.

In tiny penguin news:

A penguin has joined the list of pieces in a standard Monopoly set, along with a rubber duck and a T. rex. They replace the thimble, the boot and the wheelbarrow.

enclosure paired up. His keepers decided that, as he was now a year old, he was ready to join the centre's breeding programme, and turned to the online dating site when they realised there were no unattached females sharing his enclosure.

Computers and penguins interacted in other ways this year, as scientists set out to teach the former how to identify the latter. They want to employ AI technology to count penguins in the Antarctic, but first the robots need to know how to distinguish penguins from rocks. Members of the public have helped out, labelling penguins in various Antarctic photos in order to teach computers what they look like.

And while computers have been learning from people, people have been learning from penguins. During a cold snap in Berlin, the German Society of Orthopaedics and Trauma Surgery advised that humans should walk like penguins to avoid falling over on ice. Specifically, they recommended that people lean forward as they walk, thus moving their centre of gravity on to their front foot and reducing the risk of slipping.

PEPSI ▶

In a survey, 44 per cent of Americans who watched Pepsi's controversial Kendall Jenner advert said it made them like Pepsi more.

In the advert, Jenner is seen defusing a stand-off between police and protesters by handing an officer a can of Pepsi. Many considered this a cynical exploitation of the social justice movements that swept through America this year. Martin Luther King Jr's daughter Bernice evidently wasn't one of the 44 per cent who responded positively to the advert. She sarcastically tweeted: 'If only Daddy would have known about the power of #Pepsi.' Pepsi pulled the advert the day after it first ran.

Unfortunately, Pepsi cans demonstrably do not solve problems with the law. A protester in Portland discovered this after his offer of a can was refused by a riot police officer. Later that day, protesters turned violent and started pelting the police with – among other things – Pepsi cans.

The advert wasn't the only disaster Pepsi has had on the streets this year. Only a few weeks after it was pulled, a Pepsi warehouse in Russia collapsed, releasing 28 million litres of its products and flooding the entire town of Lipetsk.

PHONES

Smartphones spread head lice.

Following a dramatic increase in head lice cases over the past few years, a study presented at the British Association of Dermatologists revealed that children are more than twice as likely to be infected if they own a smartphone. It's assumed this is because kids put their heads together when they gather around a phone, for instance when taking a group selfie.

Mobile phones have an effect on what's going on *inside* children's heads, too. A report published by the University of Texas noted that participants performed 10 per cent less well on a memory test and 5 per cent less well on a maths test when their phones were on their desks, compared with when they were left outside the room, regardless of whether the devices were face down, face up, turned on or turned off. The students even underperformed when the phones were in a bag that was out of sight but still in the same room.

Because of phones' distracting effects, police have been cracking down on those who use them while driving. In Devon, they even took to spying on people in cars from the top deck of double-decker buses, which gave them

Donald Trump's aides have been wishing that no one had his number. He keeps giving his personal, unsecured mobile number out, for instance to the leaders of France, Canada and Mexico, when he's only supposed to share the secure one that connects to phones in the White House and his presidential car.

the perfect vantage point. Whenever they spotted drivers talking on phones or not wearing seat belts, they radioed colleagues in police cars nearby. They caught 130 wrong-doers this way within the first two days of the initiative.

Less successfully, officers in North Wales gave a burglar a mobile phone so that they could communicate with him while he was on bail. They lost track of him immediately, and the man ran up a £44,500 phone bill over the next six months.

For the number of apps Donald Trump has downloaded on to his phone, *see* **Apps**.

PIZZA ▶

Iceland's president backtracked on his wish to ban pineapple on pizza.

Guðni Jóhannesson gives 10 per cent of his salary to charity, was the first president of any country to march in a Gay Pride parade, and has a 97 per cent approval rating – but his popularity took a hit after he suggested that he'd like to ban pineapple as a pizza topping. After a week of backlash, he issued a statement saying: 'I do not have the power to make laws which forbid people to put pineapples on their pizza. I am glad I do not hold such power.'

After the story broke, YouGov conducted a survey in which Britons were asked about their pizza preferences. Fifteen per cent of people said they would ban pineapple on pizza if they had the chance. One per cent of respondents said that if they ran the world they would ban all toppings and it would be mandatory for all pizzas to be margheritas.

New Zealand's prime minister, Bill English, was told he was not fit to run a country after announcing that he put tinned spaghetti on his pizza, and Donald Trump

---

▼

When Texas was hit by Hurricane Harvey, one branch of Pizza Hut just outside Houston started delivering free pizzas by kayak.

aid that he eats just the topping off pizzas as a healthy alternative. But neither faux pas topped Jóhannesson's pineapple comment. It was especially poignant as a few months later the inventor of the Hawaiian pizza, Sam Panopoulos, died.

Panopoulus was not Hawaiian; he was a Greek immigrant to Canada who ran a Chinese fusion restaurant. Before arriving in Canada he had visited Naples, and so thought he'd have a go at combining the pizzas he'd tried there with the sweet and sour element of Chinese cuisine. He made his first pizza boxes with cardboard taken from a nearby furniture store. He could never work out why his invention divided opinion so much. 'I don't get nothing out of It,' Panopoulus said when asked about the Icelandic president's comments. 'He can do whatever he wants as far as I'm concerned.'

PLAGIARISM

People accused of plagiarism this year included Ghana's president, the US Education Secretary and Bob Dylan.

The president of Ghana, Nana Akufo-Addo, got into trouble for his inauguration speech, when he told his audience, 'I ask you to be citizens: citizens, not spectators; citizens, not subjects' – a line identical to one from George W. Bush's inaugural speech in 2001. Akufo-Addo added that 'Ghanaians have ever been a restless, questing, hopeful people', which is precisely what Bill Clinton said about Americans during his inauguration in 1993. The Ghanaian head of communications later apologised, saying it was an 'oversight' not to attribute the quotes.

Meanwhile, US Education Secretary Betsy DeVos was accused of plagiarising phrases from Obama administration officials. Defenders said this was 'a desperate attempt to discredit' DeVos. She wasn't the only Trump

Even Donald Trump's inauguration cake faced accusations of plagiarism. Duff Goldman, the baker who made the nine-tier cake for Obama's inauguration, tweeted a photo of his creation alongside a picture of the one served at Trump's inaugural ceremony. They were almost identical.

associate accused of lifting phrases from elsewhere: in 2016 a speechwriter apologised for accidentally including phrases by the previous First Lady, Michelle Obama, in Melania Trump's speech for the Republican National Convention. Also in 2016, Trump's son, Donald Trump Jr, was accused of stealing phrases from an article in the *American Conservative*. There was a perfectly innocent explanation: his speechwriter, law professor F. H. Buckley, pointed out that he had written both the original article and Donald Junior's speech, and that logically he couldn't plagiarise himself.

Bob Dylan was accused of plagiarising passages of his Nobel Prize acceptance speech from the student study-guide website SparkNotes. The speech included references to *Moby Dick*, but when a writer from the website Slate checked an apparent quote from the novel, he discovered that it actually came from the online summary, not the book. There were lots of other very curious similarities between speech and study guide. Dylan may have had an essay crisis. To pick up the $923,000 bundle of cash that comes with the award, winners have to deliver a lecture within six months of the official awards ceremony. Dylan's deadline was 10 June; he managed to deliver his lecture on the 4th.

PLASTICS

Michigan banned the banning of plastic bags.

Unlike much of the rest of the world, Michigan is not in favour of plastic-bag restrictions. The state made it illegal for any local administration to impose plastic-bag charges or limit the number of plastic bags shops can give out. It's not the first state to do so: Idaho, Wisconsin, Florida and Arizona have already passed similar laws.

Kenya swung sharply in the opposite direction, with an especially draconian new plastic bag ban. Anyone

228

caught selling, producing or even carrying a plastic bag faces four years in prison or a $38,000 fine. The country has had a particular problem with plastic bags: it used 24 million a month before the ban. Abattoirs often had to remove them from the stomachs of cattle who grazed on piles of rubbish, sometimes finding as many as twenty bags in a single cow.

Other parts of the world are combatting plastic pollution by seeking to eliminate drinking straws. The number of straws used every year would, if placed end to end, wrap around the Earth two and a half times, and each one takes 500 years to decompose. Moreover, discarded straws can harm wildlife, especially when they get stuck up turtles' noses. In the UK, All Bar One has begun phasing them out; in the US, 19 major aquariums announced they'll stop using them.

Another firm fighting plastic is Adidas, which has been making shoes out of plastic debris from the sea. Each pair of $200 shoes uses the equivalent of 11 plastic bottles that would otherwise have stayed in the ocean.

The seriousness of the ocean plastic problem was exposed when marine scientists turned their attention to tiny Henderson Island. This uninhabited coral atoll in the Pacific was found to be home to the highest density of man-made waste ever recorded, with 4,500 bits of rubbish per square metre and 13,000 new items washing up there daily. Of all the waste there, 99.8 per cent is plastic. All this pollution is having a huge impact on sea life: the average oyster on your dinner plate contains more than eight pieces of plastic.

One company has crowd-funded over £600,000 to start manufacturing edible water bottles that it hopes will replace conventional packaging. Ooho, made by Skipping Rocks Lab, is a thumb-sized blob of water contained within a membrane of tasteless, edible seaweed.

PLAYBOY

For bunnies on a priest's float, *see* **Carnivals**; for a rabbit on a plane, *see* **United Airlines**; and for a model on a mountain top, *see* **Volcanoes**.

POLLINATION

Drone bees don't pollinate flowers, but now 'drone' bees do.

Crustaceans pollinate plants. It was long thought that underwater plants such as seagrass just allowed their pollen to drift on currents, but this year scientists in Mexico found that crustaceans can act as 'the bees of the sea'.

This year a man-made drone pollinated a flower for the first time ever. Because insect numbers, and particularly bee numbers, are under threat, the hunt for artificial methods of pollinating flowers and crops is on. One experiment, conducted by a Japanese scientific institute, involved covering a tiny drone in sticky horsehairs and then flying it into flowers. The exercise was not a total success: it only worked on a very big flower, and the human pilot just smashed the drone into the flower until it was pollinated. Insects are safe from the robots for the time being.

POO, DOG

A right-wing march in San Francisco was cancelled after opponents threatened to litter the route with dog poo.

The move came amid a series of violent clashes between the alt-right and anti-fascists in the US. Not all of them went as planned. The organiser of the 'No to Marxism in America' rally, Amber Cummings, asked people not to attend, saying she had 'grave concerns' about anti-fascist violence, including the fact that counter-protesters had threatened to let their dogs poo all over the site of a nearby protest. She said they'd also vowed to send in red-nosed clowns and a giant inflatable chicken wearing a Donald Trump wig. Despite her misgivings, Cummings did still opt to protest – but on her own.

This year's dog-poo news from the UK was much less political. Residents of Bexley were told that they could buy advertising space on dog poo bags; a 'vile dog walker' was found to be throwing poo-bags on elderly residents' roofs on the Isles of Scilly; and in Ilfracombe, a volunteer complained that, thanks to irresponsible dog wners, she had been splattered in the face with dog poo 56 times while strimming the church grounds. 'I'm now looking to get a full face visor to protect myself,' she told he *Sun*.

POPE FRANCIS

Pope Francis became the first pope to act in a feature film.

Beyond the Sun is a movie that sees Pope Francis playing the role of Pope Francis. The film tells the story of four children from different cultural backgrounds who are all trying to follow the teachings of Christ. The movie was conceived by the Pope, who pitched it to two film-makers and offered to play a cameo role if they were to make it. It debuted at this year's Cannes Film Festival.

This is not the first time the Pope has shown an interest in popular culture. In 2015, he released an 11-track prog-rock album entitled *Wake Up* (*Rolling Stone* gave the album three out of five stars) and in 2008, before he became Pope, he made references to *Lord of the Rings* by mentioning Bilbo and Frodo Baggins in his Easter Mass homily.

It wasn't all show business for the Pope this year, however; some serious decisions also had to be made. For one thing, he took a stand against gluten intoler-ance, ordering all religious communities to use proper, gluten-filled wafers as part of Holy Communion. In a letter written to all the world's Roman Catholic bishops, the seriousness of the matter was spelled out: 'It is for the Bishop as principal dispenser of the mysteries of God, moderator, promoter and guardian of the liturgical life in the Church entrusted to his care… to watch over the quality of the bread.' A small compromise has been offered, though: it is permissible for communion bread to be very *low* in gluten.

POP MUSIC

James: So the summer hit of the year was 'Despacito' by Luis Fonsi and Daddy Yankee. It's become the most streamed song of all time and has been listened to 4.6 billion times. That's a total of around 30,000 years of playing time, and if you went back that far in history you'd be at a time before rope.

Anna: Fittingly, 30,000 years ago is exactly where my taste in music runs up to.

Dan: 'Despacito' has a line, 'This is how we do it down in Puerto Rico', and as a result of the song's popularity Puerto Rico's governor, Ricardo Rosselló, has named Fonsi the country's new tourism ambassador.

Andy: I think it's claimed that the song is bringing in extra tourism money, which will come in handy, because Puerto Rico declared itself bankrupt this year.

James: 'Despacito' was not the only big song of the year, but it was pretty much the only one that wasn't sung by Ed Sheeran. When his album, *Divide*, came out, it sold 672,000 copies in its first week. That was not only more than the rest of the Top 10 combined, it was more than the rest of the Top 500 combined.

Dan: Another bit of music news that came out is that while touring this year, Adele spent several minutes before every single show being wheeled around in a box.

James: That's my favourite part of that show, actually.

Anna: What does that mean, Dan?

Dan: Well, in her shows she sings in the middle of the stadium, but she needs to get there without anyone seeing her, she can't just walk through the crowd. So in some venues she gets inside a box, and they wheel her through the crowd and nobody knows it's her in there.

James: What does she do while she's waiting?

Andy: I read she has an iPad with her, so she probably plays Angry Birds or Candy Crush or something.

Anna: She had issues this year with her voice and had to cancel some concerts, and there's a theory that it's because she's singing wrong.

James: Maybe if she got out of the box she wouldn't have to shout so loud.

Andy: Well, actually, it is down to singing too loud. She has polyps on her voice box, and needs surgery, and according to researchers it's due to the fact that these days everyone sings too loudly and their vocal cords get bashed together.

Dan: There was one song that reached the charts this year that was 10 minutes of silence. It's called 'A a a a a Very Good Song', by Samir Mezrahi, and the idea is that it will always be at the top of your iTunes alphabetically, and so when you log in, it plays automatically, and you can use the silent time to choose what song you actually want to listen to.

James: That's very clever. And also good because it probably didn't damage his vocal cords much when he recorded it.

* The Vatican's univer-
sities hold regular
courses for exorcists-
in-training.

This year the Pope also gave his first TED talk, opened
a free launderette for the homeless and told priests they
shouldn't hesitate to call exorcists* more often when
they hear troubling confessions.

POTATOES

*Chinese scientists announced plans to send potatoes to
the moon to keep their silkworms alive. They also plan to
send silkworms to the moon to keep their potatoes alive.*

The mission, slated for 2018, will attempt to find out
whether life can survive on the moon, and forms part of
a wider experiment designed to establish how humans
might live there permanently. The silkworms will live in a
mini ecosystem, consisting of a small cylinder measuring
18cm x 16cm, and will produce the carbon dioxide necessary to keep the potatoes alive. The potatoes, in turn,
will be there to provide the oxygen that will help keep the
silkworms alive. The cylinder will also include a webcam,
which will live-stream the whole thing.

Back on Earth, the International Potato Centre in Peru
successfully bred a 'super potato'. Developed with NASA,
it was grown in a miniature satellite box that mimics
conditions on Mars, where days are 37 minutes and 22
seconds longer than on Earth, the atmosphere contains
very high levels of carbon monoxide, and the surface
temperature is freezing. Sixty-five species of potatoes
were tried in the experiment, but only one was deemed
'super'. Coincidentally, that variety is called 'Unique'.

PROTESTS, DIRTY

For North Korean floaters, *see* **Balloons**; for Charlotte
Church's message to Donald Trump, *see* **Inauguration**;
for faeces fighting fascists, *see* **Poo, Dog**; for a giant turd
protesting raw sewage pollution, *see* **Retirement**; for a

smear campaign against Gary Lineker, *see* **Toilet Paper, Used**; for dung under a door, *see* **Urine**; and for poopootov cocktails, *see* **Venezuela**.

PROTESTS, NON-DIRTY ▶

A US cabinet member praised Donald Trump's trip to Saudi Arabia, saying it was so successful there wasn't a single protester. Protests are illegal in Saudi Arabia.

US Secretary of Commerce Wilbur Ross, who joined Trump on the trip, said he thought it was 'fascinating' that there was 'not one guy with a bad placard'. When it was pointed out to him that this was because it was illegal to carry one (protesting in public can lead to a jail sentence of up to 15 years), Ross acknowledged that 'in theory' that could be true, but quickly returned to his point, adding, 'There wasn't anything. The mood was a genuinely good mood.'

This must have proved a welcome change for the president. Back in Washington DC, 30 per cent of all citizens have taken part in at least one protest against Trump since his inauguration.

Public protest has become a much discussed issue in America. In Minnesota, a meeting about a bill designed to discourage disruptive protesters was brought to an abrupt halt when it was disrupted by protesters. And in North Dakota, politician Keith Kempenich was so worried about protesters getting in people's way that he proposed a bill that would give immunity to drivers who accidentally ran them over. In his proposal he mentioned that that was something his mother-in-law had once almost done.

It seems nobody is safe in protests these days. In Russia, police accidentally arrested the only pro-Putin demonstrator in a crowd of anti-Putin demonstrators. He was defending the president on camera when, mid-sentence, he was dragged off by a group of police officers.

———— ▼ ————

In a diplomatic dispute between Turkey and the Netherlands, protesters in Ankara symbolically stabbed oranges in the street. They also mistakenly burned a French flag, thinking it was a Dutch one (both are red, white and blue).

Perhaps the solution is to protest without actually showing up. One German man managed this when he protested against President Erdoğan of Turkey by setting up a printer by the window in an Istanbul hotel room, and then remotely ordering it to print hundreds of anti-Erdoğan leaflets, which fluttered out to the street below. By the time police had got there to turn the printer off, he had already flown back to Germany.

PUBLIC, DON'T ASK THE ▶

The world welcomed Trainy McTrainface and Fluffy McFluffyface, but was cruelly denied Doggy McDogface.

Last year the public was allowed to vote on the naming of Britain's new polar research ship, and overwhelmingly chose *Boaty McBoatface* (*see* **Oceans**). That time, the will of the people was thwarted – the ship was named RRS *Sir David Attenborough* and the *Boaty McBoatface* name was relegated to the on-board submarine. Nevertheless, the trend has swept the world:

After a public poll, Swedish train company MTR Express named one of its new engines Trainy McTrainface, which got almost half of all votes cast. The firm said the name would be 'received with joy'.*

An extremely rare Humboldt penguin was born in the Hunstanton Sea Life Sanctuary in Norfolk for the first time. As you can't find out a penguin's sex until it's three

* Another of the trains was named Glenn, after an in-joke that everyone in Gothenburg is called Glenn. (This has a grain of truth: at one point in the 1980s, the city's football team had four players called Glenn.)

months old, they had to give it a gender-neutral name and settled on Fluffy McFluffyface.

But not all the bids were successful. An Orlando sheriff's office called on the public to name their new police dog, and suggestions included Doggy McDogface, Bitey McBiteface, Dr Borkenstein and Tool of the Oppressor. They eventually decided to call the dog Valor.

Elsewhere:

▶ When a San Diego soccer team asked the public what they should call the club, Footy McFooty Face got more votes than all 19 other candidates combined.

▶ The name of Bristol's newest city-centre bridge was put to a public vote, but Bridgey McBridgeface was deliberately kept off the shortlist. And Isle of Wight Council asked for suggestions for what to call its new floating bridge, with the caveat that Floaty McFloatface would be vetoed. In the first three hours suggestions included The Wight Floater, Sir Floatsalot and Floaty Floaterson.

▶ Eccentric tech squillionaire Elon Musk asked the Internet for a name for his new boring machine, designed to help traffic by digging tunnels under Los Angeles. Among the suggestions his followers on Twitter made were William Burroughs, David Attenburrow, Borey McBoreface ... and, perhaps inevitably, Boaty McBoatface.

The firm that operates the M25 network asked the public to name their fleet of gritters. The fleet now includes Sir Gritalot, Gruffalo Gritter, Gritty Gritty Bang Bang and Roger Spreaderer.

PUNISHMENTS

Criminals were sentenced to learn hairdressing, download Uber and make wholesome rap videos.

In Granada, a teenager who broke into a hairdresser's and stole a hairdryer was ordered to go on a six-month hairdressing course and then cut the hair of the judge

who sentenced him. The judge, Emilio Calatayud, warned the boy that he shouldn't do a shoddy job or give him a deliberately bad haircut, on pain of a criminal conviction. Calatayud does this a lot: he has previously sentenced an arsonist to work in a fire brigade, and a reckless driver to spend 100 hours with a traffic policeman.

Elsewhere in Spain, a prisoner was ordered to tweet about his crime every day for a month. Convicted of defamation, the head of Spain's Banking Services Association, Luis Pineda, was given access to social media from prison specifically so he could publicly – and repeatedly – admit his crime.

American judges proved similarly ingenious. Ohio's Judge Cicconetti started sentencing drunk drivers to download the ride-sharing apps Uber and Lyft, saying of the repeat offenders he kept seeing, 'They're not going to stop drinking, period. What you want to do is stop them drinking and driving.' And a Pennsylvania man found guilty of a gun offence was ordered to make a socially acceptable rap video. The 21-year-old offender had featured in rap videos holding a gun; in response, judge Stephanie Domitrovich said that at some point during his sentence she wanted to see him making a non-violent video with 'no guns, no drugs'.

PUTIN, VLADIMIR

It's illegal in Russia to depict Vladimir Putin wearing make-up.

In April the Russian government added 183 new items to its list of 4,199 things that it considers 'extremist', and therefore illegal to share. Item 4,071 was any picture of a Putin-like person 'with eyes and lips made up', implying 'the supposed non-standard sexual orientation of the president of the Russian Federation'. Memes of Putin in make-up first became popular in 2013, after Russia passed a law that banned teaching children about 'non-traditional sexual relations'.

Depictions of Putin-like characters were also cut from two Hollywood films this year. In these instances they were censored not by the Russians, but by the studios themselves, which were worried that including such scenes might make them targets for Russian hackers.

Putin did have one brush with Hollywood though, when he met with director Oliver Stone for an interview that aired on the Showtime channel in America. It wasn't exactly a difficult interview for Putin and we learned very little that we didn't already know: Putin is extremely paranoid about NATO, he loves judo, and he's never watched *Dr Strangelove*. The two men didn't discuss Stone's movie *JFK*, though Putin did mention the subject in an interview with NBC in June. He responded to the accusation that he rigged the US election by saying that if the US intelligence service was able to arrange and cover up the assassination of JFK, it was perfectly capable of fabricating evidence about Russian hacking.

'President Trump' is an anagram of 'Mr Putin's Red Pet'.

239

In which we learn...
What happens at Camel Camp, which scientists made the
most charming discovery of the year, why the Queen was
reported to the police, and why you shouldn't trust
David Cameron in a queue.

atar started a refugee camp for camels.

a June this year a number of countries in the Middle
ast suddenly cut off all diplomatic relations with Qatar,
laiming it was sponsoring terrorism. What triggered the
acident is not certain. One theory is that it was related to
)atar paying $1 billion to secure the release of members
of its royal family who had been kidnapped by
ranian-backed militias in Iraq. They were said
o have paid the billion dollars in cash,
carried in suitcases.

Whatever the reason, the diplomatic row
hreatened to be a huge inconvenience
for Qatar, whose only land border is with
Saudi Arabia. Qatari residents of Saudi
Arabia, the United Arab Emirates and
Bahrain were given two weeks' notice to
leave and return to Qatar. At the same time,
the Saudis stopped any goods from crossing
between the two countries – which meant Qatar
had to find a new way to import 40 per cent of its food
(*see* **Food and Drink**). The Saudis also introduced a fine
of 10,000 riyal (£2,000) for anyone watching the Qatari-
based news network Al Jazeera, and anyone expressing
sympathy for Qatar could be punished by three to
15 years in jail and a fine of no less than £100,000.
Qatari-registered animals were deported from Saudi
Arabia, and a refugee camp for at least 7,000 camels and
5,000 sheep had to be set up while officials worked out
what to do with them.

Qatar is an extremely rich country, though, and even
these severe sanctions didn't exactly have the desired
effects, at least to begin with. One banker said he wasn't
worried: 'Instead of having five maids at home, we'll
have three.'

Kazakhstan can't agree how to spell Kazakhstan.

Kazakhstan announced plans to reintroduce wild tigers. Wild donkeys and deer are also being introduced to give the tigers something to eat.

The problem is that the government wants to change from the Cyrillic alphabet, where the country is spelled Казахстан, to the Latin alphabet, but nobody can agree which letters to use. The English spelling, 'Kazakhstan', doesn't quite work, as the two 'K's are actually meant to be pronounced at the back of the throat, and there's no exact letter for that sound in the Latin alphabet.

Three possible options have been suggested for the disputed letters: a Q, a K with a squiggle below it, or a K with an inverted hat. Most Kazakhs favour the Q, which would make Qazaqstan one of only two countries to start with that letter (the other, of course, being **Qatar**). Whatever is finally agreed, some Kazakhs find the whole affair deeply embarrassing. Rasul Jumaly, a former foreign ministry official, said, 'It doesn't look very good when a country can't decide how to spell its name.'

Another country considering a name change is Macedonia, which is thinking of doing so just to keep Greece happy. Macedonia has been trying to join NATO for over a decade, but its application has always been blocked by Greece, which objects to its neighbour's name, arguing that the area historically known as 'Macedonia' was, in fact, largely in Greece. This year, with fears growing over increased Russian influence in the area, Macedonia announced that it might be willing to join NATO under a new name. Suggestions include New Macedonia, Upper Macedonia, Slavo-Macedonia, Nova Makedonija and Macedonia (Skopje). Unfortunately all these names fall foul of the one condition Greece has insisted upon: that the name Macedonia shouldn't be used.

Because both countries claim the name, the sign that greets you on both sides of the Greece–Macedonia border reads 'Welcome to Macedonia'.

QUARKS

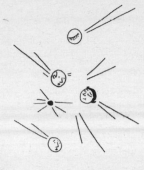

Physicists found the world's most charming particle.

You need to know only two things to understand the latest findings in subatomic physics:

1. Most particles in the universe are made of smaller things called quarks, which come in six 'flavours': up, down, top, bottom, charm and strange.*

2. Physicists are trying to find new particles by bashing existing particles together at great speed.

In a recent experiment, scientists fired lead atoms at each other, producing a 'soup' of quarks (as expected); but they also found that that soup had more 'strange' quarks than they had predicted. CERN called it 'enhanced strangeness production', and got excited, as physicists tend to do when something happens that they're not expecting.

In another experiment, a new particle called Xi-cc++ which had been predicted to exist, but had never before been seen, was found in a collision. It contains one up quark and two charm quarks, making it the most charming particle ever seen. It lasted only for somewhere between 50 millionths of a billionth of a second and 1,000 millionths of a billionth of a second. But for that fraction of a second, it was *extremely* charming.

* Strange quarks are so named because they exist for a strangely long amount of time. Charm quarks are so named because their discovery fitted in charmingly with existing theories.

QUEEN ELIZABETH, HMS

The Royal Navy's largest ever aircraft carrier was launched, without any aircraft to carry.

The HMS *Queen Elizabeth*, which set off on its maiden voyage this year for six weeks of sea trials, did so without a single aeroplane on board, because the navy doesn't yet have any. Instead the flight-deck crew were left back on land at the Royal Naval Air Service base at Culdrose,

243

where they practised pushing life-size models of F-35 planes around on the tarmac. Even at the ship's naming ceremony in 2014, the MoD was unable to get its hands on a real plane, and had to use a fake, life-size model instead

A lack of actual planes isn't the only setback from which the ship has suffered. It also has faulty doors, and the hull had to be repainted a few months before launch because it turned out that the original paint peels off in seawater.

The aircraft carrier, affectionately known as Big Lizzie, was named after the Queen in 2002 in order to safeguard the project: naval officers reckoned Tony Blair's government would find it embarrassing to scrap a ship bearing Her Majesty's name. It's capable of carrying 40 aircraft (when it gets them), a crew of 1,000, and comes with a hospital (complete with an operating theatre and dentist's surgery), police cells and even its own specially composed theme tune.

The HMS *Queen Elizabeth* is said to be the most advanced warship of all time. It's longer than the Houses of Parliament, taller than Nelson's Column, cost over £3 billion to construct, and is the largest ship ever built by the British Royal Navy. Its size and power are meant to strike fear in the hearts of Britain's enemies, although, if so, rival powers aren't letting on: the Russian military simply called it a 'large convenient target'.

It wasn't the only British navy ship to experience problems this year. In February it was revealed that the Royal Navy's new Type 45 destroyers are so noisy that enemy submarines can hear them from 100 miles away. Rear Admiral Chris Parry said crews had 'put little wooden wedges between the hatchclips and the hatches in my destroyer to stop them rattling so we could keep the noise down'.*

*The British Armed Forces also faced criticism this year when a parliamentary question revealed that 230 members of their Parachute Regiment weren't qualified to use parachutes.

The Russian navy had its share of problems, too. The *Admiral Kuznetsov* aircraft carrier, which travelled

244

through the English Channel in January, could be seen from 40 miles away, thanks to the black smoke which billowed out of it as it sailed. Half of its toilets don't work, and it needs to be towed by a tug wherever it goes.

For more sailors receiving dubious tugs, *see* **Fat Leonard**.

QUEEN ELIZABETH II

For anti-forgery codes on her face, *see* **Coins**; for not wearing a seat belt, *see* **Queen's Speech**; and for being beaten with a large vegetable, *see* **Vanuatu**.

QUEEN'S SPEECH

The Queen's Speech was delayed by two days while everyone waited for the ink to dry.

The Queen's Speech – the official ceremony in which the Sovereign reads out the laws Parliament hopes to pass – was delayed this year. Some people said it was because the Conservatives were taking a long time to reach a power-sharing agreement with the DUP. According to government sources, though, the delay was also due to the fact that it would take several days for the speech to dry on the special goatskin parchment paper used for it.

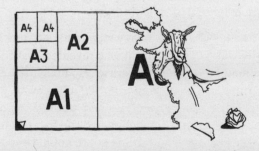

According to an expert, this wasn't the goatskin's fault. Paul Wright of William Cowley Parchment Works said that the problem lay with the ink being used, and that if the

An unknown prankster phoned 999 to report the Queen to West Yorkshire Police for not wearing a seat belt in the car on her way to deliver the speech. As West Yorkshire Police wrote on Twitter, this was not only #Not999, it was #NotEvenWestYorkshire.

government had known what they were doing they could have had it dry and ready in ten minutes flat.

The Queen can't have been best pleased by the two-day delay, as it meant she missed the second morning of her beloved Royal Ascot. Fortunately, a helicopter was on standby to whisk her away to the afternoon's horse racing.

Curiously, the 'goatskin parchment paper' the Queen's Speech gets written on doesn't actually contain any goat. It used to and it even has a watermark in the shape of a goat, but these days it's just made of high-quality paper. Unlike the Queen's Speech, the actual laws passed by Parliament *were* printed on genuine vellum (i.e. real animal skin) until this year, but from now on will be printed on paper. MPs voted to keep vellum (which lasts centuries longer), but bowed to cost-cutting pressure from the House of Lords. Tory MP Ian Liddell-Grainger said this was a short-sighted move, and that 'in a thousand years' time people will ask, "What did they do in March 2017?"'

QUEENSLAND

Queensland police successfully lowered crime rates by asking victims to stop reporting crimes.

The shocking discovery was made by the Queensland Audit Office, which discovered that 22 per cent of all the Police Service's reports from 2011 to 2016 were incomplete, inaccurate, or both.

Queensland police were 'fudging' their reports in response to mounting pressure from the government to get crime rates down. They adopted various tactics: crime data was not logged properly; 'unsolved' cases were recorded as 'unfounded'; others were labelled 'Solved – bar to prosecution'; and officers asked victims to withdraw accusations. They even sent out letters stating that if victims did not respond within seven days it would be assumed that they didn't want to take any further action. Measures are now being put into place to address these issues.

Australia also discovered this year that its most criminal name is Leon. Law firm Go To Court looked at over 25,000 crimes drawn from a database of publicly accessible records and cross-referenced them against a list of Australia's most popular names over the past 90 years. The final list consists of 500 names, with Leon coming out on top. Others include Andrew (186), Hunter (466) and Murray (76).

QUEUEING

British people queue according to unwritten rules (which are written below).

A study by University College London found that Brits queue for an average of six minutes (or five minutes and 54 seconds, to be precise) before giving up; that they are reluctant to join a queue if it has more than six people already in it; and that 6 inches is the minimum amount of space they're comfortable having between them and the other queuers.

British pride in queuing was exemplified at Wimbledon this year, where each person joining the line to get tickets was given a 29-page booklet explaining the queuing code of conduct.

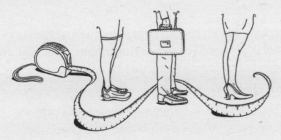

UCL summarised all this as 'the rule of six' while acknowledging that there's great variety according to the type of queue involved. People will wait longer for concert tickets, for instance, than they'll wait in a toilet queue. One caveat is that people become much less likely to leave a queue if others line up behind them. The chances of someone exiting a queue fall to almost zero when the number of people behind them builds to – you guessed it – six.

Not everyone plays by the rules. David Cameron was caught on camera breaching queue etiquette in JD Sports. After getting to the cashier and realising he'd picked the wrong-sized socks, he rushed off to fetch the right size and returned to the till, fast-tracking past about 10 other shoppers who were waiting in line. The government's integration tsar, Louise Casey, might have some tips for him. Speaking about how people could help migrants fit into British society, she commented that they should all be taught the holy trinity of British skills: 'be nice', know when to put the bins out, and queue properly.

In which we learn …
Who retired for the fourth time, what happens when you eat
1,000 coins, why Russia denied it was making a Terminator,
how centurions held Rome hostage, and which dance
can get you out of a restaurant bill.

Louisiana police offered raffle winners the chance to fire a taser at one of their officers.

The 'Tase-a-Cop' promotion was meant as an educational tool to teach children how tasers work, as well as a way to raise money for the department's Christmas charity. After the advertisement went viral, the police had to post a clarification on Facebook stating that the prize could be claimed only by adults, that the taser's electrodes would be connected to the officer beforehand rather than being 'shot' at him, and that it would all be overseen by a trained certified instructor (apparently there wasn't enough space on the advert to include such details). A number of parents expressed their concern at the prospect of their children watching a cop being tasered, but the police department sought to reassure them by saying that there were other activities on offer, too – such as water guns and a dunking booth where they could dunk a policeman.

In Oman an imam won the £500,000 first prize at a raffle run by his bank, but refused to take the money. 'They told me I was fortunate,' said Sheikh Ali al-Ghaithi, 'but it is not "fortune" to win money I have not earned. Islamic laws say I cannot keep such money, so I told my bank to keep it. It is that simple.'

RAILWAYS ▶

Railway innovations of the year included:

▶ **Country:** Ukraine

Innovation: Free journeys for poetry buffs. The Ukrainian Metro offered free journeys to anyone who could recite a poem by the country's national poet, Taras Shevchenko, on his birthday. The only drawback was that the offer applied at only three stations and for only 40 minutes at two of them. Lucky poetry reciters stood to save a maximum of 12p on their next journey.

▶ **Country:** Mexico

Innovation: The 'penis seat'. The seat, complete with protruding genitals, was introduced on Mexican metro trains, was uncomfortable to sit on and was reserved for men only. Its intention was to force men to experience the discomfort that women face when they're sexually harassed on trains.

▶ **Country:** China

Innovation: The world's first driverless, trackless train. It's fitted with sensors that respond to the shape of the road, effectively travelling on virtual tracks that negate the need for physical ones.

▶ **Country:** India

Innovation: The country's first solar-powered train – though the train will actually be pulled along by a diesel locomotive, with the solar power fuelling air conditioning and lights within the carriages.

RANSOMWARE

Ransomware caused misery to more than 300,000 computer users worldwide, but caused joy to the 590 Australians who had their traffic fines cancelled.

Ransomware is the general name for any computer virus that stops you from accessing your files unless you pay a ransom. The most notorious example of the year was WannaCry, which spread to millions of computers worldwide, including many in Britain's health service. In Australia, it hit Victoria's speed cameras when a maintenance worker inserted an infected USB stick into the system. As a result, the cameras continually turned themselves off and on again. Because the data they collected was felt to be unreliable, almost 600 fines were cancelled.

In a year when 'llamas on the line' were blamed for train delays in Kent, some passengers translated their frustration at the country's unreliable rail services to the stage. *Southern Fail: The Musical* premiered at the Brighton Fringe in June.

Serbian authorities ignited tensions with Kosovo, which declared its independence in 2008, by running a train from Belgrade across the border to Mitrovica which bore the words 'Kosovo is Serbia' in 21 languages.

WannaCry actually had its ransom paid fewer than 400 times, and so made only $120,000. But the money has not (at time of writing) been withdrawn by the virus's creators, and it looks as though it might never be, as it is kept in a couple of bitcoin accounts that are relatively easy for law enforcers to trace.

The next attack, known as either Petya or NotPetya, depending on who you spoke to, was even less successful. It made a little over $10,000 for its inventors. But, as many pointed out, those sending these attacks may have been less interested in the money than in causing as much chaos and misery as possible.

RATS

Police in India blamed rats for drinking all their confiscated alcohol.

To cut down on domestic violence and poverty, the Indian state of Bihar banned alcohol last year, and ended up confiscating 900,000 litres in just 12 months. Eventually the police had to rent extra premises to house all the contraband they'd seized, as they weren't allowed to destroy it without a court order.

And yet, when officials asked if they could examine the seized alcohol, it turned out that almost all of it had mysteriously disappeared. Officers claimed that it must have been drunk by rats, which must have nibbled off the lids. A member of the state government, Devesh Chandra Thakur, said this explanation was 'the most absurd claim that has ever been made'. In unrelated news, the president of the Bihar Policemen's Association was arrested on suspicion of consuming alcohol.*

* Rats get the blame for everything in Bihar province. After devastating floods, the water resources minister said it was all because rats had weakened river embankments by gnawing through them. Others expressed their doubts.

This isn't the only time this year that criminal rats have allegedly struck. In May, a customs officer in Udaipur was asked to produce in court some alcohol that had been seized from a resident eight years ago. He turned up with empty bottles, explaining that rats were to blame. And in March, police in the state of Maharashtra blamed rats for eating a stash of 25 kilos of marijuana being held in a warehouse.

A 2016 study found that rats drink more alcohol when they're stressed, suggesting India's rats must be the most stressed on the planet.

RECALLS

Recalls this year included double-strength gin, bony hot dogs, and a range of salads with extra bat.

A batch of Bombay Sapphire gin was recalled after it was discovered it had an alcohol content of 77 per cent, rather than the more normal 40 per cent. A spokeswoman for Bacardi, which owns Bombay Sapphire, said the extra-boozy gin was 'not unsafe to drink', but that the firm 'do not recommend consumption of the product'. Only a fifth of it was returned.

Other recalls this year included a batch of hash browns which were reported to have potentially included 'extraneous golf ball material', 3 million kilos of hot dogs which may have contained fragments of bone, and a salad range from Walmart after a dead bat was found in one packet.

RELIGION

For how to find your nearest priest, *see* **Apps**; for a DJ monk dropping beats and chants, *see* **Buddhists**; for a pastor playing Hugh Hefner, *see* **Carnivals**; for a sermon thanking God for a Premier League victory, *see* **Chelsea**; for holy toys, *see* **Fidget Spinners**; for earthquake beer made by monks, *see* **Food and Drink**; for the priest who took on the Mafia, *see* **Godfather**; for the Muslims with the keys to Christ's tomb, *see* **Jesus**; for a missing monk, *see*

A rat cafe opened in San Francisco. It's part of the San Francisco dungeons, where diners learn about the role of rats in the transmission of bubonic plague. To comply with hygiene rules, the rats are only allowed out for customers to handle once all the food has been cleared away.

Lost and Found; for a Protestant android, *see* **Robots**; and for Mother Theresa™, *see* **Trademarks**.

RESTAURANTS

For an avocado restaurant, *see* **Avocados**; for a Nutella cafe, *see* **Nutella**; for a rat cafe, *see* **Rats**.

RETIREMENT

Daniel Day-Lewis announced his retirement from acting. For the fourth time.

The first time he did so was in 1989 when, while playing Hamlet, he left the stage after making contact with his deceased father mid-performance. Eyewitnesses said he started crying and then just walked offstage without finishing the play. The second time was in 1997, when he moved to Florence to become an apprentice shoemaker. On the third occasion, in 2002, he decided to move back to Ireland to learn rural skills like stonemasonry. His latest retirement comes without an explanation, and his publicists refuse to divulge the reason. It is rumoured that he intends to become a dressmaker.

Other retirements this year include Japan's oldest female porn star, who has quit aged 80, having got into the industry 9 years ago,* and a 6-foot-tall anthropomorphic turd called Mr Floatie, who for 13 years has been protesting about the dumping of raw sewage in Canadian waters, and who was mascot to Canada's People Opposed to Outfall Pollution, or POOP.

* She can't be called the oldest Japanese porn star though, because there is an 82-year-old man who is still going strong.

RIP

People who passed away this year included: the oldest person in the world (117 – *see* **Oldest Age**); Joseph Goebbels's secretary (106); the journalist who discovered that the Second World War had started (105 – see **Holling-worth, Clare**); the creator of 'the hardest logic puzzle ever' (97); a former president of Finland who held all his press briefings in a sauna (93); the inventor of underwater television (92); a 'mildly eccentric' Tory MP who once arrived at Parliament on horseback (91); the 'Father of Pac-Man' (91); a man who claimed to have invented the Magnum ice cream* (89); the author of *The Exorcist* (89); the actor who played Batman in the 1960s (88); the actor who played Godzilla in the 1950s (88); the man who coined the word 'homophobia' (87); the creator of G.I. Joe and *ThunderCats* (84); a dictator who dressed his teddy bears as soldiers (83 – see **Noriega, Manuel**); the inventor of the Hawaiian pizza (83 – see **Pizza**); the skier who popularised crouching down as you ski (83); the last man to walk on the moon (82); the woman who popularised the word 'Ms' (78); a man who was shot in 1958, but only died from the bullet 59 years later (77); a Russian military officer who saved the world from a global nuclear apocalypse in 1983 (77); the dad of the living dead (77 – see **Zombies**); the man who brought karate to Plymouth (77); the founder of Fox News (77); the footballer who scored a hat trick in 90 seconds – the fastest ever (71); the man who created the rainbow flag symbolising LGBTQ pride (65); a man who was killed for a reality TV show that didn't exist (44 – see **Kim Jong-Nam, Assassination of**); and the founder of the Death Cafe movement (44).

Animals that passed away this year included: the oldest known killer whale (100+); the oldest aquarium fish (100+); the world's oldest hippo (65); the oldest known gorilla (60); Britain's oldest donkey (53); the world's oldest known sloth (43); Britain's oldest known wombat (31); and a Thai turtle that ate 1,000 coins (25).

… Didn't they do well.

* *Better known as James Bond actor Roger Moore.*

ROBOTS

The border between North and South Korea is guarded by robots.

The SGR-A1 robots, which are South Korean guns that have an autonomous mode, can theoretically identify the enemy and fire on them without any human input, though this feature hasn't been utilised yet. The UN has been discussing how to regulate autonomous weapons on battlefields of the future, prompting a group of more than 100 scientists and artificial intelligence experts including Elon Musk and Stephen Hawking to sign a letter calling on world leaders to ban 'killer robots'.

The letter was signed in the same week that a group of computer scientists at IOActive, a cybersecurity group, showed that a popular humanoid robot could be hacked. They took UBTECH's Alpha 2 robot, which is designed to help around the house, and programmed it to stab a tomato repeatedly with a screwdriver. In Russia, meanwhile, a 6-foot-tall humanoid robot called FEDOR was unveiled. FEDOR can lift weights, do press-ups, and fire guns with both hands at the same time. Russia's Deputy PM Dmitry Rogozin said, 'We are not creating a Terminator,' and explained that giving FEDOR the ability to fire guns was simply to 'improve its motor skills'.

Less violent robots that hit the news this year included: the BlessU-2, a robot that can issue Protestant blessings; a robot that can perform Buddhist funerary rites (*see* **Buddhists**); a robot called Sally that makes salads; a robot called Flippy that flips burgers; a robot that can turn wheels of cheese over, known as Tina the Turner; a volleyball-playing robot that has three arms; a piano-playing robot that has 53 fingers; a love-doll that can be programmed with more than 50 positions; and a robot that can carry out tiny manoeuvres in your bottom to make colonoscopies less unpleasant.

Scientists finally worked out why ancient Roman concrete is better than ours, but can't make it because we've lost the recipe.

The mystery of why 2,000-year-old ancient Roman sea walls and piers have remained standing, while modern-day concrete ocean structures corrode within years, has finally been solved. Astonishingly, it turns out that Roman concrete gets stronger over time.

Scientists at the University of Utah found that the material undergoes a rare chemical reaction. Every time the seawater corrodes a bit of it, new crystals are formed which make the structure stronger until it's rock-like. Unfortunately, despite knowing what elements make up the walls – the ingredients include, among other things, volcanic ash – we've lost the instructions on how to bake it. Scientists are now trying to reverse-engineer the process to discover how it's made. If they're successful, we could revert to using the ancient technology on our shorelines.

In other ancient Roman news, a ban on centurions standing outside the Colosseum was overturned after they won a battle with the local city council. The ban came about last year following numerous complaints that the centurions, who make their living posing for photos with tourists, were getting into fights with each other and with the tourists. However, a court overturned the ban following an appeal by the Centurion Street Artists Association, and so once again the centurions are free to roam Rome. The council haven't given up yet, saying, 'The city cannot be held hostage by centurions.'

A 2000-year-old collection of buried ancient Roman letters was found under Hadrian's Wall. Letters include one from a man named Masclus who wrote to his boss asking for time off work. Masclus has been known to historians for years, thanks to a previous letter in which he asked his boss for more beer.

RUSSIA INVESTIGATION

Dan: So one of the many people now investigating Donald Trump's ties to Russia is a man called Bobby Three Sticks.

Andy: Obviously, I'm already hooked.

Dan: Well, his real name is Robert Mueller III, hence the nickname 'Bobby Three Sticks'.

James: That's fantastic. Was he the guy who took over after Comey?

Dan: Sort of. He's now leading one of the many investigations into Trump's links to Russia, at any rate. Trump fired James Comey, the former FBI director, and claimed it was because of Comey's investigation of Hillary's emails; but a lot of people think it was because he wouldn't let the Russian investigation drop.

Andy: You know when he was fired, Comey actually thought it was a joke. He was giving a lecture to his FBI staff, and he saw it on TV in the background and he thought he was being pranked.

Anna: He and Trump didn't exactly see eye to eye; apparently when Trump kept talking to him about Russia, he went to the Attorney General, basically America's chief lawyer, and said, 'Please don't let me be left alone with him any more.'

James: Yes. And the other thing is that Comey found Trump so unnerving that when they were in the Oval Office, Comey supposedly tried to camouflage himself by wearing a blue suit and standing in front of a blue curtain.

Anna: I'm not sure I'd trust a man to be head of the FBI if he sees a curtain and thinks, 'I'm going to hide in front of that, rather than behind it.' He sounds like an idiot.

Andy: And they'd have had to be tall curtains, because Comey is 6 foot 8. He's 4 inches taller than Trump's personal bodyguard. As you'd expect, he quite likes basketball.

James: So because of this whole investigation we now know that during the election campaign Donald Trump's son, Donald Jr, met with Russians to discuss some dirt that they might have on Hillary. The guy who organised it was called Robert Goldstone, but he didn't try to keep it secret by any stretch. He even checked into Trump Tower on Facebook on the day of the meeting.

Dan: Did you know that Russia weren't only accused of meddling in the US election? They were also accused of meddling in the Stoke by-election.

Anna: Well, it was the obvious next step after the US. They tested their techniques in America and then decided to go for the big guns.

Dan: Exactly. So what happened is that fake-news makers who were previously sending out positive stories about Donald Trump were now sending out stories about Stoke.

James: I can see that anyone spreading positive stories about Stoke would immediately arouse suspicion.

Calls to the RSPCA this year came from a person who was worried about a distressed bird that turned out to be their fire alarm; another who believed they'd discovered an escaped tortoise which turned out to be made of stone; and someone who reported a wound under the tail of a stray cat that turned out to be its anus.

RUNNER, DOING A

One hundred and sixty people avoided a restaurant bill by doing the conga.

Two Canadian men were arrested after allegedly going through a McDonald's drive-through restaurant on a sofa. The sofa was being pulled by a car. As soon as the police arrived, the driver raced off, taking the sofa but leaving the two men behind. In their defence, they *were* wearing helmets. A local paper reported that actual criminal charges were 'yet to be determined'.

In February, Spain's restaurants fell victim to a 'dine-and-dash' gang who ate huge amounts of food and drink before running off. In their first hit, a group of up to 160 people paid a deposit of 900 euros, ate a 2,000-euro meal, then fled within a single minute before staff could react. According to one account, waiters didn't realise the diners were leaving 'because they seemed to be dancing the conga. They exited the restaurant in a row.' Next, the gang paid a 1,000-euro deposit at a different restaurant, ate 10,000 euros' worth of food and drink, and then disappeared in the space of five minutes. A man was later arrested on suspicion of being the gang's ringleader.

Elsewhere, an Australian rapper was arrested after he allegedly ran into the sea to avoid paying up. A Queensland court heard that the rapper, known as 2pec (real name Terry Peck), had eaten two lobsters and a baby octopus, and drunk several beers and 21 vodka oyster shots. He was pursued on jet skis by police and, after an unsuccessful attempt to hide underwater, tried to kick the officers as they apprehended him. In court, charged with stealing and assault, he claimed he had actually run out of the restaurant to help a friend who was giving birth on the beach, and that the lobsters had been over-cooked anyway.

Rwanda's president claimed victory in the country's election, a month before the ballots opened.

There are 11 political parties in Rwanda, but eight of them didn't bother fielding a candidate, instead backing the existing president Paul Kagame. In his first campaign rally, Kagame told his supporters that he effectively won this year's election back in 2015 when the country voted to amend the constitution in his favour, allowing him to be president until 2034 if he feels like it. The election went ahead anyway, and Kagame won 98.6 per cent of the vote.

This year, Rwanda became the latest country to ban the import of used clothing, in an attempt to help local textile industries. It was a particularly difficult decision, as most of the clothes are donated by American charities, and in response to the new law the USA suspended Rwanda's duty-free trade agreement. American used-clothes lobbying groups say that the ban, which already exists in Kenya, Uganda, Burundi, Tanzania and South Sudan, causes significant economic hardship to the USA's used-clothing industry.

Rwanda also announced it's delivered over 2,600 units of blood by drone over the past year as part of a new push to get medical supplies to rural areas. Doctors request blood for patients via a WhatsApp message. The blood is then loaded on to a drone that flies autonomously to the destination at up to 100km/h, texts the doctor when it's arriving, descends to 10 metres above the ground, drops the package and returns to base. The blood is attached to a parachute to ensure a safe landing.

In which we learn …
Who collected socks for Satan, who seized 6 kilos of
horse genitalia, how Zulus ended up in East Yorkshire,
and which country is now run by Mr Cheese.

Santa went on tour for the first time in 1,000 years.

One of St Nicholas's bones was allowed to leave Italy for the first time in nearly a millennium. He's been lying in a church in southern Italy since 1087, but this year a tiny bit of his rib went on tour to Russia, on a specially chartered flight.

In order for St Nick to leave at all he had to be surgically extracted: his crypt in Italy is only accessible via a 6cm-wide hole. The church hired a surgeon to look inside with a video camera and carry out a laparoscopy (aka keyhole surgery), plucking the piece of rib out with tweezers. When St Nicholas got to Russia, over a million people visited him, many of them queueing through the night.

The other big saint news of the year was that part of St John Bosco's brain was stolen, when a thief posing as a pilgrim took it from its basilica in Castelnuovo Don Bosco, Italy.* Investigators were worried it would be used for ransom or even in satanic rites, as there's almost no market for saints' brains.

Thankfully, the holy brain was eventually found in a copper teapot, and the teapot's owner was arrested. Police raided his house after finding his fingerprints at the scene of the crime. The Archbishop of Turin prayed for St John Bosco to forgive the thief, who apparently stole the relic because he thought the gold-painted container it came in might be worth something.

A bit of saint returned from space in April. The relic – a tiny fragment of St Seraphim of Sarov – was taken from its monastery to the International Space Station by Russian astronaut Sergey Ryzhikov.

* Relic thefts are not uncommon. In 1991, armed men stole the chin of St Anthony from a Padua church. The man behind the crime, underworld don Felice Maniero, later said he'd wanted St Anthony's tongue, which was more valuable, 'but those blockheads came back with the chin'.

SAND ▶

A New Zealand brewery started making fake sand out of beer bottles.

Two thirds of the world's beaches are retreating. The reason is that sand is being extracted for use in construction far more quickly than it is being naturally replenished; and since desert sand is too fine for most builders, it's being taken from beaches instead. There is a thriving sand black market. In India there's even a 'sand mafia': in the state of Tamil Nadu, 50,000 lorry-loads of sand are mined every day and smuggled to other states. The *Times of India* estimates the sand-smuggling market is worth £1.7 billion a year.

New Zealand firm DB Breweries is attempting to fight back with its invention, the Beer Bottle Sand Machine. When a bottle is inserted into the machine, a wheel of steel hammers, spinning at 2,800rpm, grinds it down. A vacuum system then sifts out the dust and the bottle's label, leaving behind 200 grams of sand substitute. The whole process takes just five seconds, and the sand generated will be supplied to construction companies, national road projects and golf-course bunkers.

The Cambodian government began its battle for the beaches, too, by announcing it was outlawing all sales of sand. For years, Cambodia has been selling its sand to Singapore (72 million tonnes since 2007), which has been using it to make itself bigger. Environmental experts have pointed out that this seriously damages coastal ecosystems, so the practice is now being banned.

Paris also made efforts to preserve sand this year when the city council decided that it would not buy the usual 3,000 tonnes of Normandy sand that it places by the banks of the Seine to create an artificial beach. Instead, it filled the space with grass and plants. The council's motives were more political than environmental. It took the decision after learning that its sand suppliers, Franco-Swiss cement maker Lafarge-Holcim, had submitted a bid to build Donald Trump's border wall.

SATANISTS

A satanist group in Florida started a 'Socks for Satan' campaign.

The Satanic Temple is a group of activists who don't actually worship the devil, but use demonic symbols to promote their campaign for the separation of religion and government. This spring they collected socks donated by the people of Pensacola and distributed them among the homeless. Fellow atheistic satanist group the Church of Satan hit news earlier in the year when they tweeted to clarify that Donald Trump is not one of them.

In 2013, the Satanic Temple attracted media attention when they tried to raise enough money to Adopt-a-Highway, hoping their name would be displayed on a road in New York. Sadly they failed, but this year they did successfully erect America's first ever satanist monument. In 2016, someone in a town in Minnesota put up a metal silhouette of an infantryman kneeling before a cross in a park, leading to objections by residents, one of whom called it a religious symbol that violated the First Amendment (the separation of church and state). After a long argument the town decided to make part of the park a 'public forum', open to any group that wanted to honour the town's veterans. The satanist group took the town up on the offer, and this year a black cube decorated with upside-down pentagrams was installed there.

According to an exorcist for the Archdiocese of Indianapolis, America has seen a rise in demonic activity, and there aren't enough exorcists to meet demands. 'The problem isn't that the devil has upped his game, but more people are willing to play it,' Father Lampert said.

SATELLITES

In August the three brightest objects in the sky were the sun, the moon and a 3-metre-wide Russian satellite.

The new Russian satellite was called Mayak, meaning 'beacon'. It was only the size of a loaf of bread while on Earth, but once in space it unfurled a pyramid-shaped mirror, one 20th the thickness of a human hair.

In June, the record for the world's smallest satellite was broken by an 18-year-old student from India. He designed the object, which was then flown up by a NASA rocket. It weighs just 64 grams, and is designed to measure radiation in space.

It reflected so much light back to Earth that it was brighter than any of the stars, the planets and even the International Space Station. By September, it had burned up in the Earth's atmosphere.

The satellite was crowdfunded, and one of the partners was the advertising company 12.digital. It horrified astronomers. Not only did such a bright light screw up all their observations while it orbited the Earth, but the company hope that the technology will eventually allow businesses to put billboards in space, which would be a disaster for stargazers.

Ghana also launched a satellite this year, the first time a sub-Saharan African country has done so. The plan is that it will monitor the country's coastline, but it is also fitted with a device that allows it to broadcast the country's national anthem from space.

SATNAV

A troupe of Zulu dancers turned up at a Yorkshire school by mistake after being misdirected by their satnav.

One of the Queen's old Bentleys was auctioned off this year. The security fittings have all been removed, and the only personal feature that remains is that the 'home' programmed into the satnav is Windsor Castle.

The Lions of Zululand are a group of dancers from KwaZulu-Natal, South Africa. On a recent tour of the UK, the dancers were meant to perform at a London school called St Ann's, but after a mix-up over addresses they followed their satnav 200 miles in the wrong direction to the similarly named St Anne's school in East Yorkshire. They arrived at 8 a.m. and approached one of the caretakers, asking, 'Is this London?' When they found out it wasn't, they did the show anyway, to a delighted and surprised group of children.

Elsewhere, a 91-year-old driver in Plymouth who followed her satnav ended up with her car lodged halfway down a flight of concrete steps; a German driver followed his until he got stuck halfway down a ski slope in Austria; and a Chinese driver followed his GPS directions halfway across a river. Independently, scientists at University College London discovered the brain activity that normally plans possible routes for a journey is completely absent when people switch from traditional maps to satnav.

SAUSAGES

For a sausage party, *see* **Dictionaries**; for an Australian who had a sausage delivered to his hot tub, *see* **Drones**; for a man armed with nothing but a sausage, *see* **Easter**; for the invention of the sausage roll, *see* **Inventions**; for an update on the state of the walking sausage, *see* **Stick Insects**; and for giant hot dogs, *see* **Tunnels**.

SCHOOLS

Schoolchildren in Bristol were made to wear signs around their necks if their shoes were too shiny.

Merchants' Academy in Bristol instituted a raft of stricter rules in July, including some that clamped down on any deviations from the school uniform. If shoes are shinier or hairbands more fashionable than the rules allow, students have to wear a lanyard with a card hanging from it that reads, 'I have 24 hours to sort out my uniform.' If they fail to wear that lanyard properly, or they don't meet the 24-hour deadline, they are sent to an isolation room for five lessons. The aim is to reduce disruption in class, and the head teacher reported the new policies were already improving students' behaviour within a month of being implemented.

This wasn't the only school to take a stand on footwear. Finden Primary School in Derby encouraged pupils to wear slippers instead of shoes. The deputy head suggested the policy after reading a paper arguing that shoeless students get better grades. The 10-year study

A group of students in Ohio were pepper-sprayed in the face for a school project. Children who want to join the military or the police took part in the 'lesson' to give them a taste of what they might be doing to other people. It also involved them being shot with a stun gun.

Pupils across the UK struggled in Key Stage 2 tests because their punctuation was the wrong shape. Teachers complained after their students lost marks for commas that pointed the wrong way, semicolons that were too large and full stops positioned slightly too high.

across 25 countries found that when children remove thei. shoes in lessons they perform better, arrive earlier, leave later, are less likely to bully each other, and are quieter and calmer. It's thought to make pupils feel more relaxed and at home, and is already common practice in Scandinavia. If the experiment goes well, the school intends to make slippers a compulsory part of the uniform.

In the US, uniform irregularities created havoc in Wisconsin when Ashwaubenon High School was evacuated after a pupil turned up dressed as Darth Vader. The student was wearing the outfit in celebration of May the Fourth – aka Star Wars Day – but a parent mistook it for something more sinister and called the police. The nearby Parkview Middle School and a local community centre were evacuated, too. The police confirmed later that there had been no actual threat, but school officials re-emphasised their 'no costume' policy to avoid such things recurring in future.

SCOTLAND

For a pirate ship in a tree, *see* **Boats**; for non-existent bairns, *see* **Donalds**; for the good name of Buckfast, *see* **Easter**; for the worst ever shot at goal, *see* **Football**; for the other Steve Bannon, *see* **Mix-Ups**; for kosher convicts, *see* **Orange Is the New Black**; for a deep-frozen single malt *see* **Whisky**; and for Nessie's current whereabouts, *see* **Zoology, Crypto-**.

SELFIES

The average millennial spent 2.2 days of the year taking selfies.

That's a full hour a week, and it was the finding of a survey commissioned by eyewear company Frames Direct. The selfie craze led police to warn that if people took photos while voting in the general election, they might inadvertently reveal another person's vote, and the photographer could face a fine of £5,000 or six months in prison. Not only that, the *Irish Medical Journal* suggested that hospitals should list 'selfie-related wrist injury' on admission forms as a unique patient issue, as it happens so often. In 2016, for instance, the authors of the article found that it happened four times in a single week in Galway alone.

Police in Canada also warned against selfies this year, specifically asking people not to take photos with an enormous moose that went on the run in Calgary, Alberta; while a zookeeper at Chessington World of Adventures created a 6-metre selfie stick so she could take photos with giraffes. And former England footballer Alan Shearer, meanwhile, broke the world record for the most selfies in three minutes this April. He managed 134.

Some life insurance companies want to use people's selfies to calculate their premiums, saying that by looking at their faces, they can tell how likely the person is to die in the next few years.

In Iran, a Lionel Messi lookalike was detained by police and had his car impounded because so many people wanted to take a selfie with him. He first found out about his doppelgänger during the last World Cup when his dad told him not to come home. 'I was confused at first, but then my dad asked me, "Why did you score a goal against Iran?" I said, "But that wasn't me!" He just responded that he was very furious.'

SEX CHANGES

For a fish that changes its gender, *see* **Abdications**; for a nursery rhyme favourite who became a woman, *see* **Farming**; and for the fictional cat who had a sex change, *see* **Wikipedia**; and then another, *see* **Wikipedia**; and then another, *see* **Wikipedia**; and then another, *see* **Wikipedia**; and then another, *see* **Wikipedia**; and then yet another, *see* **Wikipedia**; and then another, *see* **Wikipedia**; and then had another, *see* **Wikipedia**; and then another, *see* **Wikipedia**; and another one, *see* **Wikipedia**; and another one, *see* **Wikipedia**; and then another, *see* **Wikipedia**; and then another, *see* **Wikipedia**; and then another, *see* **Wikipedia**; and then yet one more, *see* **Wikipedia**; and then once again, *see* **Wikipedia**; and then another, *see* **Wikipedia**; and then another, *see* **Wikipedia**; and then yet another, *see* **Wikipedia**; and then finally one more, *see* **Wikipedia**.

SHARK ATTACK

Groups of killer whales have been ganging up on great white sharks off the South African coast, removing their livers, and then leaving the sharks to die. Biologist Alison Towner said, 'Two orcas will take a pectoral fin in their mouth and pull open a shark together to extract the liver.' Apart from their missing livers, the sharks that washed up were almost completely intact.

The UK's first ever shark attack left the victim with a cut on the thumb and a bruise on the leg.

Rich Thomson was surfing in South Devon when a metre-long shark, probably a species called a smooth hound, clamped its teeth around his leg. Mr Thomson punched it in the head and it swam off, leaving him with a large bruise on his leg (the skin wasn't broken, thanks to the protection of his wetsuit) and a badly cut hand.

Paul Cox, the head of Shark Trust – a charity that aims to educate people about the animal – was quick to defend the shark. 'I personally wouldn't describe this as an attack,' he told reporters, 'because it creates an impression that's out of context. It's an interesting and slightly unusual incident involving one of the 30 or so types of shark that we're lucky enough to have living in British Seas.'

The shark was the least of Rich Thomson's problems, though: 'I went home and told my wife I was late because I had been bitten by a shark,' he told the BBC. 'She said, "I've heard that one before."'

SHRINKFLATION

Brits now get 10 per cent fewer toilet-paper wipes for their money.

The Office for National Statistics released a report in August which showed that more than 2,500 products are not as big as they used to be: toilet rolls, coffee, chocolate and fruit juice are now all being sold in smaller sizes but for the same price. The practice is known as 'shrinkflation'.

The KitKat Chunky has been on a bit of a diet in recent years, with its weight dropping from 48 grams to 40 grams; a Pepperami is now a bit less of an animal – falling from 25 grams to 22.5 grams; and a standard roll of Andrex toilet tissue is also smaller, shrinking from 221 sheets to 200 this year.

A box of Coco Pops has shrunk in weight from 800 grams to 720 grams, but oddly you actually now get more pops in your packet – 16,500 rather than 14,500. That's because they have less sugar than they used to; and this in turn has been a reason given by many companies for shrinkflation. They're not necessarily making their packets smaller due to an increase in costs, or to increase profits, they argue: it's to fight the obesity crisis.

Many people blamed Brexit for the shrinking products, and it's true that the Brexit vote has made many ingredients more expensive to import, but actually it's a practice that's been going on for years. In 2015, the consumer group Which? lodged its first ever 'super-complaint', alleging that grocers were fooling shoppers with 'dodgy multi-buys, shrinking products and baffling sales offers'.

Nestlé launched a new range of Walnut Whip chocolates with no walnut on top. The company said the product will 'offer consumers more choice', but nut experts pointed out it could be a cost-saving measure, since walnut prices have risen by 20 per cent.

In that same year, the *Daily Mail* reported that teabags, washing powder and bread were shrinking.

Burton's Biscuits, which makes Wagon Wheels, is very clear that its biscuit has never suffered from shrinkflation, despite many claims to the contrary. Burton's says that 'most often our first Wagon Wheel experience is in childhood and hence our hands are smaller.' Donald Trump has never to our knowledge complained about the size of his Wagon Wheels.

SMART-

For a smart fridge, *see* **Languages**; for a smart drone, *see* **Lasers**; for a smart dildo, *see* **Lawsuits, Non-Trump**; for a smartphone, *see* **Phones**; for a smart brolly, *see* **Umbrellas**; and for a smart arse *see* **Yoga**.

SMUGGLING

Objects smuggled in 2017 included 4 tonnes of eels, 330 exotic tortoises and 6 kilos of horse genitals.

This year a huge, pan-European police operation to smash two international eel-smuggling networks ended, having seized 4 tonnes of glass eels* and arrested 48 people. Eels are critically endangered, but black marketeers sell them overseas as a culinary delicacy for up to £6,000 a kilo. Extra patrols have now been sent to the River Severn to deter eel smugglers.

* A glass eel is a name for a young eel, so called because it's transparent. The US Fish and Wildlife Service also cracked down on glass eel smuggling rings this year in an exercise called Operation Broken Glass.

Elsewhere, Malaysian authorities seized 330 highly rare tortoises worth over £200,000, smuggled from Madagascar in boxes labelled 'stones', and staff at JFK airport in New York found 140 kilos of yak meat hidden among sweaters and clothes. In Virginia, customs staff seized 19 kilos of horsemeat, including 6 kilos of horse genitals, from two women arriving from Mongolia. The women claimed the genitals were for 'medicinal purposes'.

Drug mules around the world have been getting more imaginative. A woman was detained in China after it was found that her suitcase was partly made of cocaine – it contained 10 kilos of cocaine injections moulded into the body of the case.

In Malaga, the Spanish police's Operation Esplit found crooks smuggling cocaine in fake bananas made of resin. And a Bristol drug dealer was ordered to pay £500,000 in costs after trying to smuggle 1.2 kilos of cocaine in a Peppa Pig tea set.

Bottom-based smuggling remains popular. In Alabama, a man was charged with carrying a concealed weapon without a licence, promoting prison contraband and receiving stolen property, after a pistol fell out of his bottom while he was being booked into a jail for drunkenness. The pistol – which was unloaded – fell out after officers noticed the prisoner was walking 'strangely'. Limestone County Jail's sheriff, Mike Blakely, said, 'It happens.'

A man in Northern Ireland was given a suspended sentence for smuggling drugs into a prison in a Kinder Egg that he'd placed in his bottom; he had tried to squeeze two up there, but found he couldn't manage it.

SNAKES

We have had it with these mother-flipping snakes found on mother-flipping planes...

'Snake on a plane cancels Emirates flight to Dubai'
—BBC News, 9 January 2017

'Snake hitches free ride on Alaska flight'
—CBS News, 21 March 2017

'Stowaway snake flies from Brisbane to New Zealand on private jet'
—ABC News, 28 March 2017

'Huge python [in landing gear] at Rajiv Gandhi International Airport causes scare'
—*Deccan Chronicle*, 21 May 2017

'Tourist discovered at Bali Airport with a suitcase full of valuable snakes'
—*Bali Post*, 28 May 2017

'Snake on plane: Python rescued from [Indian] Air Force aircraft'
—*Times of India*, 5 July 2017

'Snakes seized at JFK after flying on plane from Hong Kong, customs official says'
—*amNewYork*, 11 July 2017

SOMALIA

Somalians elected their new president – a man called Mr Cheese – in an airport.

Most of Somalia, including the capital city and seat of government, lost the Internet for three weeks this year after a commercial ship accidentally cut an undersea cable. It cost the country's economy $10 million a day, equivalent to almost two thirds of its GDP.

Because of the risk posed by terror group Al-Shabaab, voting had to be held in one of the country's safest buildings – Mogadishu airport. Not only that, on the day itself a traffic ban was imposed throughout the capital. Major roads were sealed off and everyone had to walk to work.

The procedure was not exactly democratic: the only people who could vote were the country's 300 MPs, and they, in turn, had been chosen by just 14,000 tribal elders. The process was also extremely corrupt: investigators estimated that at least $20 million changed hands to buy people's votes.

The new president, Mohamed A. Mohamed, used to work in Buffalo, New York, where he had an office job at the New York State Department of Transportation. Sadly there appears to be no connection between Buffalo and his nickname, 'Mr Cheese' (he got the name Farmajo, derived from the Italian word 'formaggio', from his father, but it's not clear why). He was previously Somalia's prime minister in 2010, but was pushed out of office after a ear, and returned to his old job in New York, where his colleagues baked him a cake to welcome him back.

SPEECHES

Donald Trump's speeches have been turned into a book of poetry.

Bard of the Deal was edited by Hart Seely, whose previous work includes *Pieces of Intelligence: The Existential Poetry of Donald H. Rumsfeld*. Amazingly it wasn't the first anthology of Trumpian poems on the market: as far back as February 2016 a book called *Make Poetry Great Again* was available on Kindle in Norway.

Translators around the world have said it is very hard to translate the words of Donald Trump, because he doesn't speak in actual sentences. Bérengère Viennot told the French version of *Slate*, 'The poverty of his vocabulary is striking.' And interpreters in Japan were confronted with a tricky question: how to translate 'nut job' when Trump fired the FBI director James Comey. They settled on *henjin*, meaning 'eccentric', rather than *atama ga warui*, which means 'stupid', thinking that the latter was inappropriate for someone of Comey's stature.

According to a 2017 study of the 2016 US election, the six words most specific to Donald Trump were (in order) 'I', 'Very', 'Tremendous', 'Nobody', 'Going' and 'Mexico'.

A paper from Carnegie Mellon University concluded that the grammar in Trump's speeches is 'just below 6th grade level' (children aged eleven and under).

SPICER, SEAN

Sean Spicer stole a mini fridge from his junior staffers.

On the day that Spicer resigned as White House press secretary, the fridge theft story was revealed in an article by *Wall Street Journal* reporter Michael Bender. Bender reported that a month into the job, Spicer sent an aide to his junior employees to request that they hand over the mini fridge in their office. They refused to do so, and Spicer was subsequently spotted dragging it down the White House driveway towards his own office after they'd all gone home.

275

SOLAR ECLIPSE

James: This year there was a big eclipse, as the moon blocked the sun. But did you know that the moon also blocked the sun on Twitter?

Dan: No way.

James: It's true. NASA has two Twitter accounts: @NASAMoon and @NASASun, and the moon one tweeted: 'HA HA HA I've blocked the Sun! Make way for the Moon. #SolarEclipse2017.'

Anna: That's excellent work by whoever runs NASA's social media accounts. So, everyone's been talking about the effects on people, but a solar eclipse has a big effect on animals, too.

Andy: They go crazy, don't they?

Anna: They sure do. And this eclipse was no different. At Nashville Zoo the giraffes ran around their enclosures, the rhinos ran to their pens because they thought it was bedtime, and all the flamingos huddled together. But the zookeeper said that she wasn't sure if the eclipse was to blame, or if it was the 7,000 shrieking people who were watching the animals to see what would happen.

Dan: That's a good point. Apparently bats are affected as well – they fly out of their cave for the three minutes of the eclipse.

James: What happens when the sun comes out again?

Andy: I think they just go back, and think, 'That was a short night.'

Dan: The eclipse did confuse some humans, too. The Perot Museum in Texas was hosting a viewing party between 12 p.m. and 2 p.m. on August 21st, the day of the eclipse. But one mother replied, 'Most kids go back to school that day, can it be done on the weekend?'

Anna: Do you know what was the number one single on iTunes during the eclipse? 'Total Eclipse of the Heart', by Bonnie Tyler.

James: She should have sung 'Total Eclipse of a Seventy-Mile Strip of the Contiguous United States'.

Anna: I guess she couldn't make that scan. But Bonnie Tyler herself was actually on a cruise ship, singing the song. And as the song is normally four minutes, 28 seconds long, and because totality lasted for three minutes, they had to miss out one of the verses.

Andy: Well, one way they could have increased the length of the eclipse is by travelling east alongside the shadow. NASA sent some jets up into the sky to do that; and they saw the eclipse for more than seven minutes, so they could have listened to the original song and the shortened version as well.

James: Yes. I read about the NASA trip. One reason they went up there is because it's darker, and so they can see the sun's corona better. They wanted to make some measurements to work out why the outside of the sun is hotter than the inside.

Dan: That's amazing, but I wouldn't want to be on that plane. Surely you'd worry that it would tip over with everyone running to one side to watch the eclipse.

Andy: Knowing my luck, if I'd been on that plane I bet I'd have been stuck on an aisle seat and the guy next to me would have closed the blind and gone to sleep.

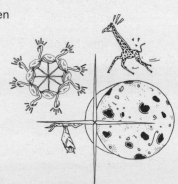

2017 wasn't the first time Spicer had worked for a president. He served under George W. Bush as the White House Easter Bunny, dressing up as a giant white rabbit as part of the administration's Easter celebrations, and spending the day entertaining children on the lawn.

Sean Spicer chews *and swallows* 35 sticks of cinnamon-flavoured gum every day before noon. He reassured the *Washington Post* that he'd spoken to his doctor about it and been told it wasn't a problem.

'Sean Spicer' is an anagram of 'I sense crap'.

Sean Spicer was an extremely visible presence, and often a figure of ridicule, throughout his time working for Trump. Before he quit the administration, Trump didn't let him meet the Pope, even though he knew that he really, really wanted to. Spicer is a devout Catholic, and meeting His Holiness was on his bucket list of things to achieve while he remained in office, according to a White House official who spoke to CNN.

It was assumed he'd join Trump for his papal audience in May, but when the moment came, the only people Trump invited to share the room with himself and Pope Francis were his wife, Melania, and his daughter Ivanka. And his son-in-law Jared Kushner. Plus Secretary of State Rex Tillerson and National Security Adviser H. R. McMaster, as well as Communications Advisor Hope Hicks, former bodyguard Keith Schiller, and White House Social Media Director Dan Scavino. One insider, when asked to comment on the fact that Spicer had been left off the list, said, 'Wow. That's all he ever wanted.' Even his harshest media critics expressed sympathy for him. *New York Times* reporter Glenn Thrush, who had a famously bad relationship with Spicer, tweeted that he found the slight 'incredibly depressing'. Happily, three months later, Spicer did get to to meet the Pope.

For things Sean Spicer definitely didn't do, *see* **Bushes, Hiding in**; for other people carrying white goods around, *see* **Marathon, London**.

SPIDERS ▶

Fifty-six new species of spider have been identified by dipping their genitals in gold.

A team of scientists discovered the species during a single 10-day expedition in Queensland. They included a tarantula the size of a human face with legs the width of a biro, and a spider with a colourful fold in its back that t can fan out like a peacock. One way scientists confirm that they're new species is by dipping their genitals (the spiders', not the researchers') in liquid gold, so that they show up more clearly under an electron microscope and can be compared better with the genitals of existing species. The team's arachnologist, Robert Raven, has arachnophobia and estimates he's been bitten 100 times.

In New York, another team of scientists observed spiders that walk like ants to avoid being eaten, because ants often bite, sting and are generally undesirable as food. The ant-jumper spider scuttles in a zigzag pattern, just like ants do, and lifts up its two front legs every few seconds to disguise them as antennae. In other leggy arthropod news, researchers discovered a species of sea spider* that breathes through its legs. In fact, one ecologist noted that 'they do all their business in their legs', storing their eggs, their guts and even their gonads there.

Members of the general public have also been encouraged to seek out spiders this year – specifically one of the world's deadliest, the funnel-web spider. A zoo in Australia asked people to stop killing funnel-webs and instead help to milk them. The Australian Reptile Park needs funnel-web spiders handed in by members of the public in order to manufacture antivenom. The zoo milks the creatures for their toxins, and then uses the resulting fluid to make the antidote by 'firing it through a very large rabbit', according to park ranger Mick Tate. The rabbit, while remaining unharmed, produces antibodies to fight the toxins, and these antibodies are then extracted and used to make the antivenom. It has saved 1,500 lives since it was introduced in 1981 but there's now a shortage, hence the zoo's request. In one interview, Tate tried to persuade listeners to help with the programme by pointing out that 'the potential to be badly envenomed or even die is certainly still there.' While this does explain the need for the project, it perhaps wasn't the best way to convince members of the public to get involved.

Spiders have eaten more meat than humans have this year. New research found that while humans eat around 400 million tonnes of meat and fish annually, spiders globally consume up to 800 million tonnes. Put another – more disturbing – way, if spiders ate human flesh they could devour the world's population (330 million tonnes) more than twice over every year.

*Not technically a spider.

The world's fastest man is going into fast food.

Scientists have found that when he sprints, Usain Bolt's left foot stays on the ground for 14 per cent longer than his right foot.

At the New Zealand World Masters Games, a 101-year-old woman won gold for the 100 metres in the 100-years-and-over category. She was the only entrant.

Usain Bolt, the greatest sprinter of all time, retired from the track at this year's World Championships in London, and he hopes to become a restaurant magnate. He announced that his 'Tracks and Records' brand, which opened its first outlet in Kingston, Jamaica in 2011, will come to the UK, and will be operating at 15 locations here by 2022.

The final year of Bolt's career didn't quite go according to plan, as he was beaten in his last 100-metre race by former drugs cheat Justin Gatlin, and he was also stripped of one of his gold medals from the 2008 Olympics. That wasn't Bolt's fault: Nesta Carter, one of Bolt's colleagues in the 4 x 100-metre relay, tested positive for the drug methylhexaneamine, which meant that Bolt's medal had to be returned – despite the fact that methylhexaneamine was not named as a banned substance until 2010.

Doping test technology usually lags a few years behind the production of performance-enhancing drugs, hence the reason you can be banned from the sport and stripped of your medals nearly 10 years after the event for taking drugs that weren't then explicitly illegal. But that doesn't stop experts from predicting what will be the next step. This year Lauren Petersen, a scientist who founded the Athlete Microbiome Project, predicted that athletes will soon be taking faeces as performance-enhancing drugs. There's a microbe found in the human body called prevotella, which helps your muscles to recover from hard work. Professional athletes have a lot more prevotella in their gut than average, so it's thought that in the future, you could take a pill that contains bacteria from, say, Usain Bolt's poo, and it will help you become a better sprinter.

STABLE

See **Strong**.

STICK INSECTS

A walking stick overtook its mum to become the world's biggest insect.

In 2014, the Insect Museum of West China found a 'walking stick' insect that was 62.4 centimetres long – a full 6 centimetres longer than the previous record-holder. The museum spent years looking for it, having been alerted to the existence of huge insects by locals. The insect was taken back to the museum, where it soon laid a number of eggs, all of which hatched into baby sticks, with even the smallest over 25 centimetres long soon after birth. This year, one of those insects has grown to overtake its mother as the world's biggest insect. It is as long as a human arm, and museum workers have found that its favourite food is strawberry jam.

Meanwhile, on an island just off the coast of Australia, another stick insect is making a comeback. The 'walking sausage' is 15 centimetres long and was once the world's rarest insect, but it is now creeping back from the edge of extinction. Officially called the Lord Howe stick insect, after the island on which it was first discovered, its other names include the land lobster and the tree lobster.

'artist's impression'

In 2001 it was rediscovered on an incredibly remote, rocky island near Lord Howe Island, almost a century after scientists thought it had died out. Researchers found just 24 individuals. They carefully removed two males and two females and have been diligently breeding them ever since. In 2006 there were 50 walking sausages. By 2008 there were 700. By 2012 the number had reached 9,000, and more are being bred in zoos all over the world. Asked whether they wanted the insects back, people on

Lord Howe Island were ambivalent, many saying that they are disgusting, and that they preferred the rats that almost drove the insect to extinction. In a recent island-wide referendum, however, the islanders voted 52 per cent in favour of wiping out the rats, thus giving them a clear and unequivocal mandate to press on with it.

STRIKES

Italian fishermen went on strike to protest against 'extremely intelligent' dolphins.

Researchers are working on a dolphin–human dictionary. So far it has only eight words for different whistles including 'bow wave ride' (when a dolphin rides the wave made by a boat) and 'seaweed'.

Fishermen on the Italian island of Lipari went on strike over the increasing problem of super-smart dolphins stealing all their fish. A spokesman said that 'they surround your boat, get in your nets, tear them apart and you are looking at 800 euros' damage in one night, apart from having no fish.' The average fishing boat used to bring in 11 kilos of squid a day; it now brings in just 1.5 kilos. The fishermen can't avoid the dolphins because they're clever enough to recognise the noise of the boats' engines and therefore follow them, waiting for their free food.

The fishermen's representative, Giuseppe Spinella, said, 'Every night in the sea, there is a war for survival… Let me be clear, we have nothing against the dolphins. But we must find a solution.' The fishermen's demands included a blockade, the removal of dolphins from fishing areas, the declaration of a state of natural disaster, and increased government subsidies.

One proposed solution was playing loud noises under-water to deter the dolphins. But this tactic didn't work for the Alaskan fishermen who were caught in a similar predicament this year. Frustrated that killer whales were stealing tens of thousands of pounds of fish from their fishing lines, they tried playing loud noises under the water, only to realise the orcas learned to associate he noise with the presence of food and treated it as a dinner bell.

Other strikers included the rat-catchers of Paris, who angrily claimed they hadn't been paid the bonus they'd been promised after carrying out a huge cull. Fifty of them – almost the whole city's pest-control unit – went and protested outside the city hall with a banner and a large dead rat. The mayor of Paris said she planned to send each of the city's rat-catchers a personalised thank-you note for their work.

STRONG

See **Stable**.

SURVEYS

Seventy-three per cent of Democrats said they would give up alcohol for life if it meant Donald Trump would be impeached.

So did 17 per cent of Republicans. The survey was carried out by Detox.net, which surveyed 1,013 men and women across the US on the question 'What would you give up for alcohol?' The study also found that 30 per cent of Republicans said they would give up alcohol for ever if it meant the media would stop writing hostile articles about the president. Worryingly, a further revelation was that 23 per cent of men wouldn't give up alcohol to halt climate change; and 7 per cent wouldn't quit alcohol even if it meant discovering the cure for cancer.

It wasn't the only interesting survey carried out this year (*see also* **YouGov**). Others that looked at how the new president has affected American lives included one by match.com that found the 2016 US election put people off dating. In January each year there's usually an uptick in people signing up to the site, but in 2017 there was a

A survey of 2,000 Londoners found that a fifth of them were scared to leave the office at lunchtime in case their colleagues judged them negatively.

decrease. Eighteen hundred people were polled to find out why, and 29 per cent of the website's liberal users said they felt less like dating since Trump's victory; 14 per cent of conservative users said the same.

Back in the UK, Premier Christian Radio conducted a survey asking listeners which politician they thought was most like Jesus Christ: 2 per cent said it was UKIP's Paul Nuttall; 20 per cent opted for Tim Farron, Jeremy Corbyn came second with 27 per cent, and Theresa May topped the poll with 45 per cent...

...which is slightly higher than the number of Americans who actually know who she is. A poll of 800 Americans found that 43 per cent could identify the current British prime minister; 36 per cent didn't know; 9 per cent answered Tony Blair; 4 per cent each thought it was Margaret Thatcher or Angela Merkel; and 2 per cent thought it was Jeremy Corbyn – the same proportion who thought it was Helen Mirren.

SWEARING*

Swearing improves your cycling.

Researchers at Keele University tested people's cycling speed and grip strength, initially as they said neutral words and then as they said swear words. People were 4 per cent better at cycling and 8 per cent better at gripping while they swore.

The subjects were allowed to pick their own swear words, which suggests that – according to another study – 'shite' would have been the one most commonly used. It's Britain's favourite swear word, based on an analysis of 500,000 online reviews. Australia's favourite is 'boob' and America's is 'sucks' according to the survey, which seems to have had a prudish definition of what constitutes a swear word. It also found that Brits are the sixth most bad-mouthed nationality, at least online, with one

Warning: may contain strong language

284

in every 1,000 words being a curse word. Cypriots topped the chart, using proportionally 10 times as many swear words as British reviewers.

Shites and boobs are technically banned now in all Sam Smith's pubs. Humphrey Smith, owner of the chain, implemented a 'no swearing' policy in all 300 of his establishments. Employees will feel under particular pressure to enforce this, given unconfirmed reports that Smith sometimes enters branches in disguise in order to check on his staff.

In which we learn …
Who floated the idea of re-sinking the Titanic, *why you*
might meet a rhino on a dating app, *why the Taliban*
are a bunch of tree-huggers, *where you'll find a singing*
dentist, *and more than you could ever want*
to know about Donald Trump.

A water fight broke out in the Taiwanese parliament.

On numerous occasions throughout the summer, the Chinese Nationalist Party (KMT) and Democratic Progressive Party (DPP) resorted to fisticuffs in the Taiwanese parliament. It wasn't just fists flying: water balloons, flour bombs, eggs and eventually chairs went through the air, too. The cause of these inflamed passions was a budget proposal for an infrastructure development programme.

Although this year's fights were particularly bad, it's not unusual for the Taiwanese legislature to descend into chaos. In 2004 a debate on military hardware purchases turned into a food fight; in 2007 one MP ended up in hospital as the two parties argued over control of the speaker's podium; and in 2006 an MP picked up a written proposal on transport links and shoved it in her mouth so it couldn't be read out – she eventually spat it out when opponents pulled her hair.

At least the fights weren't the parliament's only achievement: this year they voted to become the first Asian country to ban the consumption of dog and cat meat and the first to legalise gay marriage.

Taiwanese politician Tung Hsiang was buried in January in the southern city of Chiayi. His funeral was attended by family members, friends, and a funeral procession featuring a marching band, giant puppets and 50 pole dancers. Tung's son explained later that his father had appeared to him in a dream and said he wanted his funeral to be 'hilarious'.

TENNIS

Multiple Wimbledon matches were delayed because players had to change their underpants.

Wimbledon's dress code dictates that all visible clothes must be almost entirely white.* Officials were therefore unimpressed when they inspected the coloured pants worn by junior player Jurij Rodionov, and those of the top seeds in Junior Doubles, in front of spectators who were waiting for the matches to begin. They judged the garments illegal and requested that Wimbledon-issued,

* A coloured trim no wider than 1 centimetre around the cuffs and neck is permitted. But coloured underwear that's not initially visible, but becomes visible when the overgarments are dampened with sweat, is not allowed.

white replacement boxer shorts be promptly delivered to the courts. In the women's draw, Venus Williams's pink bra straps, which were visible during her first-round match, did not reappear after a mid-set rain delay. She didn't confirm whether she'd been told to remove the bra, understandably saying, 'I don't like talking about bras in press conferences. It's weird.'

Meanwhile, John McEnroe described as 'weird' the idea that he'd wear one-time arch-rival Björn Borg's underpants in bed. He does, however, wear them everywhere else. Borg has released a range of underwear, which McEnroe described as 'comfortable and stylish' and said he wears 99 per cent of the time.

It emerged this year that Wimbledon ballboys and ballgirls (BBGs) have to memorise a list of individual players' superstitions that hangs on the wall where they work. Rafael Nadal, for example, doesn't like walking on the white lines, so the BBGs have to avoid obstructing his path in a way that forces him to do so.

The strawberries at Wimbledon will soon be grown 30 metres beneath London. The All England Lawn Tennis Club plans to use a company called Growing Underground to produce its 62,000 pounds of tournament strawberries in future. Its farm is 178 steps down from Clapham Common tube station, in tunnels originally dug as air raid shelters in the Second World War.

TERRORISM

For staying safe in the South Pole, *see* **Antarctica**; for pretending to be bin Laden, *see* **Arrests, Human**; for a dead friend mistaken for anthrax, *see* **Ashes**; for the extremists defeated by wild pigs, *see* **Boar**; for terrorism-themed rip-offs, *see* **LEGO**; for an encounter with the mother of all bombs, *see* **MOAB**; for extremist threats to Mr Cheese, *see* **Somalia**; for the environmentally

oncerned radicals, *see* **Trees**; and for a country that can't
distinguish between journalists and terrorists, *see* **Turkey**.

THEFT

*tems stolen this year include a lunchbox, an anti-theft
dog and a stuffed chimpanzee in a top hat.*

Thefts went from the bizarre to the brazen to the bestial,
and included the following:

▶ Two men in Italy, posing as buyers, asked an art
dealer to bring a Rembrandt and a Renoir to a rented
space so they could negotiate a price for them. The
two paintings were worth about 27 million euros
combined. Once they'd agreed on a figure, the two
men left the room, claiming they were fetching a tray
of coffee. They haven't been seen since – and nor have
the paintings or the tray of coffee.

▶ A man broke into a taxidermy warehouse in London
and took £100,000 worth of stuffed animals. His haul
included a stuffed chimpanzee in a top hat, a stuffed
lion, a stuffed sloth, a stuffed giraffe, a stuffed penguin
and 13 other stuffed animals. The inanimate creatures
were all later recovered in Epping Forest, London.
Disregarding speculation that it was an attempt to
free the creatures and return them to their natural
environment, the court sentenced the perpetrator to
21 months' imprisonment.

▶ Police in Ripon, Yorkshire, confirmed they're investigating a spate of thefts of car bonnets, bumpers and
wheel arches in the area. They have warned residents
to be vigilant. No doubt they are on it, like a…

▶ A used car dealership in Fort Worth, Dallas, was
robbed so many times that the owner got a guard dog.
This didn't deter the robbers, who burgled the store
again, taking the guard dog with them.

- The owners of a jewellery store in Leeds were mugged shortly after closing up shop. Three men seized the bags they were carrying, believing they contained valuable jewellery. In fact, the contents amounted to a couple of sandwiches in some Tupperware containers.

- An Arizona man was arrested on suspicion of burglary after he tried to climb a fence, got his trousers caught, and was left hanging upside down with his pants around his ankles until police arrived. Nothing was lost but the man's dignity.

THEME PARKS

A Chinese theme park cancelled its sinking of the Titanic.

China is planning a theme park based entirely on footballer Lionel Messi. The Messi Experience Park will have 20 indoor and outdoor activities, to encourage young people in China to take up the sport.

The Chinese theme park Romandisea is currently building a 269-metre-long, life-size reconstruction of the *Titanic*,* including a ballroom, observation deck and first-class cabins for guests to stay in. It will be completely accurate: the head of the design team, Bruce Beveridge, said, 'We'll even have the correct urinals in the men's rooms.'

However, this year the park was forced to drop the idea of creating a simulated 'iceberg experience' for paying customers. The theme park's founder, Su Shaojun, had said he wanted people to experience the sinking: 'We will let people experience water coming in using sound and light effects ... They will think, "The water will drown me. I must escape for my life."'

But when relatives of the deceased made it clear that they were very unhappy about the idea, Su announced the replica sinking would not go ahead. The park later clarified that the replica would be 'respectful'. The daughter of one of the *Titanic*'s stewards said, 'I feel they could have replicated another liner – it's in poor taste.' One British Titanic Society member sympathised with the theme park, saying there had clearly been no intention to

*It's being built on the River Qi.

290

...use offence, and that most Chinese people only knew ...out the *Titanic* through the 1997 movie starring Leon-...do DiCaprio.

...eanwhile, in Japan, a theme park has started offering ... service where you can beat up bad guys. In Hirakata ...ark's 'new-style flash mobs', a pair of actors dressed like ...ugs will approach you and try to grab your boyfriend ...r girlfriend, at which point you can see them off and ...resumably impress your other half.

———— ▼ ————

The sacred Indian city of Mathura is planning a 'Krishna Land', a theme park like Disneyland but based on the Hindu god Krishna.

IES

Male Australian politicians have to wear ties at all times, unless they're wearing a safari suit.

The rule came to light this year, as parliaments around the world wondered if they should modernise and dispense with their formal dress.* The odd Australian regulation dates back to 1977 when a number of MPs decided that, due to the heat, they should be allowed to wear light, khaki-coloured clothes rather than a suit and tie. Back then, one safari-suit-wearing politician, Jack Melloy, was called a 'hippy' and told to leave the chamber, but the rules were changed and today any Aussie MP who doesn't want to wear a tie can choose the safari suit instead. Almost nobody does.

* After 300 years of wearing wigs in the House of Commons, clerks were told they could take them off. The change was approved partly to save money, partly to make the Commons less 'stuffy', and partly because clerks found them too itchy.

291

Donald Trump also commented on the subject, saying that he wanted people in the White House to be 'sharply dressed', with men wearing ties. The president famously wears his tie extremely long. It's not clear why, but Patrick Grant, creative director of the Savile Row tailors Norton & Sons, told the *Daily Mirror*: 'The way Trump's tie swings pendulously around his crotch is phallic and deeply suggestive.'

In Congress, where rules are stricter still and women are expected to wear long sleeves, more than 30 congresswomen on both sides of the aisle wore sleeveless dresses to protest, defending their 'right to bare arms'.

Ireland also looked into the dress code for the Dáil (lower house of parliament). A research paper looked at 40 parliaments around the world, and it emerged that 16 (including Portugal, Israel and the EU) had no rules, while 24 (including the UK, Spain and France) had strict regulations. In the end the Dáil did at least ban members from wearing slogans. Perhaps it should have banned ties, too: in December last year, Sinn Féin's Aengus Ó Snodaigh was making a speech on the serious topic of asbestos exposure, when he was continually interrupted by his own musical tie playing 'We Wish You a Merry Christmas' and 'Santa Claus Is Coming to Town'.

For Australian politicians with problematic foreign ties, *see* **Citizenship**.

TINDER

The last known male northern white rhino on the planet joined Tinder.

Confusingly named 'Sudan' but from neighbouring Kenya, his profile describes him as 'the most eligible bachelor in the world' and states, 'I don't mean to be too forward but the fate of my species literally depends on me.' Tinder uploaded the profile in a bid to raise £7 million for conservation and fertility treatments for white rhinos. Swiping right on him automatically donates funds towards assisted reproductive techniques for Sudan, since attempts to get him to mate have failed.

While some are swiping to help an endangered rhino, other Tinder users are not swiping at all – instead hiring someone to do the work for them. Fantastic Services is a company that specialises in cleaning and pest control, but has branched out into dating. Its Dating Debugging Service charges £30 for a consultation, after which they take over your Tinder profile and weed out undesirable matches by swiping left or right on 500 people, based on what you've told them about yourself. It costs £15 for every subsequent 500 swipes.

Tinder got a new rival when a man called Shed Simove set up an app called Shinder on which he's the only male. The app's tagline is 'Quality, Not Quantity'. Other men can theoretically sign up, but if they do they are greeted with a message informing them about Shed's hetero-sexuality, and cannot contact any women. Shed received a notice of threatened opposition from Tinder, which thought he was infringing its trademark. He also got a letter from the manufacturer Schindler requesting that he avoid making any lifts or escalators.

TOILET PAPER, USED

Every month for the last 20 years, someone has been mailing Gary Lineker a single sheet of used toilet paper.

The ex-footballer has no idea who is doing it. News of the dirty poo-mailer only emerged when cricket commentator Jonathan Agnew sent the tweet 'Can I ask the charming individual who for 10 years has sent me a soiled piece of toilet paper every Test [to] now address the envelope correctly?' His complaint was that the anonymous mailer has not been including Agnew's new MBE honour when addressing the envelope. Lineker then got in touch with Agnew to compare experiences: both, apparently, are receiving their anonymous sheets from someone in Bath.

While the identity of that particular culprit remains a mystery, Italian police officers had more luck in tracking down two other poo criminals who, for the last two years had been mailing threatening letters that often included sheets of excrement-stained toilet paper to the directors of a zoo, as well as to politicians and 'thousands of celebrities'. Police managed to analyse the handwriting on the envelopes, worked out that the perpetrators were a 71-year-old former policeman and his partner, and swooped in to make their bust as the offender was dropping one of his poo-mails into a postbox. Back at his house, police discovered 110 more envelopes pre-packed and ready to go.

TOILETS

For flushing away your loved ones, *see* **Ashes**; for ancient temple bathroom robots, *see* **Facial Recognition**; for Martian loos, *see* **IKEA**; for Don's Johns, *see* **Inauguration**; for a running toilet roll, *see* **Marathon, London**; for the students too embarrassed to defecate, *see* **Music**; for the Russian navy's faulty facilities, *see* **Queen Elizabeth, HMS**; for running out of loo roll, *see* **Shrinkflation**; for toilet-paper-hoarding politicians, *see* **Venezuela**; and for flushing in the night, *see* **YouGov**.

TRADEMARKS

Mother Teresa's signature look was trademarked by her nuns.

The saint's iconic blue-rimmed and white cotton sari was successfully trademarked on behalf of her holy order, the Missionaries of Charity, by their lawyer, Biswajit Sarkar.

wenty years ago, Sarkar also trademarked Mother
eresa's name.

he move comes after the nuns complained that busi-
esses were still using Mother Teresa's image for
ommercial gain. A school was being run in her name in
Nepal; a priest raising funds in Romania used her order's
ame; and shops near the mission's headquarters in
Kolkata told customers that any proceeds from sales
of Mother Teresa memorabilia would be donated to the
order (which they weren't). Even a cooperative bank in
ndia decided to name itself after her.

Sarkar said he would take 'severe' legal action against
anyone using the design without permission, and that
his immediate plan was to get Amazon India to remove
Mother Teresa children's costumes from sale.

Mother Teresa wasn't the only celebrity whose image was
the subject of a legal decision this year: in America Kylie
Minogue and Kylie Jenner fought over the name Kylie.
Jenner wanted to trademark it in the US, but Minogue
said it would be damaging to her brand and confuse
people because she already owns various Kylie-themed
trademarks in the US, including 'Kylie Minogue Darling'
(the name of her perfume), 'Lucky – the Kylie Minogue
musical', 'Kylie Minogue' and 'kylie.com'. Minogue's
lawyers described their client as an 'internationally
renowned performing artist, humanitarian and breast
cancer activist' and Jenner as a 'secondary reality television personality'.

A trademark ruling in the chocolate industry has cleared the way for copy KitKats. Nestlé tried to trademark the shape of a KitKat in the UK, but Cadbury argued there was nothing distinctive about it and that it should therefore be allowed to use the same shape. After months of deliberating, a 16,000-word ruling found in favour of Cadbury.

TREES

The former prime minister of Georgia has been digging up famous trees and replanting them in his garden.

Explaining that 'giant trees are my entertainment',
Bidzina Ivanishvili searches out the largest, rarest and
oldest ones in the country, digs them up, loads them

●

The 650-year-old Oak Józef, whose trunk concealed a Jewish family hiding from the Nazis during the Second World War, and which has appeared on Polish banknotes, was named 'European Tree of the Year'. It narrowly beat the Brimmon Oak in Powys, whose claim to fame is that it's now *not* going to be cut down to make way for a bypass.

A Cook Islander was crowned the first ever world champion coconut tree climber. The man scaled an 8-metre tree in 5.62 seconds, just one 100th of a second ahead of the second-place contestant.

upright on to trucks and boats, and brings them to his own personal arboretum. He reimburses the trees' previous owners, in one case swapping a eucalyptus for a computer. Sometimes the logistics cause problems: on one occasion a magnolia tree he was transporting got entangled in a eucalyptus growing on the verge, meaning the whole road had to be closed.

Trees are being used to fight climate change and pollution all over the world. In 2016, 800,000 volunteers in India planted 50 million trees in 24 hours as part of the country's Paris Accord commitment. They beat the previous tree-planting record by more than 49 million. This year, they did better still, managing 66 million trees in a single day.

China is planning to build a city of skyscrapers completely covered in trees to form 'vertical forests' that will absorb 9,000 tonnes of carbon dioxide and generate 800 tonnes of oxygen a year. In more experimental mode, researchers at Bristol University started pumping a forest full of carbon dioxide in a 10-year project to establish the extent to which plants can suck CO_2 out of the atmosphere.

Even the Taliban are doing their bit. The Islamic fundamentalists broke their usual protocol to release a rare public statement in February encouraging Afghans to plant more trees. The message was delivered in the name of the Taliban leader, Haibatullah Akhundzada, who said the undertaking would benefit the Earth and please Allah.

Some tree-planting has its drawbacks. In Aberdeenshire a council had to apologise after planting an orchard's worth of trees all over a community football pitch. A council spokesperson said, 'It would seem that we were barking up the wrong tree with plans for this site.'

TRUDEAU, JUSTIN

Canadian diplomats were told to stop using cardboard cut-outs of the Prime Minister at parties.

Since 2016, Canadian diplomats across the USA have ordered 14 life-size cardboard cut-outs of Prime Minister Justin Trudeau to display at events. These have proved very popular, but when the opposition party found that 10 consulates had spent a total of $1,900 (£1,100) on them it complained, saying the whole thing was a vanity project. The Global Affairs department quickly stepped in, asking embassies to stop using them. Opposition MP John Brassard said a two-dimensional cut-out was 'a perfect metaphor for everything that Justin Trudeau represents'. The replica Trudeaus have gone into storage.

The cut-outs were cheap compared to Canada's birthday expenditure. Canada150, the 150-year commemoration of Canadian independence, featured celebrations that included a giant dreamcatcher, giant plant sculptures, a giant flag, a giant puppet show, a giant sweater for a statue of a cow, and a giant game of snakes and ladders. The snakes and ladders cost $416,000 (£246,000), or 3,065 cardboard Justin Trudeaus.

Friends star Matthew Perry revealed that he beat up Trudeau when they were at school together. Trudeau – who once knocked out an opposition politician in a charity boxing match – offered Perry a rematch. Perry turned down the offer, saying it was unfair given that Trudeau has access to an army.

For a blatant exaggeration of size, *see* **Advertising**; for his impact on US stock prices, *see* **Amazon**; for the only app on Trump's phone, *see* **Apps**; for the many possible border-wall designs, *see* **Border Wall**; for denials of global warming, *see* **Climate Change**; for Twitterstorms over made-up words, *see* **Covfefe**; for Twitter-related synonyms, *see* **Dickheads**; for his effect on American marriages, *see* **Divorce**; for Trump's first name, *see* **Donalds**; for his impact on the safety of the planet, *see* **Doomsday**; for his new museum exhibit, *see* **Failures**; for how he spends too much of his time, *see* **Golf**; for him driving Americans to New Zealand, *see* **Immigration**; for more blatant exaggeration, *see* **Inauguration**; for his coinage of a phrase first recorded in 1819, *see* **Inventions**; for an unlikely fan of his book, *see* **Korea, North**; for more than 133 court cases, *see* **Lawsuits, Trump's 134**; for Trump's catchphrase on an anus, *see* **MAGA**; for confusing a prime minister with a glamour model, *see* **May, Theresa**; for confusing other world leaders with each other, *see* **Mix-Ups**; for his legal tussle over the iTrump, *see* **Music**; for giving everyone his number, *see* **Phones**; for a suspiciously familiar inauguration cake, *see* **Plagiarism**; for a relatively successful trip to Saudi Arabia, *see* **Protests, Non-Dirty**; for his alleged Russian ties, *see* **Russia Investigation**; for a book of his poetry, *see* **Speeches**; for what people would give up to get him impeached, *see* **Surveys**; for his pendulously phallic clothes, *see* **Ties**; for a button with its own room, *see* **Trump Tower**; if you actually *are* Donald Trump and you're reading this, *don't see* **Unpopular**; for yak and squirrel hair on Trump's head, *see* **Waxworks**; for literal fake news, *see* **White House, Winter**; for being cursed, *see* **Witchcraft**; for getting a history lesson, *see* **Xi Jinping**; for his Hogwarts house, *see* **YouGov**; for another leader who started on *The Apprentice*, *see* **You're Fired!**; and for the one person he actually could beat in the 2020 election, see **Zuckerberg, Mark**.

America's nuclear button got its own million-dollar flat in New York.

This year the White House Military Office rented an entire apartment in Trump Tower for the nuclear 'football' – the black satchel containing the device that can launch a thermonuclear strike – along with its human handlers. When the lease was eventually published, it was discovered that the nuclear button and its support team will have access to the privately owned flat in Trump Tower for at least 18 months, at a cost of $2.39 million ($130,000 a month).

US government rules dictate that the president has to have vital services – like the nuclear button – near him at all times wherever he goes. So it seemed perfectly reasonable, in theory at least, that the button should be given space in Trump's New York base. The only problem was that for the first seven months of his presidency Trump didn't spend a single night in the tower, meaning the button didn't visit until he did in August.

Trump's skyscrapers have become slightly less popular since the president's inauguration (*see* **Advertising**). Protests at various Trump buildings included a mass mooning of the Trump Tower Chicago by hundreds of protesters, dubbed the 'Rump Against Trump'.

One Direction's Liam Payne revealed that Donald Trump once kicked the band out of the Trump Tower Hotel in New York for refusing to meet his daughter, despite the fact that their manager only turned down the request because they were asleep at the time.

Scientists in Greenland are building underground labs using 40-metre-long balloons.

Jørgen Peder Steffensen, Professor of Glaciology at the University of Copenhagen, has been testing his unique lab-building method since 2012, and this year scientists adopted the technique for the first time. Steffensen says it's like making a hot dog. First a trench is dug out using

Plans were announced
for a tunnel under
Stonehenge, to ease
traffic gridlock and
remove the sight and
sound of cars from
the site. The tunnel's
intended route had to
be altered by 50 metres
after archaeologists
pointed out that as it
was planned, the head-
lights of cars emerging
from it would impede
the view of the sun on
the winter solstice, thus
defeating the object of
building the tunnel in
the first place.

a snow blower (he calls this the 'bun'), then a balloon is placed inside and inflated (the hot dog). Once fully inflated it is completely covered in snow (the condiments). Left for a few days, the snow hardens sufficiently to function as a roof. The balloon is then deflated and the engineers are left with a giant cylindrical tunnel.

So far the new technique has been a massive success, creating tunnels that are more structurally sound and longer lasting than any previous method. As a result, other polar research groups are looking into using it. A team in Antarctica has ordered two balloons and Steffensen is asking Greenland's parliament for permission to use the balloons to make ice hotels.

Another tunnel innovation this year came from Norway, where engineers solved the problem of navigating the notoriously dangerous waters of the Stad peninsula. It suffers from the highest winds in the country and has always been a nightmare for sailors (even the Vikings weren't up for crossing it, choosing instead to lift their ships out of the sea and carry them across land). After centuries of debate, Norway has decided to drill through the peninsula to build the world's first tunnel for ships.

The single-lane Stad tunnel will be 1.7 kilometres long, will cost $235 million to build, and will be able to accommodate ships weighing up to 16,000 tonnes. It will also feature emergency phones on the walls, just in case a ship gets stuck and need to call for help.

TURKEY

Turkey's president won a vote by offering his people laser hair removal.

In April, Turkey held a referendum over whether to grant its president, Recep Tayyip Erdoğan, unprecedented new powers. As part of the campaign to persuade people to vote 'yes', Erdoğan used his powers under the country's state of emergency to sign a decree allowing beauticians to carry out laser hair removal. (Previously, only medical staff could carry out the procedure.) He announced the move at a rally called 'For a beautiful Turkey, of course, yes'. The move was designed to support the industry, create jobs – and win votes. His campaign was criticised by a human rights organisation for lacking the 'fundamental freedoms' of democracy, but despite this, Erdoğan won his sweeping new powers with 51.4 per cent of the vote.

In the lead-up to the referendum, public pressure to vote 'yes' and grant Erdoğan his new powers was so great that the word 'no' – *hayir*, in Turkish – became taboo. This meant that, among other things, a group of anti-smoking leaflets was withdrawn by the Ministry of Health because they had the word 'no' on them in capital letters, and a TV company refused to screen the Oscar-nominated Chilean film *No*.* Ordinary Turks even altered their standard greeting 'have a good Friday' (*hayirli cuma*), because the first part of it sounds the same as 'no', even though it's a completely different word.

Since the attempted coup of 2016, Erdoğan's regime has sacked and locked up thousands of government employees, banned Wikipedia (*see* **Bans**) and jailed over

The mayor of Ankara demanded an investigation into an earthquake off the Turkish coast, believing it could have been artificially created by dark foreign powers trying to destroy the Turkish economy.

* Though it probably would have been banned anyway, since it's about a government losing a referendum.

170 journalists. President Erdoğan helpfully clarified that only two of the detainees had had yellow press cards, and that the rest were terrorists – although he conveniently forgot that critical journalists are often denied press cards in the first place.

TURKMENISTAN

Turkmenistan re-elected a singing dentist.

President Gurbanguly Berdymukhamedov, a former dentist, won 98 per cent of the vote in Turkmenistan's presidential election. The other eight candidates had to share 2 per cent of the electorate between them. He will be pleased – in 2012 he managed only 97 per cent.

Berdymukhamedov has a unique political style. During the campaign he sang a self-penned song to gas workers, gave desert herdsmen free TVs and consistently suppressed free journalism.

He's also a celebrated jockey and, according to state media reports, managed to win Turkmenistan's national horse race this year. The race was run on Turkmen Horse Day, just before the national horse beauty contest, a tradition that Berdymukhamedov started in 2011. And it's not the only horse-related award in Turkmenistan this year: a 40-metre-tall monument erected in the Turkmen capital Ashgabat was awarded a world record for largest sculpture of a horse's head.

The head was made to celebrate the 2017 Asian Indoor and Martial Arts Games, which took place in Ashgabat in September. To celebrate the countdown to the games, Ashgabat went car-free for a day in August. Other than public transport, the only way to get around was by bicycle or on foot, in temperatures of 40°C. Many residents of the capital weren't happy, but by way of a compromise Berdymukhamedov brought one of the country's biggest holidays forward, so that most people would

Berdymukhamedov made an anti-ISIS propaganda video in August that showed him wearing full combat gear and a pair of sunglasses while throwing knives, firing an automatic rifle and commanding air strikes. The aim was to intimidate terrorists, but it led to ridicule from his own people, who nicknamed him 'The Turkmenator'.

get a day off work and could stay home and celebrate National Melon Day.

TWEETS

Two Impassioned sentiments smashed Twitter records this year.

New record for most 'liked' Tweet:

> 'No one is born hating another person because of the color of his skin or his background or his religion…'
> —Barack Obama in response to the deadly clash in Charlottesville between white nationalists and anti-Nazi protesters.

New record for most retweeted Tweet:

> 'Help me please, a man needs his nuggs'
> —16-year-old Carter Wilkerson from Nevada, trying to get enough retweets to qualify for free chicken nuggets for a year.

TWITTER

For the only app on the president's phone, *see* **Apps**; for the word that melted the Internet, *see* **Covfefe**; for redirections to Donald Trump, *see* **Dickheads**; for TwitterPeek, *see* **Failures**; for an unintelligent tweet by an intelligence agency, *see* **Hacking**; for a tweeting recluse, *see* **Hermits**; for how Charlotte Church RSVPs, *see* **Inauguration**; for an ill-advised tweet by a movie director, *see* **Lawsuits, Non-Trump**; for the wrong Steve Bannon, *see* **Mix-Ups**; for a response to a controversial advert, *see* **Pepsi**; and for a tweeting jailbird, *see* **Punishments**.

In which we learn…
Why China's cab drivers turned into zombies, who's turning
ladybirds into umbrellas, what happens in and around
Uranus, how to produce very expensive urine, and
the fate of an enormous rabbit called Simon.

The CEO of Uber got a one-star passenger rating from one of his drivers.

Travis Kalanick, who resigned as CEO in June, got the poor review in February after getting into a fight with the driver in the back of his car. The driver complained that Kalanick was running the company badly and that he himself was losing money because of it. Kalanick retaliated by saying, 'Some people don't like to take responsibility for their own shit, they blame everything in their life on somebody else,' and stormed out, slamming the car door.

Uber also faced gender image problems this year, when a blog written by a former female employee revealed, among other allegations of sexism, that all the men in her unit had got free leather jackets, but none of the women had. The justification offered by the company was that there were so few women – six in the department, compared to 120 men – that it had proved impossible to get a bulk discount on the women's jackets. Her manager went on to explain that it was a sign of equality that he hadn't given women preferential treatment by spending more money on their individual jackets than he had on the men's. Kalanick has said that Uber improves his dating prospects, and as a result he has nicknamed the company 'Boober'.

Conversely, it was revealed that some male Uber managers pretend to be women. They sign off with fake female names when messaging their drivers because they've found that staff are more likely to agree to take on a particular job if they're being asked by a woman. The drivers themselves aren't beyond resorting to deception. In China, some of them changed their profile photos to ghost and zombie images so that when potential passengers saw their picture they would cancel the ride they'd just booked, thus earning the driver the cancellation fee.

A town in Canada has paid Uber to provide subsidised taxi journeys for its citizens because it's cheaper and easier than setting up a bus route.

A French man took Uber to court after his wife discovered he had been using it to visit his mistress. The app kept sending notifications to her phone after he used it to request a driver.

The company often stated the fact that Travis Kalanick has the world's second-highest Wii Tennis rating. He was playing on a friend's Wii (the friend was the original source for the story), when he navigated to the leaderboard to show that he was the joint-second-best player in the world. The problem with the story is that there's no such game as 'Wii Tennis' – tennis is just one of the options in the Wii Sports game – and at the time Wii Sports didn't keep a list of the highest scores in the world.

UMBRELLAS

A Chinese umbrella-sharing start-up lost all of its 300,000 umbrellas.

The company's founder, Zhao Shuping, set up the firm after raising $1.5 million in funding, but found that once people had paid a $2.79 fee to sign up, they just kept the umbrellas for themselves, and he had no way of tracking where they'd gone.*

Undeterred, the company is going to make another 30 million umbrellas available for rent across the country by the end of the year – this time with GPS installed.

Elsewhere, a Japanese scientist claimed his published paper on ladybird wings could lead to the first change in umbrella design for 1,000 years – the doesn't-blow-inside-out-on-a-windy-day umbrella.

* This is not the first time this has happened. The month before, another Chinese firm, Wukong Bicycles, which shared bikes, closed down after 90 per cent of its bikes disappeared. The founder says he now prefers to think of it as 'a charity project'.

Until now, ladybird wings have been a mystery to scientists, who couldn't work out how they fit their wings into their shells. However, Kazuya Saito, an assistant professor at the University of Tokyo's Institute of Industrial Science, has worked out that it's thanks to a complex, origami-like folding mechanism. Like a ladybird wing, the new umbrella will have only one moving part, preventing it from turning inside out at the joints – a fundamental flaw of existing brollies.

her possible applications for the research include
croscopic medical instruments, satellites, aircraft
ngs and fans.

wasn't the only exciting umbrella news announced this
ar. A 'smart umbrella' has been invented that knows
hen it is going to rain, and flashes to let you know.
ou can also find it with your phone if it's lost – and,
onversely, activate a 'phone-finder' mode in the brolly
y shaking it.

NITED AIRLINES

*he day after dragging a doctor off one of their flights,
nited Airlines' share price fell by $250 million – enough
o fly a 747 around the world 1,300 times.*

nited made global headlines when security staff dragged
9-year-old doctor David Dao off a flight in April, breaking
is nose and knocking out two of his front teeth. They
pologised and compensated him.

On the same day that Dr Dao was being dragged off his
light, a passenger on another flight being operated for
United claimed that she was forced to pee into a cup.
Nicole Harper told staff she had an overactive bladder
and she 'would either need to use the restroom or pee
in a cup'. She said the attendants took her literally and
gave her two cups. United stated, 'At no point ... did flight
attendants suggest that Ms Harper use cups instead of
the lavatory.'

United also got into trouble over a giant rabbit called
Simon. Simon was owned by former *Playboy* model
Annette Edwards, from Worcestershire. He was meant
to travel from London to the Iowa State Fair, but was
pronounced dead on arrival at (ironically) Chicago's
O'Hare Airport. United denied the rabbit had been
accidentally locked in a freezer. Simon was the son of
the world's largest rabbit, Darius.* His owner's lawyer

** Edwards has owned
the world's biggest
rabbit since 2008,
holding the record
with various different
bunnies. She says the
secret to breeding large
rabbits is to make
sure they have large
parents.*

UK GENERAL ELECTION

Anna: So, you have to pay £500 to stand in a UK election, but did you guys know that all of the deposits lost in this election went to the Queen?

Andy: No, I didn't know that.

Anna: It's true. I was reading the guidelines given to all the electoral officers, and they say, 'If a candidate does not poll more than 5 per cent of the total number of valid votes cast, their deposit will be forfeited. You must send any forfeited deposits to Her Majesty.'

James: And there were a lot of deposits lost. UKIP lost £168,500 in deposits. The Lib Dems lost £187,500 and the Greens lost £227,500. I worked out that for that amount of money, the Greens could have bought a thousand solar panels, the Lib Dems could have bought 6,700 pairs of socks and sandals, and UKIP could have bought half a million little Union Jack flags.

Andy: No wonder the Queen's so rich. It's all that mini-Union-Jack money.

Anna: Indeed. But, of course, this is all to stop frivolous candidates, and I think we can all agree that it does the job extremely well.

Dan: It sure does. I was very disappointed to read, for instance, that there was only one party which had any kind of policy about yetis in this election.

Andy: How did you manage to raise the deposit, Dan?

Dan: Actually it's a party that goes by many names, including the 'Bus-pass Elvis Party', the 'Elvis Defence League' and the

'Grumpy old Elvis Party'. This year they were the 'Elvis and the Yeti Himalayan Preservation Party'.

James: I've heard of these guys. Isn't the leader called Lord Biro?

Dan: That's right. And he promised to deal with the threat that North Korea might fire missiles towards Europe.

Anna: Very sensible.

Dan: But it was mainly because those missiles would have to fly over Tibet and they might accidentally hit the Yeti.

James: But the big character of this election was the one and only Lord Buckethead, wasn't he? He ran against the Prime Minister, and he – or someone called Lord Buckethead – has been running in elections since 1987, when he promised to destroy Birmingham and replace it with a Star Base.

Dan: He tweeted after the election that he received 249 votes, which he called 'A new Buckethead record'.

Anna: You had to feel sorry for Theresa May, didn't you? She was already having a bad night, but then she had to share a stage with Buckethead. And also a guy dressed like Elmo.

Andy: Elmo only got three votes. Buckethead absolutely mopped the floor with him.

James: Well it could have been worse for May. Tim Farron had to share a stage with a fish finger.

Dan: That's right. A guy known as Mr Fish Finger. His costume came about after someone on Twitter called @SkipLicker did a poll asking who people trusted most, Tim Farron or a fish finger. And the fish finger got 95 per cent of the votes.

said Simon might have one day outgrown even his father. United placed a 'temporary restriction on large rabbits' and paid Ms Edwards a substantial settlement.

UNITED STATES OF AMERICA

For keeping people out, *see* **Border Wall**; for drive-through drugs, *see* **Cannabis**; for a C-grade student who changed the constitution, *see* **Constitution, US**; for babies with unfortunate names, *see* **Donalds**; for the US embassy that aroused suspicion, *see* **Fakes**; for Americans trying to escape, *see* **Immigration**; for what the birth of America has to do with West Sussex, *see* **Independence**; for France's involvement in American independence, *see* **Irony**; for a patriotic anus, *see* **MAGA**; for an American president who doesn't know the name of Britain's prime minister, *see* **May, Theresa**; for a Miss USA who became an atomic bombshell, *see* **Nuclear Power Plants**; for the assassination of JFK, *see* **Putin, Vladimir**; for American non-presidents who don't know the name of Britain's prime minister, *see* **Surveys**; for keeping other people out, *see* **Visas**; for shipping mosquitoes in, *see* **Zika**; for visiting every single state, *see* **Zuckerberg**.

UNPOPULAR

For the first time in history, the percentage of Americans who approved of their president was lower than the percentage of Americans who were obese.

Trump has found himself with an approval rating of between 35 and 40 per cent throughout most of his tenure so far. But after he failed to specifically condemn white nationalists who marched in Charlottesville, this fell to 34 per cent in a survey by Gallup, marginally lower than the 35 per cent of Americans who are obese, according to the Centers for Disease Control and Prevention.

poll by Connecticut University in May that asked
registered voters to describe Trump in one word found
that the top answers were 'idiot', 'incompetent' and 'liar' –
followed by 'leader', 'unqualified', and in sixth place,
president'.

Shoppers in Leeds, meanwhile, were given the chance to
punch Donald Trump in the face when an exercise store,
Predator Nutrition, set up a punchbag dressed as the
president. Nine out of ten people chose to punch him,
while one in ten kissed him. The store said, 'The event
was a huge success and we are now looking into the
possibility of recreating it with Kim Jong-un.'

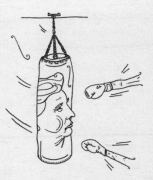

URANUS

Uranus opens up a couple of times a day, allowing wind through.

That's the finding of some new research by Georgia
Institute of Technology. It looked at the magnetic field
of the planet, and found that it flips every day as Uranus
rotates. When it flips, it opens, allowing the solar wind
to enter its atmosphere for a brief amount of time, before
closing and deflecting the particles away again.

The next thing scientists want to do is probe Uranus. This
year, NASA outlined plans to do so by 2036. The hope is
that scientists might be able to measure exactly what it is
made of, and figure out how Uranus works.

It was discovered this year that Uranus smells of farts.
Actually, generally speaking, Uranus is odour-free; it's so
cold there that gases can't really waft around. But the
smelliest chemicals there are hydrogen sulphide and
ammonia, and if the temperature rises enough, they can
form clouds that smell like rotten eggs.

This year's Glastonbury Festival was partly powered by urine.

Residents of Avebury said tourists were urinating on the village's 5,000-year-old stone circle because the public loos close too early.

A Chicago man put 'liquid faeces' under his neighbours' door to try to quieten them down. He'd previously tried urine, but that didn't work, so he told a court that he 'had to step it up'.

A special urinal, designed to harvest energy with a 'microbial fuel stack', took in about 1,000 litres of urine a day from festivalgoers. The urine deposited was kept and fed to bacteria that turned it into electricity, which was then used to power the festival's electronic display boards.

As a result of the complex legal permissions needed, only people over the age of 18 were allowed to use the urinal. Signs outside read: 'By using this urinal you are consenting for your urine to be used to create electricity. If you do use the urinal in error, you will be unable to remove your urine.'

Elsewhere:

▶ Scientists at Germany's aerospace centre announced they were growing tomatoes in tanks full of urine, a technique they hope could one day be used in space.

▶ Indiana banned the sale of synthetic urine, to make it harder for workers to cheat on drug tests. (Until recently, anyone who wanted to get around a drug test could splash out and buy 85ml of highly convincing fake urine for $30.)

▶ The Australian Medical Association's president said that multivitamins are so useless that they generally pass straight through the body, meaning that most people who take them just end up with 'very expensive urine'. AMA chief Michael Gannon said, 'You're pissing the money down the toilet for no benefit.'

In which we learn …
Who wants Prince Philip to bless their bananas, the fate of
Afghanistan's all-girl teenage robot squad, who took
their clothes off on a holy volcano, and what happens
when two male vultures love each other very much.

VAGINA, THINGS NOT TO PUT IN YOUR

See **Glitter, Ozone, Wasps.**

VANUATU

The residents of a Vanuatu island were devastated to learn of Prince Philip's retirement. They'd been patiently waiting five decades for him to visit.

* When Prince Philip announced he was retiring, British mathematician Sir Michael Atiyah said to him, 'I'm sorry to hear you're standing down.' Philip replied, 'Well, I can't stand up much longer.'

At the age of 96, the Duke of Edinburgh announced he was retiring, which means he will no longer be making any state visits.* This has upset the Kastom people of Tanna, a small island in Vanuatu, because they believe Philip is a god. In their view, a visit from him would cure all their diseases and fix their food shortages (every morning they pray to him and ask him to bless their bananas).

Philip learned he was a god in 1974, and acknowledged the honour by sending the village a signed photo of himself. In return the Kastom sent him a traditional pig-killing club. Philip then sent another photo of himself holding the club.

Had Philip ever visited Tanna, the Queen would undoubtedly have been advised not to join him. According to a biography of Philip by Tim Heald, were the Queen ever to witness him publicly drinking kava, the local brew, local etiquette dictates that she would have to be instantly executed by a single blow to the head with a vegetable root.

VENEZUELA

An actor known as Venezuela's James Bond tried to overthrow the government in a hijacked helicopter.

In June, a helicopter flew low over Venezuela's supreme court and the pilot fired shots and threw grenades at the building. Nobody was hurt, but it was quite a scene. Julio Borges, president of the opposition-led assembly, said, 'It seems like a movie.' And it turns out that he was closer to the truth than he thought. The man who flew the helicopter is called Oscar Pérez, who, as well as being a former policeman, activist and helicopter pilot, is also an actor. Perez starred in the 2015 action film *Suspended Death* in which he jumped out of a plane with a large dog strapped to his chest and took on bazooka-wielding kidnappers. A magazine article from the time referred to him as 'Venezuela's James Bond'.

Times are hard in Venezuela. The country has the world's largest oil reserves (it overtook Saudi Arabia last year), but the fall in the price of oil and severe mismanagement by the president, Nicolás Maduro,* has meant that the economy has collapsed. A thousand dollars bought in local currency when Maduro was elected in 2013 is worth just $3 today. Even though Venezuela upped its minimum wage by 50 per cent this year, due to runaway inflation it's effectively a pay cut of 17 per cent.

Maduro tried to give himself near-dictatorial powers, claiming that it was necessary in order to provide stability, so the people protested, taking to the streets for much of the year. Protesters threw both Molotov cocktails and jars full of faeces that they nicknamed 'poopootov cocktails'.

Venezuelan police arrested brownie and croissant bakers in an effort to tackle food shortages. The law now says that bakers need to make a minimum amount of bread in order to ensure food for the people, and cannot waste the ingredients on higher-priced treats.

* Maduro blames US interference. He also blames opposition leaders, for conspiring to cause poverty – accusing them, among other things, of hoarding toilet paper so ordinary people face shortages.

VIDEO GAMES

For one that doesn't exist, *see* **Bans**; for a virtual political campaign, *see* **French Presidential Election**; for putting them in your mouth, *see* **Nintendo**; for a dubious leader-board claim, *see* **Uber**; and for how sex is incompatible with gaming, *see* **Xbox**.

VISAS ▶

A summit on sustainability in Africa took place without any delegates from Africa.

A week after South Sudan's president promised 'unimpeded access' to aid workers to encourage them to come and fight the famine there, he increased the cost of aid workers' visas from $100 to $10,000.

The USA and Russia both introduced social media checks on their visa application forms. The US form states that it's not compulsory to give details of your Twitter, Instagram or other accounts, but that you may not get a visa if you fail to comply with the request.

There were meant to be at least 60 African delegates at the African Global Economic and Development Summit in California, but they were barred from entering the US due to tightened US visa restrictions. Organiser Mary Flowers said she was very disappointed: 'Usually 40 per cent get rejected but the others come. This year it was 100 per cent.'

African business leaders weren't the only ones to be excluded from the US this year. Other people denied visas included:

▸ A Tibetan women's soccer team

▸ A 15-year-old Australian-Iranian boy on his way to space camp

▸ An eight-year-old Indian boy on his way to the screening of a film he'd starred in

▸ An all-girl team of teenage Afghan robot builders

While the robot-building schoolgirls from Afghanistan were initially denied visas, their robot was allowed in. After a public outcry, US Border Control eventually relented and let the girls in, too.

When another group of roboticists were denied American visas for 2017's Computer–Human Interaction conference, the organisers provided them with an ingenious solution. Delegates were able to participate remotely, piloting robots that transmitted live feeds of the scientists via screens on top of the machines. The robots would line up during talks, so the delegates could watch the speaker, although one robot had to shuffle out of the room mid-lecture when its screen broke. The robots

could also be driven around networking events, meaning that they could mingle with other delegates, both human and robot.

VOLCANOES

Scientists discovered that a volcano on Mars once erupted non-stop for 2 billion years.

Astronomers discovered this by analysing an apple-sized Martian meteorite found in Algeria. It was made of volcanic rock and was 2.4 billion years old. Other meteorites that landed here from the same part of Mars are also volcanic, made from cooling magma, but were formed much more recently – about 500 million years ago. This suggests that the same spot was erupting and generating these volcanic rocks for 2 billion years – one seventh as long as the universe has existed.

Meanwhile, on Earth, in scenes reminiscent of 79 AD, Mount Vesuvius glowed orange, was enveloped in smoke and scattered ash on the surrounding village – but it wasn't due to an eruption. Massive fires, caused by a combination of arson and hot, dry weather, spread across its slopes and obscured its peak. Corpses of cats found at the site prompted accusations that the Mafia had set fire to them and released them into the undergrowth, either to halt construction projects in the area or to burn illegal landfill.

In New Zealand, a *Playboy* model angered the Maori community this year by hiking up an extremely sacred volcano and sharing a nude photo of herself near the top of it. The summit of Mount Taranaki is considered to be a burial ground for the local tribe's ancestors, and the mountain as a whole is thought of as an ancestor. The model, Jaylene Cook, said she wasn't being disrespectful because she didn't take the photo right on the summit, which is the really sacred part. A Maori spokesperson, however, said that what she did was the equivalent of someone taking a nude photo at St Peter's Basilica.

VULTURES ▶

Two gay vultures in Amsterdam became parents.

According to Amsterdam Royal zookeeper Job van Tol, the birds nested together, bonded together and mated together, but could never raise a chick. So when zookeepers found an abandoned egg, they gave it to the vultures to hatch. It was the zoo's first successful hatching in five years.

The news for vultures in the wild isn't so good. In Zimbabwe, 94 were killed by ivory poachers, who regard them as a threat to their livelihood. They fear that if they don't kill the vultures, then police will see the birds circling the carcasses of the elephants the poachers have slaughtered, giving away their position.

Vultures in the Canary Islands have been drawing attention to themselves by wearing face paint. Some of the birds have been observed colouring their heads in red mud-baths, which researchers say is an attempt to show that they're 'special'.

In which we learn ...
Where you can get an anti-pervert flamethrower,
how a century-old whisky was brought back from the dead,
why Garfield underwent a sex change (and then 19 more
sex changes), and who used a computer to shave Superman.

WALES

For a dog that chased a stick too far, *see* **Drones**; for a politician's 'very English' Welsh wife, *see* **French Presidential Election**; for JH11 HAD, see **Licence Plates**; for a hiking book that triggered a General Election, *see* **May, Theresa**; and for a felon with a hefty bill, *see* **Phones**.

WALLS

Germany announced it will build a wall around the Berlin Wall.

Next year the German government will erect a protective barrier in front of the remaining relics of the Berlin Wall, to stop tourists chiselling bits off or writing their own graffiti on top of the existing graffiti (which now qualifies as historic artwork). The current plan is for a 1-metre-high barrier on both sides, with signs in several languages asking people not to break off bits of the wall.

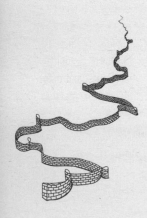

Other countries have been engaged on more ambitious wall-building projects (*see* **Border Wall**). The Turkish government built the longest border wall in the world: a 556-kilometre structure between Turkey and Syria, covering most of the border between the two countries. The ultimate aim is for it to run along the whole 911 kilometres, which will make it the second-longest structure in the world after the Great Wall of China.

One wall that won't trouble the Great Wall of China's record is the kilometre-long wall that has been built between Peru and Ecuador. It has caused controversy, though: Peru recalled its ambassador from Quito in protest, arguing that despite Ecuador's assurances that it was a flood precaution, it would just mean that any flooding that does happen will occur in Peru.

One of the few nations to rule out building a wall was South Africa. Some South Africans wanted a huge wall on

he border with Mozambique to eliminate cross-border
crime. However, the deputy president, Cyril Ramaphosa,
said, 'We are a nation that does not build walls. We do not
believe in building walls. And that defines who we are.

And besides,' he added, 'we don't have the money.'

WARNINGS

For extreme violence, *see* **Game of Thrones**; for scenes
of a sexual nature, *see* **Kinky**; for flashing images, *see*
Northern Lights; and for strong language, *see* **Swearing**.

WASPS

*Women were warned not to put wasps' nests in their
vaginas.*

Gynaecologist Dr Jen Gunter published this sensible
advice on her blog after discovering that a product called
manjakani, which some claim enhances vaginal tight-
ness, was being sold by various online stores. Manjakani,
or oak galls, are the tumour-like growths that an oak
tree produces when a wasp injects its larvae into it; the
galls enclose the developing larvae until they're ready
to emerge. Gunter warned that pulverising manjakani
and inserting them into vaginas a) would be ineffective
as there's no evidence they can tighten vaginas, and
b) could be potentially harmful. The galls contain tannic
acids, which can dry out the vaginal wall, making it
susceptible to abrasion and tearing. This, in turn, can
encourage STDs to spread more easily.

It was a tough year for gall wasps. While their homes
were being pulverised and inserted into people's genitals,
their bodies were being possessed by a newly discovered
species. The parasite, named the crypt-keeper wasp,
deposits its larvae in a gall alongside young gall wasps.
When a larva hatches, it burrows into the head of the

The president of Costa
Rica, Luis Guillermo
Solís, was giving a live
TV interview in June
when a wasp flew into
his mouth. He chewed
it, swallowed it, took a
drink of water and then
carried on the interview.

gall wasp and controls its mind from within. Usually a gall wasp, once it's fully grown, chews its way out of the host tree. But when it's possessed by the crypt-keeper, it chews a hole that's too small, and gets its head wedged in it. While it's trapped there, the crypt-keeper eats its head from within and makes its own way to freedom through the trapped gall wasp's skull.

In yet more bad news for wasps, entomologists at University College London and the University of Gloucestershire encouraged members of the public to start drowning wasps in beer. As part of the Big Wasp Survey, the scientists hoped to find out more about British wasp populations by persuading people to send them dead ones for analysis. The Big Wasp Survey published tips on how to make alcohol traps for the creatures, explaining that it was simply 'harnessing the public hatred of wasps' in order to discover more about them. Although charities like Buglife objected to the planned slaughter, the project should actually conserve wasp populations in the long term by showing researchers where certain species are in decline, and which ones need protecting.

WAXWORKS

The day after the 45th US president was inaugurated, an auctioneer in Pennsylvania flogged the previous 44.*

* Actually, there were only 43 wax presidents for sale, as Grover Cleveland served as both the 22nd and 24th, and the Hall of Presidents and First Ladies in Gettysburg decided it was only worth sculpting him once.

The Hall of Presidents and First Ladies in Gettysburg closed late last year due to falling visitor numbers, and so the life-size models of everyone from Washington to Obama went under the hammer. All of the First Ladies of the United States were also up for sale, but they weren't life-size. They were made a third of the size of their husbands to save on wax.

Abraham Lincoln was the most expensive president sold by auctioneer Randy Dickensheets. His waxwork went for $9,350, while James Monroe was the cheapest at just

to be his friends. The bride and her family became suspicious when none of them could explain how they knew him. They eventually admitted they'd been paid the equivalent of £9 each to pose as his friends for the day. The groom, Mr Wang, was investigated on suspicion of defrauding his bride's family out of 1.25 million yuan (nearly £150,000) during their courtship. The silver lining for her was that their marriage was invalid because although he'd claimed he was 27, he turned out to be 20, and in China the minimum age at which men can marry is 22.

WHISKY ▶

A whisky was brought back from extinction thanks to Ernest Shackleton.

The new whisky has been named Shackleton, and is based on a lost recipe produced in the early 1900s by Mackinlay & Co. In 2007, three cases of century-old whisky were found frozen into the ice at Shackleton's Antarctic base camp. They had lain there since his 1907 expedition. Despite having been under the ice for exactly a century, the whisky itself hadn't frozen and was still drinkable.

Whyte & Mackay, which now owns Mackinlay & Co., decided to replicate the whisky. A crate of it was sent to Scotland and handed over to master blender Richard Paterson, aka 'The Nose'. Paterson is a master distiller who last year celebrated 50 years in the industry. His skills at tasting and blending whiskies are so valuable that his nose was once insured for £1.6 million.

Paterson sampled the whisky by inserting a syringe between the cork and the bottle neck, and extracting enough liquid for the purposes of analysis and imitation. It took him months to recreate the blend. Once Paterson was done, the original bottles were returned to Shackleton's hut in Antarctica and placed back under the hut, as part of a programme to protect the legacy of Antarctic exploration that took place between 1898 and 1915.

Every single drop of the original whisky will remain undrunk – except for one small vial, that is, which now sits in the pocket of a man called The Nose.

WHITE HOUSE, WINTER ▶

The walls of the winter White House are covered in fake news.

Time magazine asked the Trump Organization to take down a fake version of its cover that hangs on the walls of Donald Trump's Florida property, Mar-a-Lago.

A reporter noticed the mocked-up magazine cover while visiting one of Trump's golf clubs. It soon emerged that it also hangs in three others, including Mar-a-Lago. *Time* requested that they be removed, and published an article entitled 'How to Spot a Fake *TIME* Cover'. The framed front covers, supposedly from 2009, show a photograph of Trump accompanied by the words 'Trump is hitting on all fronts' and 'The "Apprentice" is a television smash!' In reality, that edition featured Kate Winslet on the cover.*

* Trump claimed this year that he has been on the cover of Time *'like, 14 or 15 times', and that this is a record that will never be broken. In fact, he had been on the cover 11 times when he made the claim. Former president Richard Nixon featured on it 55 times.*

Trump, incidentally, spends about a quarter of his time at Mar-a-Lago, so lobbyists who want to get his attention have obtained its IP address and started geotargeting their online materials to the estate. The president and his staff in the property are now flooded with adverts very specifically meant for them while they're there.

Curiosity about what actually goes on at Trump's properties has led Democrats to introduce a bill demanding greater openness. The bill is called Making Access Records Available to Lead American Government Openness Act, though it's better known by its acronym,

MARALAGO. What we do already know is that the place is health and safety hazard: in April, inspectors recorded 3 violations of food safety there, including incorrectly prepared fish, and raw meat kept at temperatures too high to be safe.

Arguably, Mar-a-Lago is finally fulfilling the purpose its original owner, Marjorie Merriweather Post, intended for it. She left it to the US government in her will, hoping it would become a de facto winter White House. Unfortunately, no president wanted to live there and it was on the verge of being demolished when Trump discovered it. His offer of $15 million was initially rejected, so he bought the land between the Mar-a-Lago and the ocean and threatened to build a hideous house (his own admission) there in order to block Mar-a-Lago's sea view. This drove the price down, enabling Trump to purchase it in 1985 for $5 million.

Trump's decision to pull America out of the Paris climate agreement may cause Mar-a-Lago's value to depreciate further. Projections released this year by the National Oceanic and Atmospheric Administration suggest that most of the property will be underwater by 2100.

———— ▼ ————

Mar-a-Lago isn't Trump's only Florida purchase. The *Guardian* revealed that he also owns a quarter of an acre of isolated, unprofitable, mosquito-ridden land in the poorest part of Florida. No one knows why. He bought it for $1 from a woman who owned a studio specialising in lingerie shoots. When the *Guardian* tried to contact her, she not only failed to respond, but also immediately closed her Facebook and Instagram accounts.

WIKIPEDIA

Garfield had 20 sex changes in two days.

In an interview a couple of years ago, Garfield the cat's creator said the cartoon character is 'not really male or female'. When satirist Virgil Texas recently came across the interview, he went to Wikipedia and changed Garfield's gender to 'None'. An edit war then broke out. Over the next 60 hours his/her/their sex switched back and forth constantly, until Wikipedia's administrators lost patience and suspended all editing on the page.

Wikipedia also suspended editing of its Calibri page after it turned out the history of the font was being used as

* As a result of this
font scandal, Pakistan
is now sans-Sharif.

evidence in a huge Pakistani corruption investigation that led to the resignation of Prime Minister Nawaz Sharif.* Sharif's daughter Miriam, who was herself being investigated for corruption, showed a court documents dated 2006, typed in Calibri font. However, Calibri only became available in 2007. When this fact emerged, another edit battle began, with supporters of Sharif updating the page to say that the font had been available since 2004, presumably in order to get the PM out of trouble.

Machines have editing wars on Wikipedia, just like humans. Oxford University researchers have found pairs of bots that have been undoing and redoing each other's work for years, sometimes arguing over extremely small points of grammar. The fights they have are often down to their nationality: it turns out that bots behave differently depending on which country they were built in. German bots are the least argumentative, while Portuguese are the most quarrelsome. English Wikipedia bots undo each other's work three times as often as English Wikipedia humans.

All this confusion might explain why China just made its own version of Wikipedia that doesn't allow editing. It's been set up by the publishing house that produces the physical *Encylopaedia of China*, and the government intends it to be a rival to Wikipedia. A team of 20,000 government-approved experts and academics has been employed to write it. No one else will be allowed to contribute.

WINE

French and Spanish ministers called for a truce in the 'War of the Wines'.

France and Spain's agricultural ministers were forced to meet to defuse the furious battle French vintners have been waging against imports of cheap Spanish plonk. The

French think Spanish winemakers have been cheating by giving their bottles misleadingly French names and putting pictures of baguettes on them.

This year, protesters from France's militant vintner alliance CRAV (Comité Régional d'Action Viticole, or Regional Action Committee of Winemakers) continued their protests, which consist of attacking tankers of Spanish wine and throwing cocktails (Molotov, specifically) at premises that store it. In March, the French

agriculture minister appealed for calm after seven tankers full of wine were poured onto the ground. Two months earlier, CRAV found a tanker suspected of carrying foreign wine, interrogated the driver, and, on learning that it was Spanish, dumped it all over the highway.

This conflict has been rumbling on for some time. Last year French farmers hijacked Spanish wine lorries and poured 90,000 bottles' worth of wine down the drain while local French gendarmes stood by and watched. Elsewhere, balaclava-clad winemakers in a port town in Languedoc cracked open vats of imported wine, flooding the streets and people's homes with thousands of litres of cheap booze.

There was a bit of good news for drinkers of both French and Spanish wine after a US study on mice suggested that red wine prevents muscles from ageing. It's down to

Thanks to the US trade embargo, it's hard to get crucial winemaking equipment in Cuba. So instead of using airlocks during fermentation, Cuban winemaker Orestes Estevez rolls a condom over the top of each bottle. It stands up as the wine ferments and gives off gas – when the condom goes limp the wine is ready.

The oldest known bottle of Bordeaux was found under a mound of dirt in a French wine cellar, where it had been hidden for 270 years. It took over four years of testing the bottle – chemically examining the glass, stopper, shape and wear and tear without opening it – to verify that it dates back to 1750.

a chemical compound called resveratrol. Unfortunately, to get the equivalent amount of resveratrol to the mice in the study, the average human would need to drink at least 2,000 bottles of wine a day.

WITCHCRAFT

Canada's government is trying to legalise 'pretending to be a witch'.

▼

Two constituencies in Papua New Guinea's election had to have recounts after some candidates alleged witchcraft had been used to suck votes out of the ballot boxes.

The C-51 bill is an attempt by the liberal government to tidy up old legislation, some of which dates back to colonial times. Among the laws that they propose scrapping is one that states that it is illegal to 'pretend to exercise or to use any kind of witchcraft, sorcery, enchantment or conjuration'. So if C-51 passes, it will no longer be illegal to pretend to enchant people or to practise 'crafty science' for fun, although it'll still be illegal to use these methods to commit fraud. The change of law will mean that, as well as dabbling in the occult, people will be able to participate in duels, sell a 'crime comic', and advertise drugs as a way to restore 'sexual virility' – all of which are currently illegal.

Witchcraft also made a comeback over the border in the USA this year, where Blink-182 singer Matt Skiba, who claims to be a witch, claimed that his spellcasting was responsible for the failure of an upmarket music event (*see* **Fyre Festival**). And around the world, on the summer solstice, witches cast a spell to 'Bind Trump', calling on demons to cause him to fail.

Meanwhile, in Portugal, FC Porto accused rivals Benfica of paying a witch doctor to help them win football matches. They say that Dr Armando Nhaga was paid 1,000 euros for every game Benfica won in the domestic league and 10,000 euros for every game they won in the Champions League group stages. The magic did seem to work as Benfica won the league for the fourth year a row, though in the first game that Nhaga was said to be employed, Benfica actually lost 4–0 to Borussia Dortmund. Most football fans would have been able to predict that result, but rather than blaming it on the form of the two teams, the witch doctor said that the Benfica team had not informed him of the correct time that he needed to cast the spell.

WONDER WOMAN

This summer a fired UN ambassador became the world's biggest superhero.

Wonder Woman was the largest grossing film of the summer. Before this, in early 2016, the character was named an honorary UN ambassador. However, unlike the cases of Winnie-the-Pooh, Tinkerbell and the red Angry Bird (all UN ambassadors themselves), there was an immediate backlash, with over 40,000 people signing a petition against the appointment. The main objection was that it would be better to find a real-life woman to be an ambassador for the empowerment of women and girls. As a result, the United Nations fired her from her role.

In signing the contract to make *Wonder Woman 2*, the director Patty Jenkins – fittingly, given the film's content – became the highest-paid female movie director ever.

This would have been a huge disappointment to her creator, William Marston. When first promoting her, he said, 'Frankly, Wonder Woman is psychological

* Marston was furious when, in 1942, Wonder Woman joined DC Comics' Justice League (whose members included Batman, Superman and The Flash) and the DC writer made her the society's secretary. When all the male superheroes headed off to war, she stayed behind to answer the post.

propaganda for the new type of woman who should, I believe, rule the world.'*

Gal Gadot, who played the lead role in the film, said the training she did for the movie was tougher than the two years of compulsory service she did in the Israeli army. Not only that, she was five months pregnant when she filmed reshoots for the film. Her Wonder Woman outfit was chopped out around the stomach and replaced with green cloth so they could CGI out her baby bump.

A similar bit of airbrushing occurred in the new *Justice League* movie (which also features Gadot as Wonder Woman). It has also been claimed that Henry Cavill, who plays Superman, had to do reshoots sporting a massive moustache, as they coincided with the filming of his new *Mission Impossible* movie. As a result, the studio had to shave Superman virtually with CGI.

WORLD RECORDS ▶

For flaming stuntmen, *see* **Game of Thrones**; for long-distance runners in fancy dress, *see* **Marathon, London**; for one-fingered piano-playing, *see* **Music**; for the footballer who's the biggest poser, *see* **Selfies**; for a coconut climbing champion, *see* **Trees**; and for a giant horse's head, *see* **Turkmenistan**.

In which we learn …
How an astronaut is leading us to pirate gold, why
'Stallion83' deserves his nickname, which world leader
looks like a fictional bear, and why it's not
worth stealing a giant xylophone.

A man looked for sunken gold using a treasure map made in space.

* He was also the first
astronaut to sleep in
space. Not only this,
he's also the only one
known to have slept on
the launch pad. He did
so during countdown,
and co-workers had to
shout his name several
times over the commu-
nications link to wake
him up.

In 1963, Gordon Cooper, the first astronaut to pilot a solo space mission,* was aboard his spacecraft, looking for nuclear sites by monitoring magnetic signals on Earth. He kept getting anomalous readings from under the sea in the Caribbean, and concluded they must be caused by sunken Spanish treasure from the golden age of piracy. So, as he orbited the Earth 22 times, he made a map of where they were. He didn't tell anyone until just before he died in 2004, when he shared the map with his treasure-hunter friend Darrell Miklos. Miklos went looking for the treasure this year and has so far found nothing but an anchor that may, or may not, be from one of Columbus's ships.

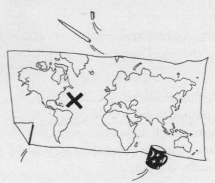

Back on dry land, police urged art dealer Forrest Fenn to call off the hunt for his buried treasure after a second person died searching for it. Seven years ago, Fenn hid a chest full of gold nuggets, jewels and gemstones, now worth about $2 million, somewhere in the Rocky Mountains and wrote a cryptic poem that he says provides the clues for where to find it. Many have tried, but no one has yet succeeded in solving his riddles. Colorado pastor Paris Wallace died this year as he braved the difficult terrain looking for the chest and so police have advised people to stop looking for the booty. Wallace's wife (a fellow treasure hunter) disagrees, and believes the search should continue.

One man who wasn't searching for gold but got lucky anyway was piano tuner Martin Backhouse. He can now retire early because he found $500,000 worth of loot inside a piano. This is particularly fortunate as he recently developed tinnitus, making it hard for him to work. The piano belonged to a couple who had owned it since 1983, before donating it to the local college last year. They never realised it contained a hoard of 19th- and early-20th century gold coins wrapped in some old Shredded Wheat packaging until the college employed Backhouse to tune it. He initially mistook the treasure for moth repellent.

XBOX ▶

Stallion83, who held the Xbox scoring record for 11 years, was knocked off the top spot because he was too busy having sex.

All users of Xbox products can accumulate points by completing certain tasks in their games. This gives them a 'Gamerscore', which indicates more about their devotion to playing games in general than it necessarily does about their skills at a particular game.

The most devoted gamer of all time is undoubtedly Ray 'Stallion83' Cox, who has had the top Gamerscore for 11 years. But this year, because he got married and went on honeymoon, he was away from his console for long enough to be overtaken by another player: Stephen 'smrnov' Rowe.

After returning from honeymoon, Stallion83 worked to get back to the top, and after a few weeks of dedicated gaming he did so, reaching 1.6 million points before tweeting: 'Now back to having all the sex.'

Winnie-the-Pooh was censored in China because he looks too similar to Xi Jinping.

Reporters were allowed to accompany Xi Jinping when he visited an army barracks in Hong Kong, but they received written instructions in advance that they weren't allowed to bring pens, books, umbrellas (a symbol of the region's pro-democracy movement) or opium.

For seven years, between the ages of 15 and 21, Xi Jinping lived in a cave. Under Chairman Mao, his family was sent to live in the tiny, windowless room cut into a rural hillside. The lifestyle is still relatively common: over 30 million people in China live in caves today.

Memes noting the physical similarities between the Chinese premier and honey-obsessed bear first spread across social media in 2013. In 2015, the most censored image in China was one of Xi standing up in a car with his head through the sunroof, alongside Pooh in his own toy car. Now, Chinese social media users are having problems making any reference to Pooh on the Internet. Posts that mentioned him on Weibo, China's equivalent of Twitter, were suddenly forbidden, and gifs of the bear disappeared from the messaging forum WeChat. The government hasn't confirmed the reason for the ban, but we know that Xi hasn't taken kindly to humorous comparisons in the past: online references to the Chinese food staple, steamed buns (*baozi*), were censored because they've been used as a nickname for Xi ever since he was photographed eating one in 2014.

The letters 'RIP' were also blocked on social media in China in July, after the death of famous government critic and Nobel Peace Prize winner Liu Xiaobo. Weibo banned anyone not only from posting 'RIP', but also the word 'Nobel' or the candle emoji.

Xi Jinping also hit the headlines in April when he met Donald Trump. Afterwards Trump said that until the two of them had spoken, he'd assumed that China could easily deal with the threat of North Korea. However, Xi had explained the background of relations between China and North Korea to him: 'After listening for ten minutes, I realised it's not so easy,' Trump said.

In excellent news for writers of A–Z current affairs books, there was some xylophone news.

A man in Virginia was arrested for stealing a 1.5-metre xylophone from a children's playground. The instrument was bolted to the ground, but as it was worth a remarkable $4,000 it's not too surprising that it was pinched. However, it must have been quite hard to find a buyer on the black market: when the police found the perpetrator, a week later, he still had the xylophone in his possession.

Astonishingly, this wasn't the only xylophone crime in the US this year. A woman from Florida was arrested for attacking a man who wouldn't stop playing a xylophone. The lady told police that she had asked him to stop. When he refused she 'dumped a pot of cold cooking grease on him'.

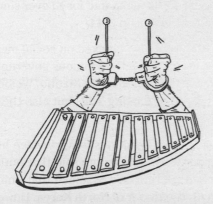

In which we learn…
How to win a boat race on a bike, why a giant yellow
crayon toured America, which farmyard animal is
best in a yoga class, and whether Usain Bolt
could escape a T. rex.

ew Zealand won the world's biggest yachting race – n exercise bikes

very racing yacht has a number of crew members known s grinders. Their job is to manually rotate the winches known as coffee grinders) that raise the sail and move he boom (which controls the sail's angle). The job is usually done by hand, but in this year's America's Cup, he Emirates Team New Zealand squad attached the grinders to pedals and brought in professional cyclists o do the work.

It's not just cycling that can help on a yacht. The high-tech sailing boats of the America's Cup have so much aeroplane technology in them that the captain of the US team got a pilot's licence to help him better understand his boat.

It worked. They won the America's Cup by an impressive seven races to one against the reigning champions Oracle Team USA. Their tactics shocked the yachting world. But as one of the Kiwi team, Olympic bronze-medal-winning cyclist Simon van Velthooven, told reporters, 'If you have half a brain and you know that your legs are stronger than your arms, why wouldn't you give it a go?'

And it's not just power. If you're doing the winching with your legs then it leaves your hands free to do other things, such as operate the wheel that lifts the boat above the water,* It's unclear what will happen in the next America's Cup in 2021. Either every other team will have to consider cycling in the race, or – perhaps more likely – the practice will be banned.

This is important because water is denser than air. If you can lift your boat into the air and only have small planks touching the water then you can almost fly in your yacht. The planks are known as foils and are also used in foil-boarding (see Obama, Barack).

YELLOW

A yellow crayon went on a farewell tour.

Crayola announced this year that they would be retiring their yellow Dandelion crayon after 27 years' loyal service. 'Dan D.', as it is known to some, went on a nation wide tour of America to say goodbye (or at least someone dressed as a giant crayon did). The announcement was supposed to be kept secret until National Crayon Day,* but after some boxes emblazoned with the slogan 'Dandelion is retiring' were sent out early, it was leaked on Twitter by Boston resident Frank Hegyi. He told the *Boston Globe* that his mother had instructed him to keep the news quiet, fearing that they'd get death threats, but he chose to break the news anyway.

Dan D. was replaced with a new shade of blue, the first new pigment discovered in over 200 years. The colour itself is called YInMn blue (short for ytrrium, indium and manganese), but the crayon's name was chosen by the public from a shortlist that included Bluetiful and Dreams Come Blue (Bluetiful eventually won). Suggestions that didn't even make the shortlist included: Sacre Blue, Blue Da Ba Di, Bluey McBlueface and Covfefe.

Tourists complained about a man parking his 'ugly' yellow car in the picturesque village of Bibury, with vandals even scratching the word 'MOVE' on his bonnet. Possessors of yellow car owners rallied in the owner's support, and 100 yellow cars drove through the village in a motorcade.

* *31 March, in case you're wondering, the same as National Bunsen Burner Day.*

YOGA

You can now buy a pair of pants that double as a yoga instructor.

The 'smart' yoga pants will gently prod you to help you know when you've got your limbs in the right positions. The company that produces them, Wearable Experiments, is already planning its next product: a smart sports bra that will do the same and tell you when to exhale.

The newest trend in yoga this year is 'goat yoga'. A herd of goats wander around sessions, nuzzle people, jump on their backs and chew their hair: organisers say the animals help to produce 'feel-good hormones'. It's not certain what the goats think of it, but we do know that elsewhere yoga pants are being used to keep goats calm. Environmentalists are taking goats off the island of Redonda in the Caribbean by helicopter because they have no food on the island and have been starving to death. To keep them calm in the chopper, the environmentalists put yoga pants on the goats' heads.

It's not just goat yoga that's on the rise. You can do puppy yoga in Brisbane, cannabis yoga in California, Beyoncé-themed yoga in Chicago and beer yoga in Germany. The last of those is exactly as it sounds: it's yoga performed with a pint. Poses include 'Drunken Warrior' and 'Earn Your Beer'.

YORKSHIRE

A group of Yorkshiremen donated their voices to a man who is losing his.

Jason Liversidge from Scarborough suffers from motor neurone disease (the same illness that affects Stephen Hawking) and will lose his speech in the coming years. But new technology will allow him to keep his accent. Scientists used recordings of a speech he gave at his sister's wedding, plus those of other Yorkshire men who donated their voices, so that he will be able to keep his identity once the machine takes over his speech. It's certainly an accent worth keeping: in a survey of employers conducted this year, 80 per cent said that someone's regional accent can affect their chances of getting a job. After 'the Queen's English', the Yorkshire accent was the one most associated with intelligence.

YOU'RE FIRED!

Dan: Did you know that Donald Trump was not the first host of *The Apprentice* to be sworn into office this year?

James: Oh God... Lord Sugar isn't the King of England now, is he?

Dan: Well, no, but you're not that far off. João Doria became mayor of São Paulo on January 1st, and he used to be the host of the Brazilian *Apprentice*. Though, unlike Trump, Doria hasn't carried on firing an employee almost every week.

Andy: Yeah, Trump's been on a firing spree. Steve Bannon, Reince Priebus, Anthony Scaramucci, Sean Spicer...

Anna: Steve Bannon was one of the biggest, but now he's left the world of politics he might return to the World of Warcraft. He used to be an investor in a company that went into virtual worlds, found virtual objects and sold them for real money.

Dan: That's right. He also profited from the sitcom *Seinfeld*, didn't he? I think he made about $2 million after investing in the company that made it.

Andy: He's invested a lot in the arts, and he wrote a sci-fi remake of *Titus Andronicus*, which featured intergalactic travel and 'ectoplasmic sex' between a human and a space queen.

Dan: What? He actually sat in a room, wrote that script and said, 'Here's something that will make me lots of money?'

Anna: Don't pretend you wouldn't watch that film, Dan.

Dan: No, I'm not really into Shakespeare's early work.

Andy: Trump also fired Chief of Staff Reince Priebus. Priebus did an interview with Bannon, where the two told the world that they were great pals and worked well together. But when

Bannon put a friendly hand on Priebus's thigh, Reince instinctively batted it away like a very annoyed wife. It was such an awkward moment.

Dan: Another guy fired by Trump was Anthony Scaramucci. After being sacked, he signed up with a Hollywood PR firm. He's thinking that he could use his fleeting fame to his advantage, but the firm is called Fifteen Minutes, so that doesn't bode well for his long-term prospects.

James: Well, he's not exactly a stranger to short-term jobs. He lasted 10 days in this one. He told the press afterwards, 'I didn't think I was going to last too long, but I thought I would last longer than a carton of milk.'

Anna: At least he has a sense of humour. I looked into it, and his 10 days as communications director was the shortest on record. Before that, the record belonged to Jack Koehler, who served for 11 days in the Reagan administration before it turned out that he'd been in a Nazi youth group.

Dan: Crikey. Well, going back to *The Apprentice*, Trump actually tried to trademark the phrase 'You're fired!' in 2004, but it was rejected because it was thought to be too close to a board game called 'You're Hired!'.

Anna: There was also an objection by a pottery shop in Chicago with the name 'You're Fired!'.

James: He should've tried changing his catchphrase slightly differently, like 'You Are Fired!'.

Andy: Well, going by the last year, it looks like he's going to get a lot more chances to say it.

As well as conducting high-profile political polls, YouGov also learned people's views on sandwich shape, Hogwarts houses and when to flush the loo.

On 31 May, YouGov released a controversial poll, referred to as 'shocking' (*New Statesman*), 'brave' (*Guardian*) and 'stupid' (*Spectator*), that correctly predicted the general election would lead to a hung parliament. It was the only polling company to foresee this. On the same day, it published another poll that found that 23 per cent of people think the 1980s was the best decade for music and 22 per cent think it was the 1960s, while only 4 per cent think it was the 2000s and 2 per cent think it's been the 2010s.

Other truths YouGov revealed in 2017 include:

▶ 68 per cent of people in the UK have their washing machines in the kitchen, compared with only 9 per cent in the US.

▶ 35 per cent of Brits think they could outrun a T. rex.*

▶ 8 per cent of Brits and 7 per cent of Americans worry about people posting hurtful things about them online, compared to 34 per cent of French people.

▶ 60 per cent of Brits make rectangular sandwiches while 28 per cent make triangular ones.

▶ A quarter of young Brits got sunburnt during the heatwave in the first weekend of April.

▶ Harry Potter fans think that the celebrity most likely to be in Slytherin is Donald Trump; the one most likely to be in Hufflepuff is Mary Berry; the one most likely to be in Ravenclaw is David Attenborough; and, slightly unimaginatively, the one most likely to be in Gryffindor is Daniel Radcliffe.

* They're probably right. Scientists concluded this year that the average T. rex top speed was about 1mph faster than the average human top speed, so the speedier runners among us could have outpaced them. In fact, the T. rex couldn't run at all. New computer modelling of their movement has revealed that if they'd tried to, their legs would have snapped under their own weight.

▶ Only 5 per cent of 18- to 24-year-olds think it's fashion-able to wear muddy jeans (*see* **Jeans**).

▶ British people overwhelmingly prefer dogs to cats.

▶ Brits are equally split on whether or not to flush the toilet if they go in the middle of the night.

In which we learn …
Why mosquitoes got robot parents, how Chicago will survive
a zombie apocalypse, why death may just be a minor
inconvenience for Robert Mugabe, which beast is
traumatised by breasts, and how 2017 got the last word.

ZHOU, YOUGUANG

The world lost a former scarecrow who improved China's literacy rate by more than 600 per cent.

Zhou Youguang (1906–2017), who died aged 111, was the 'father of Pinyin', a method for writing Chinese in the Roman alphabet. Thanks to his system, China's capital, 北京, could be written as 'Beijing'. In fact, it was down to Zhou's system, introduced in 1958, that we now call it Beijing. Prior to the standardisation of Pinyin, the city was known to the West as Peking.*

It is thanks to Pinyin that China's illiteracy rate, which stood at 85 per cent in 1958, is now just 5 per cent. Despite this, Zhou wasn't seen a national hero. In fact, during Mao's Cultural Revolution Zhou was sent away to be 're-educated' and was exiled to a farm where he was given a job as a scarecrow, literally chasing birds from farmers' fields.

Following his 'rehabilitation' in 1985, he became part of a team that translated the *Encyclopaedia Britannica* into Chinese. He then worked on the second edition, and continued translating articles until the day he died, completing one article a month.

It was this translation work that caused Zhou to become very critical of the Chinese government: he noticed the lies it was feeding the public by learning the truth in the encyclopedia. His controversial views led to many of his books being banned (he wrote over 30). However, he was never deterred from stating his opinions. 'What are they going to do,' he asked the BBC, aged 106, 'come and take me away?' His works include *The Shock Wave of Modern Culture, Chinese Characters and the Question of Culture* and *One Hundred Years Old, But Publishing a New Book.*

Zhou died on 14 January in Beijing, in a hospital called Peking Union.

* Over its 3,000-year history, city locals have called it Peiping and Beiping, but never Peking, which was a name given to it by French missionaries and then taken up in the West.

Google fought zika by releasing millions of sterile mosquitoes.

Google's science arm, Verily, has created a robot that can incubate mosquitoes and infect them with the naturally occurring *Wolbachia* bacteria, which sterilises male insects. The robot can also sort males from females, and roughly 1 million sterile male mosquitoes can be raised a week.

In a 20-week trial, sterilised males were released from vans that drove around the streets of Fresno, California. The hope is that they will inundate local females with their useless sperm, thus leading to a massive drop in the mosquito population and a simultaneous decline in mosquito-borne diseases like the zika virus. If the trial is a success, the plan is to raise and then release 20 million sterile males. Residents needn't worry about being bitten by the extra mosquitoes, as they have also been bred not to bite.

In Zimbabwe, it's customary to give a couple cash on their wedding day, but the country is suffering such a severe shortage of banknotes that local banks have started renting out card machines so people can transfer cash electronically instead.

Robert Mugabe's wife named Robert Mugabe's corpse as the successor to Robert Mugabe.

Robert Mugabe said he is keen to stand in the 2018 Zimbabwean presidential elections, by which time he'll be 94. He suggested that if he dies before the polls, his wife, Grace, should stand in his place, but Grace said that she would rather his corpse became president. She changed her mind a few months later, however, saying that perhaps he should name a successor instead.

Mugabe celebrated his 93rd birthday with a 93-kilo cake shaped like Zimbabwe, and a party that cost $800,000, even though 5 million of his citizens are currently dependent on food aid. The party also featured banners thanking the president for 'optimising the use of your resources for our people'.

Whether it's Robert, Grace or someone else, the Mugabe family are going to figure in public life for a while. This year, for example, one of the new appointees to the country's censorship board was Mugabe's daughter Bona. The board is responsible for monitoring films, books, and pole dancers, making sure their dances are not indecent. One of Bona's colleagues in her new role is former minister Aeneas Chigwedere, a man whose own son sued him two years ago on charges of witchcraft and 'possessing goblins'.

ZOMBIES

Illinois named October 2017 its 'Zombie Preparedness Month'.

The idea behind this, according to the state legislature, was that 'If the citizens of Illinois are prepared for zombies, than [*sic*] they are prepared for any natural disaster.'

Spain, however, will be in trouble if zombies attack. This year, the country's opposition asked what plans the government had in place in the event of a zombie apocalypse. The hope was that the government's inability to respond to this would highlight their general lack of answers to anything. Instead, the government came up with the considered answer that Spain has: 'no specific protocols for such an event because by that moment little can be done'.

The man who we can thank for our current epidemic of zombie films died this year. George A. Romero's 1968 masterpiece *Night of the Living Dead* was the first low-rent, high-thrill zombie film. It's worth noting, though, that while the protagonists in his movie had all the attributes of modern zombies – hostile, hungry and

A study at Leicester University considered how quickly a zombie outbreak could spread. According to 'A Zombie Epidemic', published in the *Journal of Special Physics Topics*, by day 100 of an outbreak, just over 100 lucky (or unlucky) humans would be left.

unconsciously walking to the next victim – he actually called them 'ghouls'. In an article published by *Vanity Fair* just before he died, Romero explained how he disliked modern zombie flicks such as Brad Pitt's *World War Z*. 'I can't pitch a modest little zombie film, which is meant to be sociopolitical,' he said. 'I used to be able to pitch them on the basis of the zombie action, and I could hide the message inside that. Now, the moment you mention the word "zombie", it's got to be, "Hey, Brad Pitt paid $400 million to do that."'

ZOOLOGY, CRYPTO-

A New Zealand scientist announced a hunt for the Loch Ness Monster's dandruff.

Neil Gemmell, Professor of Genetics at University of Otago in New Zealand, travelled to Scotland this year to talk to cryptozoologists ahead of his scheduled hunt for the Loch Ness Monster in 2018. He plans to bottle up some of Loch Ness's water to analyse it for environmental DNA (eDNA), which comes from the excrement, skin cells, urine or dandruff that organisms constantly shed, and leave behind in their habitat. If Gemmell finds any DNA that he can't identify, it could be a clue to Nessie's existence. Of course, he doesn't expect this to happen – rather, he's using the monster hunt as a way of publicising this method of analysis, and to discover more about non-crypto life under the surface of Loch Ness.

Professor Gemmell's announcement came as welcome news to the Nessie community, which hadn't had the best start to the year. Gary Campbell, the keeper of the Loch Ness Monster Sightings Register, said he believed Nessie had gone missing. She hadn't been seen in over eight months. It was particularly concerning given that in 2016 there were more sightings than any other year in the 21st century, which Campbell said was thanks to smartphones and webcams (one sighting having been made by a man in America watching a live stream from his computer). Much to the community's relief, 2017's dry spell came to an end in late April when a self-confessed sceptic* from Manchester submitted a (predictably grainy) photo.

Other cryptozoology spots this year include one made by a prominent sasquatch hunter who runs a Facebook group called Bigfoot 911. John Bruner, from North Carolina, published what he believed was absolute proof of Bigfoot on camera. He claimed the photo, snapped while he was hunting in the Appalachian Mountains, captured a creature that stood over 8 feet tall. However, after he published the photo a wandering shaman came forward and identified himself as the beast in the picture. Gawain MacGregor had been walking in the forest on the night of the incident, dressed head to toe in animal skin, and conducting his own search for the mythical (or not) creature. The members of Bigfoot 911 still deny that they photographed the shaman, and insist the creature they saw 'moved with speed unmatched by any human'.

Meanwhile, on another Facebook page, North Carolina police posted: 'If you see Bigfoot, please do not shoot at him/her, as you'll most likely be wounding a fun-loving and well-intentioned person, sweating in a gorilla costume' (see also **Marathon, London**).

ZOOLOGY, NON-CRYPTO-

For CPR on an aardvark, see **Aardvarks**; for controlling populations with sausages, see **Airdrops**; for a surfeit of hogs, see **Boar**; for how borders affect animals, see **Border Wall**; for condoms that look like otters, see **Condoms**; for cattle acting like lemmings, see **Cows**; for a drastic alternative to mating, see **Dragonflies**; for the plans of the Carpinator, see **Fish**; for fluorescent amphibians, see **Frogs**; for sperm orbiting the Earth, see **Mice, Space**; for a spread that stops squirrels spreading, see **Nutella**; for weird creatures of the deep, see **Oceans**; for recreational drug use in parrots, *see* **Opium**; for birds mistaken for rocks, *see* **Penguins**; for a reptile mistaken for a stone, *see* **RSPCA**; for animal attacks, *see* **Shark Attack**; for avian asps, *see* **Snakes**; for gold members, *see* **Spiders**; for rhino conservation, *see* **Tinder**; for a bird with two dads, *see* **Vultures**; for a species that had a bad year, *see* **Wasps**; and for sterilising mosquitoes, *see* **Zika**.

ZOOS ▶

A zoo in Russia sued a company for giving a raccoon an unnatural interest in human breasts.

▼

A zoo in China is charging people £100 to clean up polar bear poo. As well as paying for the privilege of sweeping the dung from the enclosures and preparing the creatures' food, you get to take a selfie with the bear and post it on social media afterwards.

The Moscow petting zoo lent Tomas the raccoon to a production company, thinking he would be used in a regular advertisement. When he was returned, they found that he was traumatised, withdrawn – and attracted to women's breasts. It turned out he'd been used in what the zoo called an 'erotic photoshoot' in which he snuggled up with a naked woman. Zookeepers suspect he was lured to her breasts with treats, with the result that he now associates them with food. The advertising company said the lawsuit was absurd, and complained about Tomas's behaviour, saying he was constantly running away during the shoot and had chewed up the actress's underwear.

Another objectionable use of zoo animals emerged in Thailand, where a safari park just outside Bangkok put on orangutan boxing shows for tourists. The apes were dressed in boxing shorts and gloves, placed in a ring and trained to kick and hit each other. Other apes wearing bikinis stood at the ringside, holding up round cards. Animal rights groups (unsurprisingly) called for the practice to be banned.

Animals don't always need human encouragement to start fighting each other. In fact, a baboon war that had been raging at Toronto Zoo for more than two years required human intervention to end it. The war began in 2015 after the matriarch died, triggering a succession crisis where baboon factions fought to install their candidates as the dominant 'queen'. The violence led to dozens of injuries and multiple surgeries, with one monkey having to have part of her tail amputated. Zookeepers eventually gave the baboons hormonal contraceptives to regulate their tempers and reduce rivalries. A new queen, Kalamata, has finally emerged and a truce seems to have been reached, at least for now.

ZUCKERBERG, MARK

Facebook, which has been accused of peddling 'fake news', accidentally reported its founder was dead.

A glitch in the system meant that a memorial was posted on Mark Zuckerberg's Facebook page, along with those of 2 million other users. Zuckerberg was very much alive though, and on a huge tour of all 50 states of America. He said he was undertaking this so that he could meet 'ordinary Americans', many of whom are Facebook users, in order to improve his website. Most people, however, assumed that the tour was a precursor to him announcing a presidential bid in 2020. His claims to the contrary didn't convince many people, as it was pointed out that he was travelling with former official White House photographer Charles Ommanney, who was official snapper for both George W. Bush and Barack Obama.

If Zuckerberg does become president, he will be the youngest person to get the job. He's got a long way to go to convince the American public though. In a July poll asking who would win in an election between him and Trump, Zuckerberg only managed to poll 40 per cent, meaning that at that moment he wouldn't even beat the most unpopular president in US history.

Mark Zuckerberg revealed that Facebook has a secret division at its California headquarters that is working on mind-reading technology. The experiments to crack telepathy are being conducted in Facebook's mysterious 'Building 8', which employs over 60 scientists.

The Oxford English Dictionary *added a new last word.*

As of this year, the very final entry in the *OED* is 'Zyzzyva' (pronounced 'zih-zih-vah'). It's the name of a genus of tropical weevils found in South America. Before 'Zyzzyva' took over, the last word in the dictionary was 'zythum', which was a kind of beer brewed in ancient Egypt. Other new entries in the summer 2017 intake included 'bare-backing', 'devil's shoestring', 'ginge', 'hygge', 'unclenched' and 'zoomable'.

The *OED* doesn't know why 'Zyzzyva' has 3 'z's, 2 'y's, one 'v' and only one 'a'. The word was coined by an Irish entomologist in 1922. It could be that it was intended to mimic the noise the weevils make; then again, it could have been chosen deliberately to be annoying and secure a position right at the very end of an alphabetically ordered book.

For another word that appears at the extreme end of dictionaries, *see* **Aardvarks**.

LATE NEWS

There are a lot of people we'd like to thank.

Our colleagues at QI – Alex Bell who chewed over many ideas with us and brought crucial design inspiration to the table, as always; Anne Miller who provided heaps of ideas and news stories, without which this book would have been poorer; and Alice Campbell-Davies, who painstakingly read through the manuscript, making sure that we didn't say see **Insects** when, of course, we meant see **Stick Insects**. And to the wider QI family: Coco Lloyd, James Rawson, Liz Townsend, Freddy Soames and Natascha McQueen, who all chipped in at vital moments too.

Our editor, mentor and wrangler, Nigel Wilcockson, who knew there was a book in us two years before we did, and who coached us into producing one we could be proud of. He's done ten jobs at once, and done them all better than we could have hoped. Scientists are currently studying how he managed to deal with all four of us and still, somehow, maintain a sunny disposition throughout.

Our thanks also go to everyone at Cornerstone and the rest of the fantastic team at Penguin Random House: Rowan Borchers, Fergus Edmondson, Laura Brooke and Francesca Russell. Natascha Nel delivered a stonking cover and Lindsay Nash was a brilliant designer, and both were remarkably tolerant of our constant back-and-forthing over the tiniest of details. Thanks, too, to our superb illustrator, the doughty Adam Doughty, who never batted an eyelid when we sent over requests for him to draw (for example) an aardvark receiving mouth-to-snout.

To all the Harkin, Murray, Ptaszynski and Schreiber family members – thank you for buying at least 30 copies of this book each to give to your friends this Christmas. And thank you for not giving them the receipt, so they can't exchange it for something else.

Thanks, most importantly, to John and Sarah Lloyd, QI's founder-managers and fountainheads of advice, encouragement and understanding. When we first told them about the idea for the podcast – something that would probably make no money and chew up a lot of our work time – they said 'go for it', because what they value more than anything is a good idea. Without them both, there really would be no such thing as *The Book of the Year*.

Who could have known that when we first gathered around a microphone those three-and-a-bit years ago that it would eventually lead to a book? We have only managed to get this far because each week a group of people from all over the world press play on the latest episode we've posted online. To those listeners, we want to say thank you so much, and we promise that if you keep listening, we'll keep dorking out. May the Mongolian Death Worm bless you all.

That's it, that's all of our thanks. A lot of early errors were caught by our publishers, early readers and well-wishers: any that remain belong to us four alone (mainly Dan). If you spot any inaccuracies, we warmly encourage you to write in to us on podcast@qi.com or @nosuchthing on Twitter, and we'll make sure to apologise in the introduction to the Book of the Year 2018.